'This volume is a timely and rich resource for modern constitutionalists. The essays are engaging, incisive and offer broad political and legal perspectives on one of the central questions in contemporary constitutional debates.'

Professor Adrienne Stone, *University of Melbourne, Australia*

'Recent developments in constitution-making and amending practices have implicated a range of methods of encouraging direct public participation, through crowd-sourcing, referenda, and more. This book examines the ways that these developments accentuate a range of fundamental issues dealing with the constituent power, sovereignty, and deliberation, through conceptual analysis and empirical studies. An important contribution to an increasingly important discussion.'

Professor Mark Tushnet, *Harvard Law School, USA*

'This book reveals both good and bad practice, and problems of how to cope with citizen choices that are not mandated at formal election times. The book is timely and well written and appeals to a broad cross-section of readers from political science to constitutional lawyers. It is highly recommended.'

Professor John McElldowney, *Warwick University, UK*

Participatory Constitutional Change: The People as Amenders of the Constitution

This book explores the recent trend of enhancing the role of the people in constitutional change. It traces the reasons underlying this tendency, the new ways in which it takes form, the possibilities of success and failure of such ventures as well as the risks and benefits it carries. To do so, it examines the theoretical aspects of public participation in constitutional decision-making, offers an analysis of the benefits gained and the problems encountered in countries with long-standing experience in the practice of constitutional referendums, discusses the recent innovative constitution-making processes employed in Iceland and Ireland in the post financial crisis context and probes the use of public participation in the EU context. New modes of deliberation are juxtaposed to traditional direct-democratic processes, while the reasons behind this re-emergence of public involvement narratives are discussed from the aspect of comparative constitutional design. The synthetic chapter offers an overview of the emerging normative and comparative issues and provides a holistic approach of the role of the people in constitutional change in an attempt to answer when, where and how this role may be successfully enhanced. The work consists of material specifically written for this volume, and authored by prominent constitutional scholars and experts in public participation and deliberative processes.

Xenophon Contiades is Professor of Public Law, School of Social and Political Sciences, University of Peloponnese and Managing Director of the Centre for European Constitutional Law-Themistocles and Dimitris Tsatsos Foundation, Athens, Greece.

Alkmene Fotiadou is Research Associate at the Centre for European Constitutional Law, Athens, Greece.

Comparative Constitutional Change
Series editors:

Comparative Constitutional Change has developed into a distinct field of constitutional law. It encompasses the study of constitutions through the way they change and covers a wide scope of topics and methodologies. Books in this series include work on developments in the functions of the constitution, the organization of powers and the protection of rights, as well as research that focuses on formal amendment rules and the relation between constituent and constituted power. The series includes comparative approaches along with books that focus on single jurisdictions, and brings together research monographs and edited collections which allow the expression of different schools of thought. While the focus is primarily on law, where relevant the series may also include political science, historical, philosophical and empirical approaches that explore constitutional change.

Xenophon Contiades is Professor of Public Law, School of Social and Political Sciences, University of Peloponnese and Director of the Centre for European Constitutional Law-Themistocles and Dimitris Tsatsos Foundation, Athens, Greece.

Thomas Fleiner is Emeritus Professor of Law at the University of Fribourg, Switzerland. He teaches and researches in the areas of Federalism, Rule of Law, Multicultural State; Comparative Administrative and Constitutional Law; Political Theory and Philosophy; Swiss Constitutional and Administrative Law; and Legislative Drafting. He has published widely in these and related areas.

Alkmene Fotiadou is Research Associate at the Centre for European Constitutional Law, Athens.

Richard Albert is a tenured Associate Professor and Dean's Research Scholar at Boston College Law School, USA. He is currently a Visiting Associate Professor of Law and the Canadian Bicentennial Visiting Associate Professor of Political Science at Yale University.

Participatory Constitutional Change

The People as Amenders of the Constitution

Edited by
Xenophon Contiades and Alkmene Fotiadou

Routledge
Taylor & Francis Group
LONDON AND NEW YORK

First published 2017 by Routledge

2 Park Square, Milton Park, Abingdon, Oxfordshire OX14 4RN
711 Third Avenue, New York, NY 10017

Routledge is an imprint of the Taylor & Francis Group, an informa business

First issued in paperback 2018

British Library Cataloguing in Publication Data

A catalogue record for this book is available from the British Library

Library of Congress Cataloging-in-Publication Data

Title: Participatory constitutional change : the people as amenders of the constitution.
Description: Milton Park, Abingdon, Oxon ; New York, NY : Routledge, 2017. | Series: Comparative constitutional change | Includes bibliographical references and index.
Identifiers: LCCN 2016014380 (print) | LCCN 2016014458 (ebook) | ISBN 9781472478696 (hbk) | ISBN 9781315599489 (e-book) | ISBN 9781317083894 (Web PDF) | ISBN 9781317083887 (ePub) | ISBN 9781317083870 (Mobipocket)
Subjects: LCSH: Referendum—European Union countries. | Direct democracy—European Union countries. | Constitutional amendments—European Union countries.
Classification: LCC KJE5267 .P37 2017 (print) | LCC KJE5267 (ebook) | DDC 342.403/2—dc23
LC record available at http://lccn.loc.gov/2016014380

ISBN: 978-1-4724-7869-6 (hbk)
ISBN: 978-1-138-36280-2 (pbk)

Typeset in Galliard
by Apex CoVantage, LLC

Contents

Notes on contributors

Paul Blokker, Associate Professor of Sociology, Charles University Prague

Xenophon Contiades, Professor of Public Law, University of Peloponnese and Managing Director, Centre for European Constitutional Law

David Farrell, Professor of Politics, University College Dublin

Thomas Fleiner, Professor Emeritus of Public Law, University of Fribourg and former Director, Institute of Federalism

Alkmene Fotiadou, Research Associate, Centre for European Constitutional Law

Jörg Gerkrath, Professor of Public and European Law, University of Luxembourg

Clodagh Harris, Senior Lecturer of Political Sciences, University College Cork

Claudia Josi, Adjunct Professor of International Human Rights Law, Santa Clara University

Helle Krunke, Professor of Constitutional Law, University of Copenhagen

Jan-Herman Reestman, Professor of Constitutional and Administrative Law, University of Amsterdam

Jane Suiter, Research Associate, Dublin City University

Björg Thorarensen, Professor of Law, University of Iceland

Dario Elia Tosi, Associate Professor of Public Law, University of Valle D'Aosta

Acknowledgments

This volume is the first publication of the Research Group on Constitution-Making and Constitutional Change, operating under the International Association of Constitutional Law. The rationale and the aims of the volume were thoroughly discussed at the roundtable 'Constitutional Change and People', organized by the University of Luxembourg and the Research Group on Constitution-Making and Constitutional Change on 12 December 2014, attended by all the contributors.

The roundtable aimed at intervening in the debate on enhancing popular participation in constitutional amendment. What would it mean for Luxembourg to enhance civic participation in constitutional amendment? What should any established democracy take into account before constitutionally enshrining participatory devices? These questions were addressed through various aspects, to offer theoretical and practical insight to constitutional designers who consider embarking on a civic participation enhancement journey. This common thread is conspicuous throughout the chapters of the volume.

We owe much to our host, Professor Jörg Gerkrath, not only for his wonderful hospitality, but most importantly for the idea of organizing a roundtable on the subject. His contribution to the elaboration of the working hypothesis has been invaluable to the volume.

We are also indebted to the former President of the European Court of Justice, Professor Vassilios Skouris, who kindly accepted to chair the event contributing to the discussion with insightful comments.

The support of the Centre for European Constitutional Law – Themistocles and Dimitris Tsatsos Foundation has been indispensable.

Finally, we would like to thank Ion Contiades for making the writing process more intriguing.

Acknowledgments

Introduction

Participatory constitutional change

Xenophon Contiades and Alkmene Fotiadou

In film sequels the attractive villain often makes a comeback. The attraction such heroes exert on the audience make them indispensable to the narrative. It would be hard to imagine *Terminator II* without the human-looking indestructible cyborg. His icon had become so popular that it is explicable why in the sequel he uses his powers to do good. In *X-Men: The Last Stand* mutants are deprived, 'cured' of their abilities, but Magneto demonstrates that the nullification of his powers is temporary and he shall re-acquire them.[1] The previously incapacitated hero returns fully operative.

In constitutional narratives constituent power has the part of the enduring superhero. The exercise of constituent power entails the option of further sequels. The allure of the constituting power, which 'bears the marks of an unconstrained, undivided, and limitless force that verges, once again, on violence, arbitrariness, and raw facticity',[2] is unsurmountable. Much like Magneto the nullification of the constituent superpower can only be perceived as temporary. The continuity of the narrative depends upon the possibility of the superhero re-emerging in full force.

Understanding the role of the people in constitutional amendment

The grasp of constituent power is remarkable in constitutional scholarship. Constituted power seems to derive attraction as a sequel to constituent power, exactly because it entails the possibility of a new, even cameo appearance, of the attractive, yet dangerous, villain. Revisiting the relationship between constituent and constituted power is a recurring theme in constitutional amendment theory.[3] The

1 C. Jess-Cooke and C. Verevis, *Second Takes: Critical Approaches to the Film Sequel* (State University of New York Press 2010).

2 A. Kalyvas, 'Popular Sovereignty, Democracy, and the Constituent Power' (2005) 12(2) *Constellations Volume* 225.

3 See J. Colon Rios, *Weak Constitutionalism: Democratic Legitimacy and the Question of Constituent Power* (Routledge 2012); M. Tushnet, 'Peasants with Pitchforks, and Toilers with Twitter: Constitutional Revolutions and the Constituent Power' (2015) 13(3) *International Journal of Constitutional Law* 639; J. Komarek, 'Constitutional Revolutions and

image of the constituent sovereign overhangs the tendency to enhance people – driven constitutional change.

Citizen-led constitutional change is currently emerging as a distinct trend in constitutional design theory and practice. The reasons for this are manifold. Recent experiments in participatory constitution-writing in Iceland and Ireland have triggered a dialogue on the possibilities of creating new paths of constitutional change. Much discussed referendums, such as the independence referendum in Scotland, the Greek bailout referendum, the marriage equality referendum in Ireland and the UK's EU referendum have renewed the debate on the risks and assets of holding referendums on issues that have the potential of exerting major influence on constitutions. Along with the augmented use of participatory processes and referendums, an ongoing dialogue exploring the boundaries between constituent and constituted power suggests that the role of the people in constitutional change has to be being revisited.

The volume aims to offer a concise guide to popular participation in constitutional change. Throughout the chapters, the reasons for this growing tendency are sought and novel ways of creating participatory constitutional change mechanisms are explored through the examination of the features that account for the success or failure in such ventures. A crucial goal is to explore criteria for making informed and workable constitutional design choices. To do so, the volume consists of 10 contributions authored by Professors of Constitutional Law and Political Science. Each chapter follows its own rationale, focusing on different facets of the issue. Nonetheless, a common thread exists. People-driven constitutional change is addressed as a constitutional design aim.[4] Thus, across the chapters unfolds the answer to the question of what constitutional designers should take into consideration before embarking on a direct-democracy enhancement journey.

Participatory constitution-writing methods and referendums entail particular assets but also risks, while formal amendment rules follow a logic of their own. How does the enhancement of participatory constitutional change relate to the goals set by amendment formulas? Rich and extensive analysis of the issues from both a theoretical and a practical aspect is found in the book, which is divided in six parts. The first part under the title of 'The People as Amenders of the Constitution. A Synthetic Approach' (Xenophon Contiades and Alkmene Fotiadou)

---

the Constituent Power: A Reply to Mark Tushnet' (2015) 13(4) *International Journal of Constitutional Law* 1054, doi: 10.1093/icon/mov060; and Y. Roznai, 'Unconstitutional Constitutional Amendments: A Study of the Nature and Limits of Constitutional Amendment Powers' (February 2014), http://etheses.lse.ac.uk/915/1/Roznai_Unconstitutional-constitutional-amendments.pdf, accessed 10 January 2016.

4 See M. Pichou, 'Elements of Direct Democracy in the Recent Practice of European Countries: Some Thoughts à Propos the Roundtable "Constitutional Change and People"' *Constitution Making and Constitutional Change* (21 January 2015), http://constitutional-change.com/elements-of-direct-democracy-in-the-recent-practice-of-european-countries-some-thoughts-a-propos-the-roundtable-constitutional-change-and-people/, accessed 10 January 2016.

offers a synthetic approach and attempts to address this question. In this part we suggest criteria for deciding on the enhancement of popular involvement in constitutional amendment procedures. There are various ways in which people can engage in constitutional change lying along a continuum of civic engagement in constitutional amendment. A true move along this continuum towards more participation entails building workable mechanisms that fit the amendment rules and the way those rules operate in practice within a given environment. Where the enhancement of citizen engagement is to be pursued though the enshrinement of referendums within the amendment formula, the task at hand is tricky. Risks associated with the use of referendums, such as elite manipulation, can be effectively addressed with detailed regulation. Such rules, however, as part of the amendment formula may render it more stringent, distancing in practice the people from constitutional change instead of enhancing their role in it.

The synthetic chapter investigates this paradox. The paradigms used include revisiting the crowd-sourcing of the Icelandic constitution, evaluating the results of the Irish Constitutional Convention and scrutinizing sovereignty related referendums. Furthermore, juxtaposing the marriage equality referendum in Ireland to the Swiss minaret referendum allows a better understanding of the tensions between majority decision-making and fundamental rights. Investigating the impact of the enhancement of participatory constitutional change on the operation of formal amendment rules, pinning down possible risks posed to fundamental rights and assessing the actual impact of innovative attempts of citizen-led constitutional change, the first chapter examines the possibilities of the people entering the role of constitutional amenders.

Different possibilities of citizen-led constitutional amendment

The second part addresses theoretical and historical aspects of popular participation in constitutional change. Paul Blokker in 'Constitutional Reform in Europe and Recourse to the People' analyzes the theoretical rationales and normative justifications for this phenomenon, critically discussing forms of inclusion and civic participation in constitutional politics, while also addressing legal, political, popular, and democratic understandings of constitutionalism. Drawing examples from recent examples of civic engagement, Iceland, Ireland, the Netherlands, Romania, and the Convention on the Future of Europe, the chapter provides a thorough theoretical analysis of the multiple forms of civic engagement in constitutional change exploring the distance between theory and practice. In the third chapter, under the title 'A Future for Referendums in the Fifth French Republic', Jan-Herman Reestman traces the evolution of popular participation in France exploring whether referendums constitute a genuine expression of the will of the people. Starting off with the constitutional amendments introduced by De Gaulle's referendums, which changed the political environment by rendering the president the de facto leader of the country, the chapter traces changes in the function of referendums in France over the years through the lens of the

Rousseauian tradition. The function of referendums in the current political environment, where they can only take place if opposing political actors agree, is examined in view of the utility of referendums for the political actors.

The third part turns towards constitutional orders with long standing direct-democratic experience, to provide insight into the equilibrium between democracy and constitutionalism. In the chapter 'Participation of Citizens in Constitution Making; Assets and Challenges – The Swiss Experience', Thomas Fleiner explains the various channels through which the Swiss people participate in constitutional change. The enduring tradition of direct democracy offers the context in which the assets as well as the dangers of direct popular involvement emerge clearly. This chapter, by providing a comprehensive overview of the way constitutional referendums and popular initiatives work in Switzerland, traces the sources of the problems encountered. In the chapter which follows, titled 'Direct Democracy vs Fundamental Rights? A Comparative Analysis of the Mechanisms that Limit the "Will of the People" in Switzerland and California', Claudia Josi focuses on the potential risks posed by popular initiatives to the protection of fundamental rights. The chapter assesses from a comparative perspective the extent to which legislation in Switzerland and California provides substantive and procedural restrictions on direct democratic devices to ensure the protection of fundamental rights. The availability of mechanisms that strengthen minority protection and guarantee the rule of law emerges as a key concern in enhancing civic participation in constitutional change.

The fourth part of the volume presents the new trends in popular involvement. The attempt to crowd-source the constitution in Iceland following the outbreak of the financial crisis and the Irish Constitutional Convention, which brought forth the idea of 'ordinary citizens' as constitutional amenders, provide a step-by-step analysis of the obstacles that get in the way between the idea and the reality in such ventures. Good practices are analyzed, while mistakes and failures are also thoroughly assessed. Björg Thorarensen in the chapter 'The People's Contribution to Constitutional Changes. Writing, Advising or Approving? – Lessons from Iceland' explains in detail how Iceland's crowd-sourced constitution was 'killed by politicians'. The question 'what went wrong' is addressed through the assessment of all political, legal and practical factors that account for the failure. This assessment of the process, apart from the various shortcomings, also highlights the positive aspects of the experiment. From the viewpoint of constitutional law and theory, the Icelandic example provides a lesson in constitution-writing choices. The next chapter addresses what is perceived as a much more successful exercise in popular involvement, attracting nonetheless much criticism. David M. Farrell, Clodagh Harris and Jane Suiter discuss the Irish Constitutional Convention in their contribution 'Bringing People into the Heart of Constitutional Design: The Irish Constitutional Convention 2012–14'. The Irish Constitutional Convention was designed give the Irish people a leading role in constitutional change. The features of this attempt, that is, random selection of 'ordinary' citizens, mini-publics, the involvement of experts as advisors/witnesses and of politicians as 'fellow members' are explained and assessed. The elements that can render a deliberative process successful are thoroughly analyzed. Still, a distinction is drawn between process and outcomes. Does a successful process secure successful outcomes? The chapter provides evidence to allow reflection on what is considered a successful outcome with regard to constitutional change and how successful procedures can narrow the gap between narratives and practice.

The fifth part deals with the dilemma of introducing constitutional referendums in the constitution. Two different examples, Luxembourg and Greece, where the narratives in relation to the enhancement civic participation in constitutional change are getting stronger are approached. In 'The "Sudden Eagerness" to Consult the Luxembourgish People on Constitutional Change', Jörg Gerkrath probes the question what triggered the discussion about directly involving the people in constitutional change in a country where the use of referendums has been exceptionally scarce. The turn towards more participatory procedures in Luxembourg is approached through the lens of referendums past practice. The possibility of a genuine enhancement of popular participation is explored, setting the question whether referendums could block laboriously achieved compromises among members of parliament. In 'The Role of the People in Constitutional Amendment in Greece: Between Narratives and Practice', Alkmene Fotiadou explores a post-financial crisis Greek paradox. The more distant the people are becoming from the constitutional revision process, the stronger the narratives for more involvement get. The chapter discusses the current amendment formula and the recurring proposals about enshrining a constitutional referendum, through the lens of the bailout referendum of 5 July 2015 following the total lack of referendum practice since 1974. The recent referendum experience, being a textbook example of bad referendum practice due to a totally ambiguous question and absence of time for deliberation, rephrases the dilemma about enhancing participatory procedures in Greece. The authors explore whether constitutional design can achieve a major paradigm shift from virtually no popular participation in constitutional amendment to citizen-led constitutional change. They suggest that the starting point of reflection should be the current political and constitutional culture of distrust and the recent referendum malpractice episode, that indicate that no direct-democratic culture exists at the moment.

The sixth part of the volume explores EU aspects of popular participation, tracing the interaction between European integration, national sovereignty and direct-democratic procedures. Dario Elia Tosi in 'The Use of Referendums on European Topics in the Integration Process of the European Union' provides an overview of the EU referendums. The chapter delineates the different perceptions and uses of referendums in member states pinning down the place such deliberation can have in the EU context. To do so, the chapter traces developments, since the popular vote held in France in 1972 for the enlargement of the EC. In the chapter 'Sovereignty, Constitutional Identity, Direct Democracy? Direct Democracy as a National Strategy for Upholding the Nation State in EU Integration', Helle Krunke, detects a competition between the EU and its member states for democratic legitimacy, through the use of direct democracy mechanisms. Thus, she examines this trend as a part of the on-going competence struggle between the EU and the member states. The passage from 'sovereignty' and 'constitutional identity' narratives to the era of 'direct democracy' is analyzed through theory and case-studies.

Moving along the constitutional amendment participatory continuum

A recurring theme throughout the volume is the distance between narratives of popular involvement in constitutional change and the reality of its practice. Enhancing the role of the people in constitutional amendment is a complex task. Much depends on understanding the available options and deciding which one agrees best with the existing amendment model. Does the reform sought entail a big shift from the existing mode of constitutional change?

Pinning down the current role of the people in the 'participatory continuum' helps identify the present position and the degree of change sought. Understanding the constitutional culture and detecting the existence or the absence of direct-democratic reflexes is also crucial to determine whether building a new constitutional culture is necessary for the success of the endeavour. There are thus two interrelated questions that need to be answered in any constitutional order where the enhancement of civic participation is sought. The first question is which route constitutional change has been following so far and the second is whether the people are familiar with direct-democratic devices. Where an intervention in the formal amendment rules is attempted, caution is needed to ensure (a) that the traditional risks associated with referendums such as elite manipulation do no spill over to the amendment formula and (b) that the additions do not render the formula over-stringent, thus sabotaging the very purpose sought.

Moving along the continuum of popular participation in constitutional change is fraught with unexpected obstacles. The recent examples of Iceland's attempt to crowd-source the constitution and the Irish Constitutional Convention are suggestive of the difficulties but also of the future possibilities. The desire for an enhanced role of the people in the exercise of constituted power has become evident and thus the challenge is to create the appropriate constitutional change mechanisms.

Part I

A synthetic approach

1 The people as amenders of the constitution

Xenophon Contiades and Alkmene Fotiadou

Introduction

In the context of constitutional democracies it is difficult to support that constitutional change does not belong to the people. Yet, it is far from clear how the people can effect constitutional change through the exercise of constituted power and whether the people are the drivers of informal constitutional change. Conceptualizations of the constituent power often coincide with conceptualizations of the people.[1] Constituent power can be viewed as 'the body of people from whom the constitution's authority emanates'.[2] The study of constituted power, however, often revolves around its limits and the way it is exercised.

This chapter aims to explore the role of the people as amenders of the constitution. Distinguishing between narratives and reality, theory and practice, it attempts to offer an overview of the current tendency towards popular involvement not only in constitution-making, but also in constitutional amendment. The crucial question is what makes the difference between success and failure in attempts to directly involve the people in constitutional change.

A conspicuous recent trend in constitutional design and political practice is the enhancement of the role of the people in constitutional change. Referendums, including constitutional referendums, are currently making a comeback in constitutional theory and practice.[3] Although public participation in constitution-making appears to be a given, the same does not apply to constitutional amendment. Still, the emergence of novel participatory constitutional amendment procedures dictates the reconceptualization of the boundaries between constituent and constituted power. More than that, placing the focus on participatory constitutional

1 Mark Tushnet distinguishes between two conceptualizations of the constituent power: constituent power as a pure concept and constituent power as real embodied people. See M. Tushnet, 'Peasants with Pitchforks and Toilers with Twitter' (2015) 13 *International Journal of Constitutional Law* 639, 644–653.

2 http://www.texaslrev.com/wp-content/uploads/Tushnet.pdf, 1986–1987, accessed 18 December 2015.

3 S. Tierney, *Constitutional Referendums: The Theory and Practice of Republican Deliberation* (OUP 2012); A.H. Trechsel, 'E-Voting and Electoral Participation' in C. de Vreese (ed.), *The Dynamics of Referendum Campaigns–An International Perspective* (Palgrave 2007) 159–182; and F. Mendez, M. Mendez and V. Triga, *Referendums and the European Union: A Comparative Inquiry* (Cambridge University Press 2014).

change seems to represent a shift from the era of rights-centered constitutional discourse towards participatory democracy, which in turn could signal a shift in the balance between constitutionalism and democracy.

The reasons underlying this tendency vary. Accordingly vary the new ways in which it takes form, the possibilities of success and failure of such ventures, as well as the risks and benefits they carry. Understanding the current landscape entails revisiting the theoretical aspects of public participation in constitutional decision-making, understanding the benefits gained and the problems encountered in countries with long-standing experience in the practice of constitutional referendums, assessing the recent innovative constitution-making processes employed in Iceland and Ireland in the post-financial crisis context, and mapping out the use of public participation in the EU context. New modes of deliberation are juxtaposed to traditional direct-democratic processes, while the reasons behind this re-emergence of public involvement narratives must be linked to constitutional design.

What are the contemporary reasons for adopting direct-democratic modes of constitutional amendment? Do novel ways of building participatory constitutional change mechanisms exist? What are the features that account for success or failure in such ventures? Can all constitutional cultures effectively absorb direct-democratic procedures? Can the problems with the use of referendums, such as avoiding elite manipulation and framing the question, be similarly addressed in different countries? Is there a chance that the attempt to ensure more popular participation by adding a constitutional referendum to the prerequisites of the amending formula may backfire? Does this tendency towards more popular involvement mark a shift in constitutionalism, putting less emphasis on the constitutional protection of fundamental rights? Is it possible to put together a concise guide to popular participation in constitutional change?

The issues are multi-faceted. To begin with, every new political and constitutional proposal entailing a move towards a direct-democratic direction must be placed within its environment. The first question posed, requiring an answer, is whether such proposals qualify as a true move towards a more deliberative model, or are they merely a political narrative? The reasons behind this new trend vary: it may be a reaction to the financial crisis experience, or it may be rooted in the growing concern about the sovereignty loss due to European integration, or perhaps it signifies a new form of constitutional faith deepening the bond between the people and the constitution. Nonetheless, there is a distance between the theoretical conceptualizations of public participation and the reality of their practice.

Why? Sovereignty, democracy and constitutional change

The augmenting deliberative turn in established democracies can be attributed to distinct reasons.[4] The enhancement of deliberative citizen-driven constitutional

4 R.E. Goodin, *Innovating Democracy: Democratic Theory and Practice after the Deliberative Turn* (OUP 2008).

change can be viewed as a democracy – perfecting choice, or as a response to disenchantment with representative democracy, which in many cases was triggered by the financial crisis or policy failures, or as an attempt to counterbalance sovereignty loss through the participation to international entities such as the EU. From a different perspective, calls for enhancing civic participation may express a response to judge-made constitutional change, in jurisdictions where judicially induced informal constitutional change is perceived as a symptom of juristocracy.[5]

Innovative constitution-writing endeavours aimed at citizen-led constitutional change, which came as a response to the financial crisis, had a therapeutic function empowering the citizens. As such, experimental constitution-writing methods cannot be assessed only with regard to their success in producing constitutional text. Enhancing recovery efforts by reinforcing the people and restoring constitutional faith and trust in the institutions are aspects that need to be taken into consideration.

Responding to political and institutional disappointments is a corrective function aimed at filling the holes of representative democracy. Culture matters in such attempts not only with regard to their potential success or failure, but also with regard to the choice of remedy. Stephen Griffin considers direct-democratic infusions as an answer to political dysfunctions that have become apparent in recent policy disasters.[6] Furthermore, he discusses the relationship between Americans and their constitution, stating that they 'typically revere' the constitution, stressing that, as Sanford Levinson points out, Americans are more likely to attribute to the constitution good policy results than policy disasters.[7] The object of frustration is thus culturally defined and depends on the popular perception of the constitution.

Direct-democratic devices used as a response to the financial crisis provide a test area for the pitfalls of holding referendums to address unspoken sovereignty issues. The financial crisis triggered two debt referendums. Iceland and Greece subjected sovereign debt settlements to a referendum. Both referendums had underlying sovereignty issues, not in the straightforward way the issue appears in EU membership referendums, but in a more implicit and subtle way. Still, there is an important difference between the two debt referendums: in Iceland the question was clear and so were the consequences,[8] whereas in Greece the question was ambiguous, and incapable of leading to predictable consequences. Furthermore, in Iceland the referendum must be placed in the wider context of

5 Chr. Moellers, *The Three Branches: A Comparative Model of Separation of Powers* (OUP 2015); R. Hirschl, *Towards Juristocracy: The Origins and Consequences of the New Constitutionalism* (Harvard University Press 2007).

6 S.M. Griffin, *Broken Trust: Dysfunctional Government and Constitutional Reform* (University Press of Kansas 2015).

7 Ibid. 51; S. Levinson, *Framed: America's 51 Constitutions and the Crisis of Governance* (OUP 2012) 5.

8 http://www.voxeu.org/article/iceland-greece-and-political-hectoring, accessed 18 December 2015.

constitutional participatory and quite experimental procedures that expressed an overall tendency.

An additional parameter is the fiscal content of such referendums. Debt deals are fraught with fiscal consequences, therefore the pros and cons of fiscal referendums also come into play.[9] Should the people decide on taxation through referendums and how does this relate to the tax state? Fiscal referendums follow a different logic than sovereignty referendums and they are designed to impact fiscal policy directly. On the whole, there is a choice of constitutional politics to be made and it is highly questionable whether this can be a one-off choice. Nonetheless, in Icesave and the Greferendum issues were blended into a whole, which was neither about sovereignty nor about fiscal matters, but an amalgam, a fusion of notions and feelings.[10]

In the crisis-related fiscal referendums it is also possible to add the Irish 2012 referendum, where the Irish people voted 'yes' to the European fiscal stability treaty. The possibility of future bailouts was one of the important stakes of this referendum, which was however very straight-forward with regard to its result. Furthermore, from a comparative aspect, in Ireland there is a longstanding referendum culture, while there has been no sense of sovereignty loss in defiance of the people's will, since the Irish constitution provides that every concession of sovereignty must be done by way of popular referendum.[11] Thus, in Ireland holding a referendum on the fiscal stability treaty is part of the constitutional culture, in Iceland it was part of a general turn toward citizen involvement, and in Greece it was an unexpected episode since referendums are not part of the constitutional culture.

Citizen involvement in fiscal matters through referendums is a constitutional choice with multiple repercussions. The dilemma in fiscal referendums can be simplified as 'more or less state', that is, referendums may operate either as a break on tax interventionism or adversely trigger a Robin Hood[12] effect leading to redistributive policies. This dilemma does not apply when the taxation is related to debt and to external obligations. Then the stakes are more complex but, contrarily, the narratives are simpler. The predisposition of citizens does not relate to their beliefs about the role of the state, interventionism and redistribution, but has to do with their stance towards the EU, nationalist sentiments and euroscepticism. The fiscal measures put to referendum are imposed so that international

9 L. Feld, Chr. Schaltegger and J. Schnellenbach, 'On Government Centralization and Fiscal Referendums: A Theoretical Model and Evidence from Switzerland' (May 2008) 52(4) *European Economic Review* 611.

10 On identity and voting see J.A. Elkink and D. Farrell, *The Act of Voting: Identities, Institutions and Locale* (Routledge 2015).

11 See F. De Londras and S. Mullaly, *The Irish Yearbook of International Law*, vol. 8/2013 (Hart Publishing 2015) 55; F. de Londras and D. Gwynn Morgan, 'Constitutional Amendment in Ireland' in X. Contiades (ed.), *Engineering Constitutional Change: A Comparative Perspective on Europe, Canada and the USA* (Routledge 2013) 179–202.

12 M. Freitag and A. Vatter, 'Initiatives, Referendums, and the Tax State' (January 2006) 13(1) *Journal of European Public Policy* 89.

lenders can be repaid, which renders debt referendums a unique category of fiscal referendums.

Furthermore, the supra-national character of the subject matter also renders these referendums (especially the Greek one) a unique form of sovereignty-related referendum. One of the side effects of the financial crisis has been that it became obvious to all that constitutional control had slipped away from the hands of national governments. The darker side of European integration emerged. Nonetheless, there exist different ways to perceive things. If we view the financial crisis as a disaster, that is, a sudden event that seriously disrupts the functioning of a community or society and causes losses that exceed the community's or society's ability to cope using its own resources,[13] we may view bailout agreements and the grouping of international lenders (such as the European Commission, the International Monetary Fund and the European Central Bank) as a response to the inability of countries to cope using their own resources.

Debt referendums were caught in between patterns of diminishing state sovereignty. The question is: were they 'sovereign acts, self contained within the state', or a delayed chimerical cry for self-determination? It must be noted that although Icesave did not have to do with EU membership, it enhanced isolationist and anti-EU feelings and subsequently Iceland dropped its bid to join the European Union. In Greece the outcome of the referendum was equally nebulous with its question. Although the question in debt referendums is about more or less taxes, it reads more or less sovereignty. The reaction of the people thus corresponds to what Tierney describes as the people 'long excluded from what they envisage as an undemocratic process of elite bargaining' instead of voting on the substance of the issue, vote against the process 'which has preceded it'.[14]

Viewing debt referendums as a hybrid of fiscal and sovereignty referendums raises the question of their role not only within the state but also beyond it: within the context of multi-level constitutionalism.[15] Furthermore, given that a stated purpose and an applied use of their outcome (with better or worse results) was that of a negotiation tool employed deliberatively toward attaining a better debt deal, a different question is also raised. What does it mean for referendums to be used for purposes other than the traditional deliberative and participatory function attributed to them?[16]

Pinning down the reason behind the turn towards referendums as a means of inducing formal or informal constitutional change is crucial for understanding the role of the people, that is, the role they are expected to perform and the role

13 https://www.ifrc.org/en/what-we-do/disaster-management/about-disasters/what-is-a-disaster/, accessed 25 November 2015.

14 Tierney (n. 3) 262.

15 N. Walker, 'Multilevel Constitutionalism: Looking Beyond the German Debate' in K. Tuori and S. Sankari (eds), *The Many Constitutions of Europe* (Ashgate 2010) 143–168.

16 See Reestman's analysis of De Gaulle's use of referendums, that transformed them 'into a matter of personal confidence' in J.-H. Reestman, 'A Future for Referendums in the Fifth French Republic', in this volume.

they actually perform. A unique antagonism between the EU and member states with regard to the pursuance of more democracy seems to be developing. The EU appears to seek more democratic legitimacy, whereas member states appear to seek through domestic processes a re-affirmation of sovereignty. This competition could result in more civic involvement at both levels, but it could also prove to be an empty shell, more symbolic than real.[17] Much depends on cultural factors since constitutional cultures vary, even within the EU context, and so does the people's familiarity with direct democratic processes.

How? Channels of people-driven constitutional change

Popular involvement in constitutional change can take many forms. The role of the people can be constitutionally prescribed either in the amendment formula or through the constitutional enshrinement of referendums that may induce informal constitutional change. Other channels of people-driven constitutional change exist.[18] The people are often considered the driving force behind constitutional moments.[19] Furthermore, empirical constitutional analysis has raised serious doubts on the very existence of the countermajoritarian problem,[20] suggesting that seminal court decisions may be inducing change in the direction the people would want it to follow.

Nonetheless, being the driving force behind constitutional change is different from being the amender of the constitution. In order to be the amenders of the constitution, the people need to be designated amenders by the formal amendment rules, while these rules must be designed in such a way as to allow the people to actually perform this role. The roles assigned to the people by the amendment formulas vary. Several amendment formulas provide that the decision, which concludes the process of a constitutional amendment, is made directly by the people by way of referendum. Another option is obligatory referendums under specific conditions, such as failure to achieve enhanced parliamentary majorities or at the request of the opposition. The stronger form of popular participation in constitutional referendums is the possibility of popular initiative with regard to constitutional amendment. Popular participation may appear in a less straight-forward way where the amendment formula provides for the involvement of two parliaments in

17 See H. Krunke, 'Sovereignty, Constitutional Identity, Direct Democracy? Direct Democracy as a National Strategy for Upholding the Nation State in EU Integration', in this volume.

18 X. Contiades and A. Fotiadou, 'Models of Constitutional Change' in X. Contiades (ed.), *Engineering Constitutional Change: A Comparative Perspective on Europe, Canada and the USA* (Routledge 2013) 417–468.

19 B. Ackerman, *We the People: Foundations*, vol. 1 (Harvard University Press 1995); B. Ackerman, *We the People: Transformations*, vol. 2 (Harvard University Press 2001).

20 M.A. Graber, 'Foreword: From the Countermajoritarian Difficulty to Juristocracy and the Political Construction of Judicial Power' (2006) 65 *Maryland Law Review* 1; D. Law, 'Constitutions' in P. Cane and H. Kritzer (eds), *The Oxford Handbook of Empirical Legal Research* (OUP 2012) 376, 386.

the amendment process. The people then participate indirectly in the amending procedure through their vote in the general elections held between the two phases of the process. This vote is presumed to express choices on the proposals of political parties regarding the pending constitutional reform.[21]

The role designated to the people by the formal amendment rules is correlated to the aims of the amendment formula and the way it attempts to achieve the balance between continuity and change, and also between democracy and constitutionalism. The degree of citizen involvement in constitutional change depends on how constitutional-change mechanisms prescribing popular participation are applied in practice. It is important to detect if the role prescribed to the people is the role actually performed by the people with regard to constitutional change.

Adverse consequences with regard to popular participation are frequent. To begin with, referendums as part of the amendment formula render the formula more perplexed. This extra hurdle may render the amendment formula more stringent, making the constitution more difficult to change. Constitutional referendums may thus create a paradox when they work in the direction of adding stringency to the amendment formula: they distance the people from constitutional amendment, rendering formal constitutional change more intricate. Furthermore, constitutional referendums operating as mechanisms of constitutional change, in order to enhance the capacity of the people to have a genuine role in constitutional change, must meet certain requirements that rule out elite manipulation. This depends not only on the rules in place regulating referendums, but also on constitutional culture. Where citizens are not familiar with the use of referendums, the significance of the rules guaranteeing genuine popular expression and deliberation can be downplayed.

In the milder form of popular participation in the amending process, that is, through intervening elections, constitutional change proposals are not self-evidently decisive with regard to voting behaviour. The choices of the electorate are mainly influenced by the agenda of political parties on other public policy issues and also by the popularity of candidates.[22] The will of the people regarding each specific constitutional reform proposal is rarely clearly discernible, while it is not binding on the parliament vested with the task to conclude the amendment process. Thus, the participation of the people in the amendment process is rather imaginary, and corresponds to the image of the people exercising delegated power and not to genuine popular decision-making.

Formal amendment rules often attempt to furbish constitutional amendment with the symbolic force of the original exercise of the constituent power. Delegated power draws its allure from its link to the primordial constituent power.[23]

21 Contiades and Fotiadou (n. 18) 452 ff.

22 Ibid.

23 M. Loughlin, 'The Concept of Constituent Power' (2014) 13(2) *European Journal of Political Theory* 218; J.I. Colón-Ríos, 'Five Conceptions of Constituent Power' (2014) 130 *Law Quarterly Review* 306.

The recent trend of enhancing popular participation is in line with revisiting the boundaries between constituent and constituted power.

Whither? New trends in constitutional amendment

The emerging trend towards the adoption of referendums dictates approaching the topics on which referendums are held from the aspect of constitutional change. When popular involvement in constitutional change takes the straightforward, obvious form of constitutional referendums, the crucial question is whether all topics are suitable for being put to referendum. This question is neither a question about amendability, nor a question regarding the ability of the people to decide on all constitutional issues. It is a question about the characteristics of referendums and how they relate to the issues put to referendum. Can the amendment of constitutional rights be decided on by way of referendum? Can technical legal issues be put to referendum? Can the response to judge-made informal constitutional change be effected through referendums? Does popular initiative enhance the dangers linked to holding referendums on certain categories of issues, and most importantly on rights-related issues?

Referendums, constitutional change and individual rights

The use of referendums on rights issues heightens the tension between constitutionalism and democracy. The inherent dangers of using referendums, such as the risk of elite manipulation and the problem of framing the substantial issue, become more acute. Recent examples present in a schematic form what is at stake. The Swiss minaret initiative and the Irish same-marriage referendum demonstrate opposite facets of popular involvement in constitutional change in the field of rights. Both countries have a long tradition of holding referendums, so they can provide the basis for understanding how the mechanism of referendums operates in the area of fundamental rights. In a like manner, the Californian Prop 8 example is also relevant and can be directly juxtaposed to the 'marriage equality' Irish example. The analysis of these examples is crucial particularly where the enhancement of direct-democratic procedures is pursued in constitutional orders that have no longstanding familiarity with referendums. Where the direct-democratic trend in constitutional change represents a shift from placing emphasis on fundamental rights protection in favour of direct forms of popular expression, it is crucial to pin down potential risks to fundamental rights' protection.

All three examples are really about equal protection with regard to constitutional rights. Nonetheless, the minaret case had to do with religious liberty in its traditional conceptualization, whereas the recognition of the right to marry to same-sex couples has to do with the evolution of rights and the changing attitudes of the people towards them. On one hand, if a referendum leads to the recognition of a right, as happened in the marriage equality referendum, it may substantially enhance its protection for right-holders. It is easily arguable that for a same-sex couple life is definitely better in a legal order where the right to marry has been constitutionally enshrined following a referendum with high turnout, than in one where the right was recognized through judicial interpretation. Still, from the aspect of rights theory a major problem emerges where the protection of what is perceived as a fundamental right is rejected by the majority, or even worse denied to some.

The minaret case is illuminating. The proposed constitutional ban on building minarets was strongly fought against by the Swiss government, the parliament, human rights organizations, political parties and churches.[24] Furthermore, its legality was dubious. Under Swiss law the parliament may reject an initiative if it violates mandatory provisions of international law. Nonetheless, it was questionable whether religious freedom falls within the scope of *ius cogens*. The proposed amendment was approved by 57.5 per cent of the voters with a 53.4 per cent turnout. Islam is the second largest religion in Switzerland, where more than 4.3 per cent of the population is Muslim. Discrimination and the free exercise of religion is not a matter of numbers; still it is noteworthy that it affects not only a large number of residents but a considerable number of citizens as well. As such, it creates a typical example of the tension between majority rule and minority rights.

The Irish marriage equality referendum can be read as an opposite example. Ireland was the first country to introduce marriage equality into its constitution as a result of a referendum. The 62 per cent vote in favour may be attributed to a very successful 'yes' campaign, but also to the work of the Irish Constitutional Convention, which recommended holding this referendum. The Irish Constitutional Convention involved a random selection of ordinary citizens and can be viewed as one of the innovative constitution-writing experiments that emerged as a reaction towards the financial crisis.[25] In Ireland three categories of referendums exist with regard to the subject matter. The first category includes changes to the legal, political and administrative system, the second issues related with international treaties, and the third includes moral and social issues.[26] The marriage equality referendum falls within the scope of the third category. Although the very existence of this category indicates that the Irish people are accustomed to deciding on such matters by way of referendum, not all such referendums are considered to be successful. For example, the 'children rights referendum' was not considered to be successful.[27] In these referendums a lot depends on citizens'

24 See Th. Fleiner, 'Participation of Citizens in Constitution-Making: Assets and Challenges–The Swiss Experience'; C. Josi, 'Direct Democracy vs Fundamental Rights? A Comparative Analysis of the Mechanisms That Limit the 'Will of the People' in Switzerland and California', in this volume.

25 See J.A. Elkink, D.M. Farrell and Th. Reidy, 'Understanding the 2015 Marriage Referendum in Ireland: Constitutional Convention, Campaign, and Conservative Ireland' (November 2015) *UCD Geary Institute for Public Discussion Paper Series*, http://psai-pdd.org/sites/default/files/document/gearywp201521.pdf, accessed 10 December 2015.

26 Ibid.

27 See O. Doyle and D. Kenny, 'Constitutional Change and Interest Group Politics: Ireland's Children's Rights Referendum' in R. Albert, X. Contiades and A. Fotiadou (eds), *The Foundations and Traditions of Constitutional Amendment* (Hart Publishing 2017, forthcoming).

participation. In a sense, thus, conferring constitutional protection on the right at stake depends on voters showing up, which in turn has to do with information.

If marriage equality is considered one of the most important contemporary issues in the area of fundamental rights, it is crucial to discern whether the Irish example suggests that referendums provide an option for enhancing the protection of fundamental rights. Does the marriage equality referendum success suffice to convince that rights protection can be successfully 'taken away from the courts',[28] or is it an exceptional case, where the elements that account for the success can also be read as a warning against entrusting rights protection to the hands of the majority? Is the minaret or the same marriage case the right example for understanding the tension between individual rights and the use of direct-democratic devices, or do both examples highlight similar dangers?

Still, it has to also be considered that judge-made constitutional change is not only about legal doctrine, although judges are better equipped to deal with intricate legal issues than citizens. If a parallel can be made between the manner in which same-sex marriage was afforded constitutional protection in the US and in Ireland, it must be noted that by the time Obergefell[29] was issued, ruling that bans on same sex-marriage violate the US constitution, the majority of the citizens approved of allowing same-sex marriage. It is worth remembering that in the *Lawrence* case[30] Justice Kennedy suggested that Bowers[31] was wrongly decided[32] the day it was decided.[33] Although the interpretative expansion of rights is easy to conceive, difficulties arise once something is understood as a constitutional right, and the scope of its exercise, or even worse the right holders, are to be decided on by way of referendum.

The possibility of a negative vote in referendums related to fundamental rights is qualitatively different from a wrongly decided case. The denial of the majority to allow the enjoyment of specific rights to the minority is much more explicit, while it does not have the cover of misapplied legal doctrine. The recognition or expansion of a constitutional right by way of referendums can have many positive repercussions. It may enhance constitutional faith and it may bridge the gap between constitutionalism and democracy.

A different aspect emerges through the approach of more innovatory approaches to constitutional rights.[34] The recent Luxembourgish example of

28 M. Tushnet, *Taking the Constitution Away from the Courts* (Princeton University Press 2000).

29 *Obergefell v Hodges* [2015] 576 US__.

30 *Lawrence v Texas* [2003] 539 US 558.

31 *Bowers v Hardwick* [1986] 478 US 186.

32 https://supreme.justia.com/cases/federal/us/539/558/case.html, accessed 18 December 2015.

33 See J. Greene, 'The Anticanon' (2011) 125 *Harvard Law Review* 379; M.A. Graber, 'Hollow Hopes and Exaggerated Fears: The Canon/Anticanon in Context, Responding to Jamal S. Greene, "The Anticanon"' (2011) 125 *Harvard Law Review* 379.

34 J. Gerkrath, 'The "Sudden Eagerness" to Consult the Luxembourgish People on Constitutional Change', in this volume.

the attempted expansion of voting rights to foreigners is illuminating. Granting voting rights to foreigners could be constructed as a right that could indeed be granted by way of referendum but was overwhelmingly rejected by 78 per cent of voters. Foreigner voting rights would be an interesting innovation in a country where 45 per cent of the working population are foreigners, although it cannot be regarded that foreign nationals have a fundamental right to vote. The 'decoupling of citizenship and nationality' would potentially have multiple constitutional repercussions.[35] The question is whether the 'no' vote has a different impact on the position of foreigners in Luxembourg than the lack of voting rights had before it was overwhelmingly rejected. The standard problems related with the use of referendums can render the endangerment of rights more acute. Clarity of the question, availability of information, adequate deliberation when individual rights are at stake cannot be an evasive goal. When popular initiative is available, extra guarantees are also necessary to safeguard rights from being trampled on by temporary majorities.

Unsuccessful referendums impact constitutional agenda setting. When such referendums result from popular initiatives, although the people fail to impact the constitution, they may still succeed to place an issue on the political agenda.[36] When issues are set and supported by the political class and are rejected by the people, deliberation on the issue may familiarize the people with particular aspects of the evolution of constitutional rights. An argument could be construed thus to address the strong reservations against allowing referendums on constitutional change with regard to fundamental rights issues. Very much like maturing jurisprudence allows rights to evolve, referendums that fail to induce constitutional change may be viewed as a process allowing ideas to mature, not only within the limited forum of judicial thinking, but also in the public sphere. Still, this does not relieve the tension between constitutionalism and democracy, expressed in its most explicit form in referendums where the subject matter allows the majority to decide on the fate and scope of constitutional rights.

Changing the constitution through innovative constitution-writing methods

Part of the financial crisis legacy has been the introduction of experimental methods of constitution-writing, aimed at innovating the mechanisms of constitutional change. Iceland became the centre of attention of constitutional scholarship by embarking on an impressive constitution-writing experiment.[37] In June 2010, a

35 M. Finck, 'Should Foreigners Vote in National Legislative Elections?' *International Journal of Constitutional Law Blog* (13 May 2015), http://www.iconnectblog.com/2015/05/should-foreigners-vote-in-national-legislative-elections, accessed 18 December 2015.

36 Contiades and Fotiadou (n. 18) 455.

37 B. Thorarensen, 'The Impact of the Financial Crisis on Icelandic Constitutional Law: Legislative Reforms, Judicial Review and Revision of the Constitution' in X. Contiades (ed.), *Constitutions in the Global Financial Crisis. A Comparative Analysis* (Ashgate 2013) 263–283;

consultative Constitutional Assembly that had the task of revising the constitution was established by a Parliament Act. The election of the Constitutional Assembly was, however, invalidated by the Supreme Court of Iceland due to various legal defects, and the Parliament replaced it by the Constitutional Council, which was given the same consultative role as the Constitutional Assembly had been intended to perform. The proceedings of the Council were open and transparent, and became known for using social media such as Facebook, YouTube and Flickr to communicate with the public. Its proposals were unanimously approved by all delegates in the Council and submitted to the Althingi as a Bill for the new constitution of Iceland.

Many steps followed, including the elaboration of a draft by a team of experts and an advisory referendum, which with a turnout much lower than the usual turnout in general elections indicated that the people wished the proposals of the Constitutional Council to become the basis for the new constitution. The mandate of the Constitutional Council was wide, comparable to that of the Irish Constitutional Convention established in 2013. The Council decided to draft a new constitution instead of suggesting amendments to the existing one. Proposals were quite innovative and included new provisions on referendums and popular initiatives. The actual proposals became the object of severe criticism, culminating in concerns expressed by the Venice Commission.[38] The Commission suggested that the task should be completed by the Parliament, which would have time to consider all the discrepancies and problems in the proposed constitutional change.

Along the same lines the Parliamentary Ombudsman of Iceland found a major problem with the suggested innovations, because they appeared to be modelled after foreign paradigms, not readily compatible with the Icelandic reality. This view brings forth the possibility of misuses of comparative constitutional law, especially when handled by the people through participatory processes. Constitutional transplants may look appealing when constitution-writing results from a severe shock such as the financial meltdown in Iceland; more so when the political and constitutional institutions are discredited and the people have for some reason lost faith in the constitution in place.

In Iceland the constitution had been blamed for the financial crisis. Regardless of the constitution's actual responsibility with regard to the financial crisis, the way the people perceive it changed, while the fact that the document was aged and perhaps also outdated became suddenly conspicuous. Under such circumstances, when the people are suddenly given the lead in constitutional amendment, picking and choosing (and then mixing) institutions and practices that look appealing is very likely to occur. The paradox here is that the very experimental

---

B. Thorarensen, 'The People's Contribution to Constitutional Changes: Writing, Advising or Approving?–Lessons from Iceland', in this volume.

38 http://www.venice.coe.int/webforms/documents/?pdf=CDL-AD(2013)010-e, accessed 10 January 2016.

process that led Iceland's Ombudsman and the Venice Commission to express concerns became in itself an object of admiration in other countries, regarded by many as an example to follow.

Constitutional amendment is different from constitution-making, especially when it takes place within established democracies, which have longstanding legal and constitutional institutions and where a constitutional culture has already been formed. Even when an amendment aims at remedying detected malfunctions, it cannot be designed in a vacuum. The cultural context enhances the complexity of the borrowing endeavour. Two additional factors are also crucial. In countries where constitutional change, is people-driven and direct-democratic procedures are a common path of constitutional change, distrust of experts is a usual characteristic.[39] Where the turn toward direct-democratic forms of participation in constitutional amendment came as a response to the crisis, hostility toward experts could be linked to the augmented role of technocrats in tackling the results of the financial crisis. Still, the involvement of experts in people-driven constitutional amendment impacts the feasibility of the proposed changes. The absence of expert elaboration may facilitate failures, such as the Icelandic attempt to crowdsource the constitution by making it easy for politicians to 'kill' the amendment.[40] And yet, suspicion toward experts seems to accompany criticism of participatory amendment endeavours.

Questioning the success of the Irish Convention, Eoin Carolan observes that there is a chance that the positive academic commentary of the experience and outcome of the Convention is linked to the fact that much of it comes from experts who advocated and/or were involved in its operations. The examples used include David M. Farrell, who was Research Director of the Irish Constitutional Convention, Jane Suiter, who was Deputy Director, and Clodagh Harris, who was a member[41] and who have co-authored the chapter on the Irish Convention for this volume.

Does participation in constitution-writing processes negate the ability of experts to retain their skill to critically assess the very process in which they take part? The chapter in this volume on the Irish Convention presents in a balanced and critical manner the work of the Convention, discussing how successful it was. Björg Thorarensen, who has authored the chapter on Iceland for this volume, was a member of the Constitutional Committee appointed by the Parliament to prepare and organize the National Forum elaborate its results and present to the Assembly ideas on amendments to the constitution. Still, throughout her academic scholarship she maintained a critical stance viewing both the negative

39 See Contiades and Fotiadou (n. 18) 455.

40 Th. Gylafson, 'Democracy on Ice: A Post Mortem on the Icelandic Constitution' *openDemocracy* (19 June 2013), https://www.opendemocracy.net/can-europe-make-it/thorvaldur-gylfason/democracy-on-ice-post-mortem-of-icelandic-constitution, accessed 18 December 2015.

41 E. Carolan, 'Ireland's Constitutional Convention: Behind the Hype about Citizen-Led Constitutional Change' 13(3) *International Journal of Constitutional Law* 733, 734.

and the positive aspects of the Icelandic experiment.[42] A second important criticism Eoin Carolan expresses against the Irish Convention is that it allowed the coalition government to cynically 'pass the buck' of dealing with the same-sex marriage issue to an alternative institution, avoiding the political cost and inconvenience.[43] According to Carolan, besides the above the Convention delayed and ultimately defused the demands for radical reforms emerging from the crisis.[44]

Although the way citizen-led assemblies and the mini-publics work in practice may be fraught with dangers, dismissing the marriage equality referendum as a trivial reform, compared to more radical changes that could have resulted from the financial crisis, downplays its importance. It is true that constitutional responses to the financial crisis could be expected to entail major institutional and political reforms. The importance of amendments is nonetheless not always to be judged by their scope. The recognition of marriage equality is probably not irrelevant from the collective experience of the financial crisis and from the way this issue was channelled through a deliberative forum, which, despite its shortcomings, had remarkable qualities. Achieving constitutional change in marriage equality through the path of a referendum cannot be ignored as a paradigm of the potentiality of deliberation.

The possibility of the idea migrating to other constitutional orders makes it imperative to understand what made deliberation work in the direction of the majority recognising the existence of a right to marry that should belong to all. It would be thus a mistake to consider that the marriage equality amendment in Ireland was the result of a referendum, even one held in a country with a longstanding history of referendums. The marriage equality referendum must be understood as the outcome of the deliberative process of the Irish Convention. It is thus a matter of perspective: the Irish Convention can be viewed from the aspect of how wide the scope of the constitutional changes it resulted in or, adversely, the marriage equality amendment can be viewed from the aspect of the elaborate participatory process that led to the referendum that resulted in the amendment.

What the Icelandic and Irish recent experiments in citizen-led constitutional amendment have in common is that they both stemmed from the financial crisis. The experiment in Iceland was originally greeted with enthusiasm, while the Irish Convention did not originally attract positive reactions. Multiple and important differences exist between the two attempts. The constitution of Iceland was adopted in 1944, when the union with Denmark was broken, making minimal amendments to the previous constitution to effect the passage from constitutional monarchy to a republican form of government. Parts of the Icelandic

42 B. Thorarensen, 'Why the Making of a Crowd-Sourced Constitution in Iceland Failed' *Constitution Making & Constitutional Change* (26 February 2014), http://constitutional-change.com/why-the-making-of-a-crowd-sourced-constitution-in-iceland-failed/, accessed 20 December 2015.

43 Carolan (n. 41) 739.

44 Ibid. 746.

constitution, especially as regards the executive and its relation to the Althingi, and the provisions on the judiciary, had remained more or less unchanged from the time that Iceland was granted its first constitution from the Danish Monarch in 1874. The constitution thus did not include notions such as 'democracy', 'nation', 'parliamentary rule' or 'government'.[45] By contrast, the constitution of Ireland vests the final say in constitutional change to the people, and civil society plays a crucial role in constitutional change, where political elite-driven and judge-made change also play a vital role.[46]

Innovations in the paths of constitutional change do not happen in a vacuum. They are attempted within a specific constitutional culture and aim to achieve major or minor changes to the pre-existing model of constitutional change. New mechanisms of change may be created, and the design of procedures matters as much as the context within which they shall operate. This entails understanding the constitutional and political culture in place and how it interacts with the change in the environment that triggered the attempted reform.

Referendum culture and direct-democratic reflexes

The new wave of referendums and the recent deliberative turn[47] in constitutional change brings forth the question whether the role of the people in constitutional change can be enhanced by the adoption of referendums as part of the amending formula. The ultimate criterion for evaluating formal amendment rules is whether they achieve the goals they set out, which is largely dependent on how well they connect with the constitutional and political culture. Enshrining a constitutional referendum may serve an expressive function with regard to the role of the people.[48]

Nonetheless, it is highly possible that such an addition could have adverse consequences, augmenting the stringency of the formula and thus the rigidity level of the constitution, or remain unused, or even open up new possibilities of elite manipulation of the amendment process by transferring the dangers linked to referendums at the level of constitutional amendment. Tierney detects three major inherent problems associated with the use of referendums: elite manipulation, the 'deliberation deficit' and the 'majoritarian danger'.[49] For the purposes of

45 Thorarensen, 'The People's Contribution to Constitutional Changes' (n. 37).
46 Contiades and Fotiadou (n. 18) 456–457.
47 R.E. Goodin, *Innovating Democracy: Democratic Theory and Practice after the Deliberative Turn* (Oxford University Press 2012).
48 R. Albert, 'The Expressive Function of Constitutional Amendment Rules' (2013) 59 *McGill Law Journal* 225.
49 S. Tierney, 'Europe is Entering the "Age of the Referendum", But There is Nothing to Fear for European Democracy if Referendums are Properly Regulated' *Scottish Constitutional Futures Forum* (3 September 2014), http://www.scottishconstitutionalfutures.org/Default.aspx?tabid=1767&articleType=ArticleView&articleId=4188, accessed 10 January 2016.

amendment formula design these problems must be placed within the framework of each particular constitutional and political culture, and also within distinct constitutional amendment models.

To facilitate making informed constitutional design choices it is crucial to apply criteria for making such choices workable. Are there specific parameters that constitutional designers should take into consideration before embarking on a direct-democracy enhancement journey? Where people already have direct-democratic reflexes, the task of incorporating a direct-democratic process as part of the constitutional amendment process is easier, or at least less risky. Direct-democratic reflexes can be defined as the automatic reaction of the people to the characteristics of a given referendum, such as its subject matter, the wording of the ballot question, the way the campaign is conducted etc. For example, it is hard to imagine the Greek referendum of 5 July 2015 to have taken place in Ireland;[50] not merely because of the existence (or the lack) of rules and procedures, but most importantly because the people are familiar with the rules of the game. A referendum question characterized by tremendous ambiguity would not convince the citizens in Ireland that they would be able to express themselves, whereas they would expect some independent committee to review it.

When a common denominator exists, comparison between referendum processes may impact their legitimacy. EU membership referendums are characteristic, putting forth the issue of lack of coherency between procedural safeguards in connection to elements of constitutional culture. National constitutional cultures in the EU are quite different from one another. Is it acceptable for referendums used to decide EU membership not to be subject to common standards of referendum practice? And how would this unification of standards be achieved, taking into consideration that some EU member states have a longstanding referendum culture, whereas in some other states no direct-democratic reflexes even exist?

It is thus important to distinguish whether the aim of constitutional design is to change the constitutional culture or, where the people are already accustomed to civic participation through the use of referendums, the goal is to incorporate this form of civic engagement in the amendment process. In the absence of a referendum culture, the introduction of new formal amendment rules has also a culture-building function. It is thus crucial to determine the exact type of change that is pursued in the existing status of citizen involvement in formal constitutional change. Different degrees of citizen involvement in constitutional amendment lie along a continuum of constitutional amendment engagement: intervening elections, participation-deliberation through new forms of discourse (social media, constitutional assemblies and mini-publics), advisory referendums, binding referendums, citizens-initiated referendums (popular initiative). Milder forms of participation, such as mandatory intervening elections between amendments,

50 On the Greek referendum see A. Fotiadou, 'The Role of the People in Constitutional Amendment in Greece: Between Narratives and Practice', in this volume.

may be enhanced through the introduction of parallel procedures establishing new forms of deliberation.

Greater changes in the type of citizen participation may be effected through a move along the continuum of citizen engagement in constitutional amendment. Still, such shifts entail the introduction of novel elements in the existing correlation of mechanisms of constitutional change, prescribed by the amendment formula and the combination of procedural and material limits it sets out. The amendment formula often attempts through these mechanisms to regulate constitutional change as a simulation of the original constitution-making moment.[51] Sometimes such attempts result in unexpected consequences, rendering the constitution more difficult to change instead of creating the envisaged bridge between constituent and constituted power. Where the constituent moment includes a referendum, the attempt to simulate the original constitutional moment and reproduce the constitution-making enthusiasm of the time may lead to the inclusion of referendums in the amendment formula.

There is a dual goal in enshrining referendums in the amendment formula, meeting the prerequisites of democratic deliberative referendums, and meeting the requirements of an efficient amendment mechanism that achieves the targeted rigidity level. The two goals are connected yet distinct. Prerequisites for holding democratic referendums may be met through good design of referendum rules and yet their addition to the amendment formula may render the amendment formula more stringent. The function of referendums depends on their detailed regulation. The type and bindingness of rules that regulate the referendum, who has the power to hold and initiate a referendum, how and by whom is the clarity the question and the availability of information guaranteed, how is the campaign conducted (including issues such as funding, time-length, purdah period, government involvement etc.), and the existing sanctions in case of violations[52] must be viewed not only as guarantees of the referendum process, but also as part of the amendment process. This adds a new conceptual lens as the function of referendum rules is viewed as a constitutional amendment mechanism.

There are many ways referendums can be incorporated into the structure of formal amendment rules, as they may become part of a single-track or a multi-track amendment procedure.[53] Referendums as constitutional amendment mechanisms impact the rigidity level of the constitution, the legitimacy of constitutional change, and ultimately the path constitutional change follows. The example of Denmark is quite characteristic. The Danish amendment formula prescribes a popular vote requiring approval of at least 40 per cent of the voting population. This requirement at first glance appears to enhance the role of the people in constitutional change. In practice, however, the 40 per cent threshold

51 Contiades and Fotiadou (n. 18) 419.
52 Tierney (n. 49).
53 R. Albert, 'The Structure of Constitutional Amendment Rules' (2014) 49 *Wake Forest Law Review* 913.

renders the mobilization of the citizens a very demanding task and the dangers of political failure too high, so the design of citizen involvement in formal constitutional amendment, instead of strengthening participation, enhances rigidity and sidetracks constitutional change toward other paths.[54]

Different constitutional design strategies are employed for the making of formal amendment rules and for the regulation of referendums. The optimal would be thus to combine these different strategies or at least harmonize them, so that the goals pursed by the amendment rules are not fettered by the referendum rules and vice versa. For example, holding a double referendum may be a good referendum practice in terms of deliberation on certain occasions; still it may be a poor design choice for an amendment formula.

Constitutional amendments are constitutional rituals, and so are referendums. As such they both have strong symbolic power; each however symbolizes distinct things. Formal amendment rules have multiple functions and strive to achieve the balance between continuity and change, whereas referendums are meant to be tools of deliberative civic engagement. At the symbolic level those aims are different but compatible. At the practical level achieving conciliation is more demanding. To ensure genuine citizen-led constitutional change, the amendment formula must integrate the procedural guarantees of referendums with the procedural and material limits of amendment.

Lack of direct-democratic reflexes, linked to absence of a referendum culture, augments the requirements for safeguarding through rules the deliberative, democratic character of constitutional referendums. Nonetheless, the more procedural rules are added in the amendment formula, the more the chances of perplexity and stringency get. By adding more stringency to the amendment formula referendum rules may produce adverse consequences, in which case what is designed as a means to give the constitution back to the people ends up adding extra rigidity to it.

Conclusion

The answer to the question who are the true drivers of constitutional change is an elusive one. Constitutional amendment mechanisms operating in different legal orders channel constitutional change through various paths, while multiple actors compete for the final say.[55] The recent turn toward the use of constitutional referendums has opened up the possibility of alleviating the tension between constituent and constituted power by empowering the constituted power holders. Can the constituted power vested in the people be truly exercised by the people?

54 Contiades and Fotiadou (n. 18) 456; H. Krunke, 'Formal and Informal Methods of Constitutional Change in Denmark' in X. Contiades (ed.), *Engineering Constitutional Change: A Comparative Perspective on Europe, Canada and the USA* (Routledge 2013) 73–92.

55 See Contiades and Fotiadou (n. 18) 422 ff.

The temptation of reading too much or too little into recent experiments in constitution-writing, such as the Icelandic crowd-sourcing and the Irish constitutional assembly, is strong. The increase of such attempts in combination with the increase in the use of referendums in established democracies suggests that, despite the risk of failure, a change in the exercise of the constituted power is taking place. If, however, people-driven constitutional change is to be enhanced, the study of formal amendment rules must be combined with the study of referendum rules.

The constitutional rigidity level becomes a referendum regulation concern, whereas elite manipulation becomes an amendment formula concern. The first steps towards deliberative constitutional change is the diagnosis of the current state of popular involvement in constitutional change, including mapping out the way the amendment formula is applied in practice and the role of the constitutional and political actors involved in its operation. Any distance between how the amendment formula was intended to operate and how it operates in reality must be detected at this point. The second step is history taking with regard to referendums in order to determine whether a referendum culture exists and to note if there is a history of good or bad referendum practice. The final step is making a list of the alternatives for enhancing popular involvement in constitutional amendment, to decide which ones fit better the existing amendment model, and rejecting options that are prone to malfunction or are more likely to remain but narratives.

Part II

Popular participation in constitutional change

Theoretical and historical aspects

2 Constitutional reform in Europe and recourse to the people

Paul Blokker

Constitutionalism in Europe is in turmoil. This is not only because of the European integration project and its constitutional claims, but also due to important changes in the form and role of constitutions in European societies (as well as globally). One could, as Francesco Palermo does, speak of an age of 'constitutional acceleration', that is, the 'intensification of recourse to (the instrument of) revision in order to update the constitution'.[1] Ginsburg and Dixon, more generally, relate the prominence of constitutional change and constitution-making in recent times to the 'third wave of democracy' that commenced in the 1970s and which occurred in southern Europe and later central and eastern Europe, but that in a way, in particular from the 1990s onwards, also affected the constitutional design of 'established' democratic states.[2] Constitutional dynamics are thus not restricted to new democracies in the making, but also involve established democratic regimes. What interests me here in particular is how the 'trend over this period has been one of increasing public participation in the constitutional design process'.[3]

In this chapter, I will look at one recent tendency in constitutional politics, that is, a (possibly increased) emphasis on a recourse to popular participation in the reforming of constitutional orders. There are now quite a lot of examples in contemporary Europe in which constitutional revision and amendment is orchestrated in such a way as to include the voice of the people. A transversal set of arguments included in these projects of constitutional revision is that they provide an explicit response to civic discontent and structural democratic deficiencies and that reforms can only be successful if citizens and/or civil society are able to participate. In recent years, examples of such projects have taken place in Iceland, Ireland, the Netherlands, Romania and, not least, the Convention on the Future of Europe. In addition, in the UK proposals are currently being made to set up

1 F. Palermo, 'La "manutenzione costituzionale": alla ricerca di una funzione' in F. Palermo (ed.), *La Manutenzione Costituzionale* (CEDAM 2007) 1–18, 15.

2 T. Ginsburg and R. Dixon (eds), *Comparative Constitutional Law* (Edward Elgar Publishing 2011) 3.

3 J. Blount, 'Participation in Constitutional Design' in T. Ginsburg and R. Dixon (eds), *Comparative Constitutional Law* (Edward Elgar Publishing 2011) 38.

a Constitutional Convention that is to include citizens, following two decades of constitutional reform that included allusions to democratizing the constitutional order.

The tendency towards a recourse to the people is curious in a number of ways. First of all, arguably the main tendency in European constitutional orders since 1945 has been a turn away from the people towards a form of 'juristocracy' in what has been called 'new constitutionalism'.[4] Second, in a related way, while the most significant constitutional changes in Europe, related to 1989, were in important respects about the re-establishment of self-government, in most if not all cases of central and eastern European constitutionalism, the emphasis has been on legalistic, rigid and entrenched constitutions in which there is an only relatively weak attention to civic democratic engagement.[5] Third, the emergence of constitutionalism beyond the state – arguably most developed in the European context – appears to involve an unbalanced emphasis on legalistic understandings of constitutionalism, which emphasizes aspects of the rule of law and a regulative dimension, but generally complicates relations with democracy and self-government. In this regard, many scholars appear to 'theorize away' the problem of democratic legitimation in post-national regimes.[6]

While democratic involvement in constitutional politics appears, then, to be an uphill struggle, at the same time it seems difficult to deny that some form of counter-tendency towards 'a popular constitutionalism' or 'counter-constitutionalism' (the term is Richard Albert's)[7] is increasingly visible. This counter-trend is related to democratic innovation and legitimacy as well as to the contestation of purely technocratic and legalistic governance, and it seems prominent in a number of constitutional reform projects in Europe. In this chapter I want to, first, discuss different degrees of sensibility in constitutional theory to forms of inclusion and civic participation in constitutional politics, concisely engaging with the dimensions of constitutional subjectivity and forms of collective autonomy. I will search for these dimensions in what I will call legal, political, popular and democratic

4 R. Hirschl, 'The New Constitutionalism and the Judicialization of Pure Politics Worldwide' (2001) 75 *Fordham Law Review* 722; A. Stone Sweet, 'Constitutions and Judicial Power' in D. Caramani (ed.), *Comparative Politics* (OUP 2008) 217–239.

5 See P. Blokker, *New Democracies in Crisis? A Comparative Constitutional Study of the Czech Republic, Hungary, Poland, Romania and Slovakia*, Series: Routledge Advances in European Politics (Routledge 2013).

6 Cf P. Dobner, 'More Law, Less Democracy? Democracy and Transnational Constitutionalism' in P. Dobner and M. Loughlin (eds), *The Twilight of Constitutionalism?* (OUP 2010) 141–160; S. Besson, 'Deliberative Demoi-Cracy in the European Union' in S. Besson (ed.), *Deliberative Democracy and Its Discontents* (Ashgate 2006) 181. See, for example, G. Teubner, *Constitutional Fragments: Societal Constitutionalism and Globalization* (OUP 2012); M. Kumm, 'The Cosmopolitan Turn in Constitutionalism: On the Relationship between Constitutionalism in and Beyond the State' in J. Dunoff and J. Trachtman (eds), *Ruling the World? Constitutionalism, International Law, and Global Governance* (Cambridge University Press 2009) 258–324.

7 R. Albert, 'Counterconstitutionalism' (2008) 31 *Dalhousie Law Journal* 1.

understandings of constitutionalism. In a second step, I will turn to a number of recent examples of citizen involvement in constitution-making in the cases of Iceland, Ireland and Romania. Finally, I will conclude that the recourse to the people is often more apparent than real and that in only a few instances does civic participation in constitutional politics live up to the requirements set by normative democratic theory.

Constitutionalism and the people: A theoretical inquiry

Legal constitutionalism

From the legal-constitutionalist perspective, the constitution is a legal document that can be largely understood as providing the preconditions for democracy. Democracy can only function as such if democratic politics abides by the constitutional limitations set for it. The constitution – and increasingly so the idea of an included set of entrenched fundamental rights – provides an independent and superior law that secures the working and outcomes of democracy. One of the key assumptions of legal constitutionalism is that it is in principle possible to reach a reasonable consensus on what such preconditions of democracy ought to be and how they should be translated into a language of rights and fundamental law.[8]

A good example of legal constitutionalism is Ronald Dworkin's substantive view of constitutional democracy. In the words of Frank Michelman, for Dworkin democracy does not mean that 'the people of a country ought to decide for themselves all of the politically decidable matters about which they have good moral and material reason to care',[9] but rather means that 'government subject to conditions – we might call these "democratic conditions" – of equal status for all citizens'.[10] From this perspective, it is in principle possible to arrive at a pre-political set of 'essential preconditions for democracy', the 'right' abstract principles,[11] 'right rights'[12] or 'best answers'[13] that all can rationally agree to and which identify what democracy is ultimately about.[14] Indeed, Ronald Dworkin's concern is with 'what democracy, accurately understood, really is'.[15] For Dworkin, constitutionalism means a 'system that establishes individual legal rights that

8 R. Bellamy, *Political Constitutionalism: A Republican Defence of the Constitutionality of Democracy* (Cambridge University Press 2007) 3.
9 F. Michelman, *Brennan and Democracy* (Princeton University Press 1999) 6.
10 R. Dworkin, *Freedom's Law: The Moral Reading of the American Constitution* (OUP 1996) 17.
11 R. Dworkin, 'Constitutionalism and Democracy' (1995) 3(1) *European Journal of Philosophy* 2.
12 Michelman (n. 9).
13 Bellamy (n. 8).
14 One of the most well-known formulations of such an idea is that of an 'overlapping consensus', J. Rawls, *Political Liberalism* (Columbia University Press 1993); cf. Bellamy (n. 8) 101–102.
15 Dworkin (n. 10) 15.

the dominant legislature does not have the power to override or compromise'.[16] In this sense, the 'constitutional conception presupposes democratic conditions. These are the conditions that must be met before majoritarian decision-making can claim any automatic moral advantage over other procedures of collective action'.[17] Since a consensus on the right norms can be presupposed in a well-designed constitutional democratic system, there is no need to change such norms in the future, only to ensure their correct implementation. In other words, it is possible to depoliticize principled, constitutional questions and take these out of the democratic political process altogether, because a rational consensus has been reached or can be presumed on those questions once a constitution is in place.

The relevant constitutional subject in Dworkin's substantive view, that is, those who are able to make their interpretation of the constitution and its principles count, is ultimately restricted to Supreme Court judges. While general debate about constitutional principles includes 'professional lawyers but also the public at large in newspapers and popular journals',[18] the 'Supreme Court has the last word'.[19] According to Dworkin, it should ultimately be higher judges who identify and interpret key constitutional principles, as they are more reliable than political majorities in terms of doing this.[20] One could interpret this as meaning that democratic politics is 'regarded not only as something apart from law, but as inferior to law. Law aims at justice, while politics only looks to expediency. The former is neutral and objective, the latter the uncontrolled child of competing interests and ideologies.'[21] According to Dworkin, '[i]n some circumstances . . . individual citizens may be able to exercise their moral responsibilities of citizenship better when final decisions are removed from ordinary politics and assigned to courts, whose decisions are meant to turn on principle, not on the weight of numbers or the balance of political influence'.[22] Thus Dworkin finds it beneficial that the 'public participates in discussion', but lays the final 'adjudicative responsibility with the judges, whose decision is final, barring a constitutional amendment, until it is changed by a later judicial decision'.[23] Citizens' expression of their views on constitutional principles is essential in this view, but since citizens (or politicians) are not able to transcend a political, particularistic understanding, judges need to guide the way to a 'clean', purely moral understanding of these principles. As Michelman puts it, 'you have to admit the practical possibility that

16 Dworkin (n. 11) 2.
17 Dworkin (n. 10) 23.
18 R. Dworkin, *Is Democracy Possible Here?: Principles for a New Political Debate* (Princeton University Press 2006) 156.
19 Ibid.
20 Bellamy (n. 8) 3.
21 J. Shklar cited in M. Goldoni, 'Two Internal Critiques of Political Constitutionalism' (2012) 10(4) *International Journal of Constitutional Law* 929.
22 Dworkin (n. 10) 30.
23 Dworkin (n. 11) 10.

an independent judiciary will tend to get closer to the truth than would the great body of the people or their elected tribunes in legislatures'.[24]

According to the substantive view, self-government does not mean that citizens should be engaging in making their own rules, including the fundamental rules, but rather means that persons are able to identify with laws made through a majoritarian process, while judicial review secures the rational preconditions for this process.[25] In other words, self-government is supposedly not about the actual authorship of the laws, including the laws of law-making,[26] but rather about the realization of and recognition by any individual citizen that formal politics maintains 'by its actions' 'due respect for [one's] own moral and intellectual singularity, and for the interest [one] accordingly take[s] in both the contents of collective outcomes and [one's] capacities to influence them'.[27] Dworkin argues that 'we must ask . . . what rights must be reserved to an individual citizen if submitting to the will of the majority of his fellow citizens in other circumstances is to be consistent with his dignity'.[28] Self-government is not the realization that a citizen can directly participate in majority rule. It is rather, as Michelman understands it, a 'feeling of satisfaction or even pride that you take in lawmaking that is done by an organization that treats you and your independence and your interests with the kind of respect that is due to a member'.[29] Thus, on Dworkin's 'partnership view', 'constitutional rights protecting an individual's freedom to make ethical choices for himself are not compromises of democracy but rather attempts to guarantee it'.[30]

The emerging view of the constitution is that it is a relatively static, permanent framework, which is only to a very limited extent open to political and civic influence, in the form of amendment, revision or otherwise. The legal-constitutionalist view in essence understands the constitution as a 'meta-norm', which is not implicated in, as it transcends, substantive views on the common good, and provides a 'neutral framework that rests on a separation of the right from the good'.[31]

Political constitutionalism

The most visible contender for a legalistic theory of constitutionalism, which as we have seen endorses *inter alia* judicial supremacy and the strong entrenchment

24 Michelman (n. 9) 19, 23.
25 Ibid. 31.
26 Ibid. 24–25.
27 Ibid. 30–31.
28 Dworkin (n. 18) 146.
29 Michelman (n. 9) 32; cf. J. Waldron, 'The Core of the Case Against Judicial Review' (2006) 115 *Yale Law Journal* 1345.
30 Dworkin (n. 18) 146.
31 R. Bellamy and D. Castiglione, 'Democracy, Sovereignty and the Constitution of the European Union: The Republican Alternative to Liberalism' in Z. Bankowski and A. Scott (eds), *The European Union and Its Order* (Wiley-Blackwell 2000) 174–175.

of rights, is the theory of political constitutionalism.[32] The political-constitutionalist conception takes a wholly different view of the role and substance of the constitution and its relation to democratic politics. Its dispute with legal constitutionalism starts from the observation that the

> need for [an] alternative and more political approach arises from the *contested* nature of rights. Despite widespread support for both constitutional rights and rights-based judicial review, theorists, politics, lawyers and ordinary citizens frequently disagree over which rights merit or require such entrenchment, the legal form they should take, the best way of implementing them, their relationship to each other, and the manner in which courts should understand and uphold them.[33]

Rather than understanding the constitution as a 'right basic norm', political constitutionalists understand the constitution as providing a basic framework for resolving disagreements over the right and the good. This also means that foundational norms should always be subject to reconsideration and reformulation. In other words, the constitution is not seen as in need of an entrenched set of fundamental principles, but rather as the framework for the articulation of and deliberation over conceptions of self-government and the common good. As Bellamy aptly expresses it: '[W]e could see constitutions not as constraints imposed upon democracy but as the limits that a mature democracy places upon itself.'[34] The relation between democracy and constitutionalism in political constitutionalism is not based on the need for 'pre-commitments' or extra-political guarantees and the idea of superior judgmental capacity (of judicial experts). Rather, the emphasis is on the idea of political equality and a thrust towards the inclusion of a wide range of people's judgments.[35] Political constitutionalism starts from the idea that reasonable disagreement is an integral part of democracy. The critique of legal constitutionalism is that a 'failure to acknowledge the disagreements that surround constitutional values, and the resulting need for political mechanisms to resolve them, can itself be a source of domination and arbitrary rule that impacts negatively on rights and the rule of law'.[36]

The political view of the constitution opens a door to the influence of politics on the law in that it emphasizes the negotiation of differences and a continuous quest for mutually agreeable conditions. Political constitutionalism does not attempt to sever democratic politics from questions of justice and right, but, in full acknowledgement of the impossibility of settling constitutional questions and

32 See, most prominently, J. Waldron, *Law and Disagreement* (Clarendon Press, OUP 1999); Bellamy (n. 8).

33 Bellamy (n. 8) 16; emphasis added.

34 Ibid. 91; emphasis added.

35 See M. Goldoni, 'Two Internal Critiques of Political Constitutionalism' (2012) 10(4) *International Journal of Constitutional Law* 926.

36 Bellamy (n. 8) 145; cf. Waldron (n. 32).

rights issues once and for all, it makes the relation between politics, and rights and legality visible by means of a continuous political engagement with acceptable interpretations. In this respect, however, political constitutionalism risks being less inclusive and participatory than it claims to be on the basis of its full recognition of pluralism. As Marco Goldoni has rightly pointed out, the view of constitutional subjectivity or agency in political constitutionalism is reduced to the parliament.[37] Political constitutionalists hold that it is the legislature that is ultimately best able to represent (always anew) the irreducible diversity of viewpoints in society. Indeed, 'so long as a system of equal votes, majority rule and party competition – however interpreted – offers a plausible system for giving citizens an equal say in the ways collective arrangements are organized – including those of the democratic process – then a self-constituting democratic constitution that avoids dominating through arbitrary rule will have been secured'.[38] Existing, representative arrangements are thus also preferred as means of constitution-making, while extra-institutional actors and politics are looked at with a certain scepticism: constitutions are structuring, enabling devices in that 'it is a matter of what a constitution affirmatively makes possible out of what would otherwise be the loose and lurching and dangerous politics of the streets'.[39]

The main criticism of political constitutionalism is of its insistence on norm entrenchment and judicial review in legal constitutionalism. The argument is – rightly, from a democratic viewpoint – that constitutional arrangements should not be imposed on a democratic society, but should rather be the result of reflections of '*the people whose society is to be governed by these arrangements*'.[40] Constitutions institutionalize 'legislatures, large institutions, manned (peopled) in a certain way and invested with public authority so that they can act credibly in the name of us all'.[41] The way in which self-government is perceived is, however, not entirely unrelated to Dworkin's view in that it is not so much the actual possibility of civic engagement in actual (constitutional) politics that is stressed, but rather the realization that representative institutions offer the best arrangements for the preservation of individual dignity (in the case of Dworkin) or respect for different viewpoints (Waldron).

The political-constitutional approach takes a more flexible view of the constitution than the legal-constitutional one, but at the same time understands the primary constitutional subject largely as the parliament, as the most adequate forum for debate on and decision-making regarding foundational rules and principles.

37 M. Goldoni, 'Political Constitutionalism and the Value of Constitution Making' (2014) 27(3) *Ratio Juris* 387.
38 Bellamy (n. 8) 220–221.
39 J. Waldron, 'Constitutionalism – A Skeptical View' in Th. Christiano and J. Christman (eds), *Contemporary Debates in Political Philosophy* (Blackwell 2009) 267.
40 Ibid. 11; emphasis in original.
41 Ibid. 20.

Popular constitutionalism

A set of constitutional theories that endorses more extensive popular engagement with constitutional politics than is provided either by legal or by political constitutionalism is that of popular constitutionalism. A very influential theory in this branch is Bruce Ackerman's idea of dualistic democracy. In Ackerman's reading of American constitutional history, politics can be understood in a dual sense, that is, as consisting of normal politics (normality) and constitutional politics (exceptional circumstances). In periods of normal politics, it is political officials who engage in politics, constrained by the 'constitutional forms imposed during rare periods of constitutional creativity', while ordinary citizens do not or hardly engage in political matters. It is in periods of exceptional constitutional politics that 'mobilizational forms of mass engagement . . . dominate the constitutional stage'.[42]

In popular constitutionalism, the constitutional role of citizens is not reduced to the receiving end, as in legal constitutionalism, nor to a purely indirect role through parliamentary prerogatives, as in political constitutionalism. Rather, citizens' initiatives are relevant for changing the existing constitutional architecture, even if only rarely so, that is, 'under well-defined historical situations'.[43] In Ackerman's view, the citizens' role is not always available but occurs in specific 'constitutional moments' in which a 'heightened constitutional consciousness' informs a high level of civic mobilization in favour of constitutional change.[44] Such moments often involve some sort of crisis: '[t]he events catalyzing a dramatic rise of political consciousness have been as various as the country's history – war, economic catastrophe, or urgent appeals to the national conscience'.[45] The role of citizens comes through in such moments in which normal politics gives way to higher law-making, but such moments can only be successful if a civic 'movement earns the constitutional authority to claim that, in contrast to countless ideological fractions competing in normal politics, its reform agenda should be placed at the center of public scrutiny'.[46]

In Ackerman's dualistic approach, the role of the citizen is, however, largely confined to one of support and mobilization. Ackerman's discussion of the constitutional convention refers to an illegal vehicle in which 'informal and unauthorized propositions' emerge, but which is ultimately grounded in a popularly elected convention which is made up of revolutionary elites.[47] The public has a supportive rather than a proactive function in this constitutional theory. In

42 B. Ackerman, *We the People* (Belknap Press of Harvard University Press 1991) 171.

43 Ibid.

44 B. Ackerman, 'Neofederalism?' in J. Elster and R. Slagstad (eds), *Constitutionalism and Democracy* (Cambridge University Press 1988) 153–194.

45 B. Ackerman, 'Higher Lawmaking' in S. Levinson (ed.), *Responding to Imperfection: The Theory and Practice of Constitutional Amendment* (Princeton University Press 1995) 66.

46 Ackerman (n. 42) 266.

47 Ibid. 174.

relation to his 'neo-Federalism', Ackerman suggests the working of a 'life cycle of a successful movement in constitutional politics' that begins with 'sufficiently deep and broad support among the private citizenry', but then moves on to the proposal stage (which brings in the established political parties or the president), mobilized popular deliberation (in the appropriate political institutions) and legal codification (with an upfront role for the Supreme Court).[48] Ackerman's idea of a two-track system includes a higher law-making track that 'imposes specially rigorous tests upon the political movements that hope to earn the heightened sense of democratic legitimacy awarded to spokespersons for the People'.[49] In other words, much of the civic input is reduced to – during an early phase – support for an initiative, while in later stages the constitutional project, driven by 'revolutionary elites', becomes entirely dependent on 'institutional trial' or 'testing'.[50] As Ackerman claims:

> Only after the innovators carried their initiative repeatedly in deliberative assemblies and popular elections has our Constitution finally awarded them the solemn authority to revise the foundations of the polity in the name of We the People.[51]

And elsewhere Ackerman states that 'it is no easy thing for a transformative political movement to maintain control over the presidency, Congress and the Court for a decade or two to elaborate and consolidate a fundamental change of our constitutional principles'.[52] No separate democratic procedures or channels for citizen participation are suggested (such as a civic initiative for amendment or a deliberative forum of a civic-constitutional assembly).[53] Civic involvement seems mostly to be subjected to the endorsement of a cause by revolutionary elites as well as the goodwill of formal political and institutional representatives that leads them to take up such a cause. Indeed, 'parties have played a strategic role in almost all important exercises in constitutional politics',[54] while constitutional politics also 'very heavily relies on the good judgment of courts' (284). As Sanford Levinson puts it, 'Ackerman's principal interest is in decision-making by political leaders (and, necessarily, elites) who make decisions in the name of the

48 Ibid. 266–267.
49 Ackerman (n. 45) 65.
50 Ackerman (n. 42) 267; (n. 45) 65.
51 Ackerman (n. 45) 64.
52 B. Ackerman, 'De-Schooling Constitutional Law' (2014) 123(8) *Yale Law Journal* 3104.
53 Ackerman does admit to the contemporary importance of rethinking American constitutional revision practice in the light of instruments of direct democracy, not least the referendum (see Ackerman [n 45] 356–357, fn 12). Recently, Sanford Levinson has, however, pointed to Ackerman's 'faith in a fundamentally anti-democratic constitution' while at the same time he pays little attention to state constitutions that often allow for referendums and popular initiatives (S. Levinson, 'Popular Sovereignty and the United States Constitution: Tensions in the Ackermanian Program' (2014) 123(8) *Yale Law Journal* 2644).
54 Ackerman (n. 42) 282.

People rather than in such decision-making by the People themselves.'[55] Indeed, the '"popular sovereigns" may be like a Greek chorus or Shakespearean groundlings, but the focus is on the actions of the kings and their courts'.[56]

What emerges from this brief discussion of popular constitutionalism is a view in which the People matter, but at the same time they perform a largely supportive role for elites who identify the People's voice in 'revolutionary' projects of constitutional revision. While Ackerman importantly distinguishes between government and the people, the constitutional theory mostly describes the importance of popular support for constitutional revision projects, without which such projects would appear as privatistic assaults on the constitution.[57]

Democratic constitutionalism

In a final theoretical interpretation of constitutionalism I wish to discuss, a critical, radical democratic or agonistic dimension is at the forefront. The argument in 'democratic constitutionalism' is that contemporary or modern constitutionalism is deficient in terms of its democratic nature. On Joel Colon-Rios's view, democratic constitutionalism 'rests on the idea that ordinary citizens should be allowed, to the extent to which it is practically possible, to propose, deliberate, and decide on important constitutional transformations through the most participatory methods possible'.[58] The thrust of democratic constitutionalism is against a one-sided understanding of constitutional democracy in which constitutional order and stability take priority over the possibility of the ruled interfering in the setting of the rules. The main problems in contemporary constitutionalism involve its depoliticizing/juridifying tendencies. Whereas the critique of political constitutionalism, and to some extent that of popular constitutionalism, tends to remain confined to a 'test of reality' of the existing constitutional order, largely reproducing its ontology, democratic constitutionalism's critique addresses the foundations of the existing constitutional paradigm.

Democratic constitutionalism understands modern constitutional orders as having significant problems with democratic legitimacy, in that a constitutional meta-dimension overshadows a democratic meta-dimension. A democratic-constitutional approach attempts to critically analyse unbalanced constitutional forms and orders as well as indicating ways of rebalancing them. What is significant is that democratic constitutionalism points to practices beyond existing institutions and sees as relevant a 'multiplicity of sites' where citizens can

55 Levinson (n. 53) 4.

56 Ibid. 9.

57 J. Colon-Rios 'The Second Dimension of Democracy: The People and Their Constitution' (2009) 2(2) *Baltic Journal of Law & Politics* 17.

58 J. Colon-Rios, 'The Three Waves of the Constitutionalism-Democracy Debate in the United States: (And an Invitation to Return to the First)' (2011) 1(4) *Victoria University of Wellington Legal Research Paper* 23.

engage in democratic practice.[59] Democratic constitutionalists question the legal-constitutionalist understanding of constitutional law as 'impermeable to the passions of mass politics', that is, it can only be 'changed and interpreted by those occupying positions of power'.[60] They argue that such a restricted view of the relation between the citizenry and the constituent power 'can only be compatible with an extremely limited conception of democracy'.[61] The suggestion is that 'ordinary citizens'' lack of opportunities to recreate 'their' fundamental laws and to engage in acts of democratic reconstitution brings into question the democratic legitimacy of the constitutional regimes under which they live.[62] There is a strong call in democratic constitutionalism in favour of the inclusion of citizens among the constitutional subjects so that they can 'propose, deliberate and decide upon important constitutional transformations through extraordinary mechanisms that work independently of a constitution's ordinary amendment procedure'.[63]

A radical democratic view of constitutional democracy claims that democracy should entail a more direct and substantive participation of citizens in the democratic process, including constitutional politics. Democratic or civic constitutionalism shares with political constitutionalism an emphasis on the open-endedness of the democratic process and the ultimately open-ended nature of rights. But for civic constitutionalism this means that the nature of the constitution itself is understood in a radically different way from modern constitutionalism's foundationalism. That is, whereas modern constitutionalism understands 'constitution making as an "act of completion", the constitution as a final settlement or social contract in which basic political definitions, principles, and processes are agreed, as is a commitment to abide by them', civic constitutionalism entails a 'conversation, conducted by all concerned, open to new entrants and new issues, seeking a workable formula that will be sustainable rather than assuredly stable'.[64] While the foundational nature of modern constitutionalism is not dissolved completely, the idea of a 'final act of closure' is replaced by one of flexibility and a 'permanently open process'.[65] This derives from an unwillingness to tie down democracy to choices made by previous generations and the recognition of the continuously changing nature of society and identity, as well as the realization that it is ultimately impossible to ground foundational principles once and for all.

59 J. Tully, *Public Philosophy in a New Key* (Cambridge University Press 2008) 98.

60 J. Colon-Rios, *Weak Constitutionalism: Democratic Legitimacy and the Question of Constituent Power* (Routledge 2013) 200–208.

61 Ibid. 208–815.

62 Ibid. 223–230.

63 Ibid. 223–237.

64 V. Hart, 'Democratic Constitution Making', Special Report (United States Institution of Peace, July 2003), 2–3, http://www.usip.org, accessed 15 June 2015; cf. S. Chambers, 'Contract or Conversation? Theoretical Lessons from the Canadian Constitutional Crisis' (1998) 26 *Politics and Society* 143.

65 Hart (n. 64) 3.

Civic constitutionalism departs significantly from political or republican constitutionalism in that it judges representative constitutional politics as insufficient. Indeed, according to the latter, the 'democratic arrangements found in the world's established working democracies are sufficient to satisfy the requirements of republican non-domination'.[66] Instead, civic constitutionalism endorses a more open democratic settlement which aims at the 'extension of democratic process to include, free, open, and responsive discussion of the constitutional settlement'. This provides the framework under which 'diverse and disagreeing groups can live, while continuing to engage in a freely accessible debate about that settlement itself'.[67]

In democratic or civic constitutionalism, democratic politics is understood in its radical sense as the 'rule of people extended to all matters . . . including the creation and recreation of the fundamental laws'.[68] Here, the democratic dimension of constitutional democratic legitimation clearly has priority, even if the constitutional ordering type of legitimacy is not abandoned. To this effect, civic constitutionalism is potentially open to a wide range of pluralistic influences.

Examples of conventions

I will now turn to a number of cases of involvement of citizens in projects of constitutional change and constitution-making in Europe. Three cases – those of Iceland, Ireland and Romania – indicate important shifts away from a rigid, legalistic view of constitutionalism, with its insistence on expert-based or elite-based constitutional politics, and in some cases also from political constitutionalism, with its emphasis on the pre-eminent role of parliament in constitutional politics. The cases relate to forms of constitutional reform in which both legality and legitimacy are continuous, and which have an emphasis on established rules of revision (even if these are sometimes abandoned in practice), in contrast to more radical, rupturing forms of change in cases of, for instance, transitions from authoritarian to democratic systems.[69] All three cases include some forms of more incisive civic engagement, as imagined in popular or, more directly, in democratic constitutionalism. These cases might serve as important empirical 'testing' of the theories explored above.

Iceland

The Icelandic case is unique in that it is the only instance of a 'consolidated' modern democracy in which a full-blown constitution-making process was (co-)

66 Bellamy (n. 8) 260.
67 Hart (n. 64) 5, 3.
68 Colon-Rios (n. 57) 23.
69 See A. Arato, 'Conventions, Constituent Assemblies, and Round Tables: Models, Principles and Elements of Democratic Constitution-Making' (2012) 1(1) *Global Constitutionalism* 173.

initiated and executed by (formally) ordinary citizens. In this regard, Icelandic constitutional politics comes closest – even if not in all respects, as we will see below – to the democratic-constitutional idea. The mobilization of the citizens in the wake of the severe economic crisis that resulted from a financial collapse at the end of 2008 could be understood in Ackermanian terms as having led to 'universal alarm'. The economic crisis led to a 'heightened constitutional consciousness' of the citizenry, which, through widespread protest, made a variety of claims, including radical constitutional change. In Iceland, the constitutional subjects, or rather protagonists, were clearly the people in some form: a multitude gathered in frequent protest actions, in particular in Reykjavik's main square in front of the Icelandic parliament, Althingi; civic associations that promoted radical constitutional change, such as the Democratic Movement and the Citizens' Movement, which emerged in the midst of the crisis; and individual political entrepreneurs such as Hordur Torfason, a musician who sang protest songs outside parliament on a daily basis from 2008 onwards.[70] Baldvin Bergsson has observed that a veritable 'social movement' emerged from the protests against the implications of the financial crisis in 2008–9, even if the initiatives to effect constitutional change were coming from distinct individuals and civic associations, such as the Constitutional Society.[71] The call for change was not merely one of 'constitutional engineering' or 'maintenance' but included invocations of radical change in the form of an entirely novel constitution.[72] For instance, in 2009 the Citizens' Movement argued as follows:

> We must make radical democratic reform to ensure that the events of the last months [the economic and political crises, pb] will not repeat themselves . . . We must build from the bottom up. To ensure this is possible we need to instigate a constitutional [assembly]. A constitutional [assembly], if done correctly, would initiate a discourse on what kind of society we want, what values we wish to uphold and how we want to distribute power to those that seek to represent us in government. Post collapse, the build up and investigation needs to be put on a certain path – we believe a *constitutional [assembly]* is that path.
>
> (Citizens' Movement 2009; emphasis added).

70 cf. R. Bater, 'Hope from Below: Composing the Commons in Iceland' (2011) *Open Democracy*, https://www.opendemocracy.net/richard-bater/hope-from-below-composing-commons-in-iceland, accessed 2 December 2011.

71 B. Bergsson, 'The lessons of the Icelandic attempt to constitutional revision' (Conference paper, 'Constitutional Challenges within the EU and Beyond', Central European University, Budapest, 14 March 2014).

72 This needs to be seen not only in the light of calls for a moral regeneration of Icelandic society in the context of the financial crisis, but also in the context of the 1944 constitution that had never been significantly changed and is very similar to the 1874 Icelandic constitution. The latter was a copy of the Danish constitution and reflected Iceland's suzerain status with regard to the Danish Crown. In other words, the 1944 constitution can only with great difficulty be regarded as an expression of collective Icelandic autonomy.

But citizens and social movements were not only the initiators of critique and change. Citizens played a constitutive part throughout the attempt at constitution-making that was set up in the wake of the protests. It should be noted here that according to some observers, calls for constitutional change had emerged at various times in recent decades, and therefore some fertile political ground for radical constitutional change might be said to have been available when the financial crisis erupted at the end of 2008. When the government collapsed as a result of the crisis, Jóhanna Sigurðardóttir became the new prime minister; she had been endorsing constitutional change on various occasions since at least 1994. Both societal and political calls for constitutional change came together in the idea of setting up a Constitutional Council, to be made up of 25 elected citizens and to have a drafting mandate; political actors were to be explicitly excluded.[73]

The citizen-based Constitutional Council was elected in November 2010, although these elections were not unproblematic. The elections for the Council were nullified by the Supreme Court in January 2011, because of supposed procedural inconsistencies, but the Council was subsequently appointed by Althingi. The Council worked on a new draft constitution for four months in 2011, and delivered a draft by July of that year. The drafting process itself was, unusually, open to civic input and comment, not least by means of the use of new media (a website, Facebook, Twitter), and the Council does indeed appear to have taken into account individual comments by citizens in its deliberations. From the delivery of the draft onwards, however, the process of constitution-making changed rather radically, in that it was now Althingi that was supposed to deliberate on the draft and decide on its future. Althingi had been very slow in actually engaging with the citizens' draft (between 2011 and 2013 very little deliberation took place), and one reason for this might have been a certain level of alienation between the political forces and the 'bottom-up' citizen-driven project of constitutional change. The citizens were consulted one more time, in a referendum in October 2012 that contained six questions on the constitutional draft and that resulted in a relatively positive result for the project, but the citizens' draft was ultimately left mostly undiscussed until the elections of April 2013 saw the electoral victory of largely hostile political parties, the conservative Independent and Progressive parties. Even if the civic-constitutional project has not resulted in tangible, comprehensive changes, currently (summer 2015), the governing political parties are suggesting a new referendum on constitutional changes on some of the most significant issues,[74] indicating that some constitutional reform is hard to avoid in the wake of the project of constitutional renewal.

73 Citizen deliberation was also part of a Constitutional Gathering, a so-called deliberation day involving some 1,000 randomly selected citizens, held in November 2010.

74 B. Bergsson, 'Constitutional changes as a political tool: Lessons from Iceland' (Conference paper, 'The Renovation of the Modern Constitution: Contemporary Constitutional Transformations in Europe', University of Trento, Italy, 25 May 2015).

One international expert report on the Icelandic constitutional text identified 'significant input from the public' and judged its civic dimension as being 'at the cutting-edge of ensuring public participation in ongoing governance'.[75] The constitutional drafting was evaluated as 'tremendously innovative and participatory', and the final result 'as one of the most inclusive in history and well-above the mean of contemporary constitutions'. All this indicates a significant democratic-constitutional dimension in the Icelandic experiment. At the same time, if we consider Ackerman's observations, it might be true that, since the civic draft has not survived the test of the political institutions, the verification of the voice of the People shows that it has not, in fact, spoken on this occasion.

Ireland

The Icelandic case indicates important affinities with the theory of democratic constitutionalism, and might, to some extent, have influenced the constitutional revision process that emerged in Ireland in roughly the same period. The Irish Constitutional Convention that operated from December 2012 until February 2014 was about a partial revision of the Irish constitution and was not purely citizen-driven, but the process did contain significant innovations regarding citizen participation in constitutional revision.

The setting up of a Constitutional Convention in Ireland in December 2012 probably found its origins in the Oireachtas (national parliament) Joint Committee of the Constitution in late 2009/early 2010. The parliamentary committee proposed the establishment of a Citizens' Assembly along the lines of the British Colombia Citizens' Assembly as well as the Dutch Burgerforum of 2006.[76] The Assembly was understood as enabling electoral reform on a 'non-partisan basis', while the establishment of such an 'Assembly would facilitate ***greater popular engagement with the democratic institutions*** as well as enhancing the ***legitimacy*** of any proposed reform'.[77] This idea of an assembly or Constitutional Convention was equally endorsed by oppositional political parties and explicitly justified through references to citizen involvement. The centrist party Fine Gael, one of the political promoters of constitutional change in the wake of the economic meltdown, argued in its manifesto 'New Politics' that 'Ireland's broken political system is at the heart of its economic collapse' and that '[i]n any Republic the people are supposed to be supreme' but 'Ireland today is a Republic in name

75 Z. Elkins, T. Ginsburg and J. Melton, 'A Review of Iceland's Draft Constitution' *The Comparative Constitutions Project* (14 October 2012), 11, www.comparativeconstitutionsproject.org/reports-and-other-publications/, accessed 15 June 2015.

76 D. Farrell, 'The 2013 Irish Constitutional Convention: A Bold Step or a Damp Squib?' (2013), on file with author.

77 Oireachtas Join Committee on the Constitution, 'Fourth Report: Article 16 of the Constitution', Review of the Electoral System for the Election of member to Dáil Éireann (2010) p. 15, available at <http://www.oireachtas.ie/documents/committees30thdail/j-constitution/report_2008/20100722.pdf>, accessed 16 June 2015.

only'.[78] The manifesto argued for the involvement of citizens in radical change and that a 'Citizens Forum' was to 'accept submissions from all groups and members of the public on possible changes to the institutional articles of the constitution, and encourage as wide ranging a public debate as possible on these changes'.[79] Similar observations were made in a statement of the Labour Party:

> It is time for a fundamental review of our constitution. It is essential that the people be involved in the process. Labour proposes a constitutional convention, a coming together of all strands of Irish society to redraw our Constitution. The constitutional convention would include experts and specialists, but would *also include individual citizens, randomly chosen* to serve in much the same way that we choose juries.[80]

The Constitutional Convention that was set up did involve citizens in new and innovative ways. Of particular interest is how citizens were selected and how the constitutional revision process was set up.[81] The 66 citizens who were selected to participate in the Convention were selected randomly, with the help of a survey company which selected citizens on the basis of age, gender, the region they lived in, education and socio-economic status.[82] The other members of the Convention were 33 elected politicians, selected by various political parties. Experts – mostly political scientists – were also involved as mediators and advisors. The Convention process consisted of deliberative meetings roughly every month from January 2013, which would last for a weekend, with the members of the Convention voting on final recommendations. The mode of operation of the meetings was deliberative and was based on debates between politicians and citizen members held around circular tables. In some ways following the spirit of the Philadelphia Convention, the Irish Convention went beyond its explicit mandate and adopted 38 recommendations for reform, including proposals for the reform of the lower house (Dáil) and the introduction of citizen initiatives.

Initially, the Irish Convention was met with social and political indifference and critique, including regarding its merely consultative nature. But there are indications that the process has been understood more positively over time. Upon its completion in early 2014, the Convention generally received much more positive

78 Fine Gael, *Manifesto* (2011) 3, available at <http://michaelpidgeon.com/manifestos/docs/fg/Fine%20Gael%20GE%202011.pdf> accessed 15 June 2015.

79 Ibid. 4.

80 Labour, *New Government, Better Government: Changing a Broken System* (Labour 2011), http://www.labour.ie/policy/listing/12943264241775893.html, accessed 15 June 2015; emphasis added.

81 cf. D. Farrell et al., 'The Irish Constitutional Convention of 2013–14' (Conference paper, 'Constitutional Challenges within the EU and Beyond', Central European University, Budapest, 14 March 2014), on file with author.

82 Ibid. 3.

reviews.[83] In terms of the Convention's citizen involvement and deliberative nature, it corresponds to some of the thrust of democratic constitutionalism and an emphasis on the need for complementary, direct democratic instruments in modern democracies in crisis. While its purely consultative nature deradicalized the Irish experiment from a democratic-constitutional point of view, the process did result in some real impacts. In 2014, four referendums were promised on the basis of the Convention. On 22 May 2015, a first referendum was held on two issues, same-sex marriage and the reduction in the age at which a person could be eligible to run for president. The first issue, same-sex marriage, was approved by a large majority of the voters (62 per cent), whereas the second was rejected (by 73 per cent).

In contrast to the Icelandic experience, the Irish experience seems to have been a largely top-down, elite-driven experiment, remaining an exercise that was granted from above rather than initiated from below. But while it is ultimately the political institutions that execute the 'test' of the popular voice, in that the government had the final say over reforms,[84] in the Irish context this seems to have meant that it is a voice that cannot be (fully) ignored.

Romania

The Romanian case of citizen involvement involves a not insignificant attempt at wider public involvement in constitutional debate and politics, but also an unclear and very limited impact of such involvement on constitutional reform. A recent attempt at constitutional reform, starting in 2013, was not the direct result of a wider societal call for change, but rather the reaction to continuous political infighting between institutions. In this respect, the Romanian case of constitutional politics can be taken as being closer to a political-constitutional approach, but with an important twist. The recent Romanian attempts at reform follow less a pluralistic, parliamentary approach and more a majoritarian, governmentally driven process.

In the wake of a major constitutional conflict between President Băsescu and the incumbent government of Victor Ponta in the summer of 2012, the Social Liberal Union (USL) of Victor Ponta won a large majority in the December 2012 elections. This supermajority made the prospective of significant constitutional revision possible, as the Romanian amendment rule stipulates that amendments need to be approved by two-third majorities in both Houses of Parliament (Art. 151(1)). One of the main objectives of the project of constitutional reform – which started in February 2013 – stemmed from the insight that the intrinsic power struggle in the Romanian democratic system was related in particular to the cohabitation between the president and the prime minister, and in distinct ways

83 S. Suteu, 'Constitutional Conventions in the Digital Era: Lessons from Iceland and Ireland' (2015) 38 *Boston College International & Comparative Law Review* 267.

84 cf. Ibid. 268.

was facilitated by the constitution's vagueness over presidential prerogatives;[85] this power struggle is unlikely to subside. In its 2013–16 programme, the Ponta government has stated that:

> The aim of constitutional revision consists in *(re)gaining the trust of citizens* in state institutions through guaranteeing a predictable and stable conduct of institutionalized power. The stake of this step consists in strengthening Romanian democracy. The fundamental law would need to clarify the responsibilities and relations between the main public authorities and, very importantly, to achieve the integrative function. [The] Constitution and its values should become the binding element uniting the Romanian citizens with the state. The electoral legislation cannot be absent from the process of rethinking the institutional architecture. The harmonization of the legislative acts in the field and their integration in the Electoral Code, expression of a consensual approach at the level of political class and the consultation with the civil society is one of the major objectives of the Government.[86]

Ponta argued that the main objective was to build 'constitutional peace'. His articulation of the formal objective was that '[i]t is the obligation of enlightened minds and sensible people to build a long-lasting peace, that is to find those mechanisms that make sure that in a period hopefully as long as possible we will no longer have conflicts among the state powers, political, constitutional conflicts likely to disrupt the smooth running of the society'.[87]

Constitutional reform was thus primarily driven by internal political concerns and initiated by part of the political establishment. The substance of much of the reform entailed fairly modest modifications of the constitutional order, but the *process* of revision appeared to point to a promising and innovative – civic-constitutional – way of enhancing a democratic-constitutional culture in Romania. Ample space was given to public debate and pro-democracy movements, based on an earlier experience with a so-called Forum Constitutional in 2002. The two forums involved relatively wide public debate on constitutional reform, organized with the Chamber of Deputies. Public debates were held in various cities throughout Romania, and the forums provided the opportunity to submit proposals for constitutional revision on the Forum's website and to discuss publicly constitutional issues on an online forum. The final outcome consisted of a report, edited by the president of the Forum and presented to the parliamentary commission.

85 E.S. Tănăşescu, 'The President of Romania, Or: The Slippery Slope of a Political System' (2008) 4 *European Constitutional Law Review* 64.

86 Adapted from http://www.gov.ro/programme-for-government-2013–2016__l2a105576.html, accessed 15 June 2015; emphasis added.

87 See http://www.agerpres.ro/english/index.php/english-news/item/194055-PM-Ponta-Building-longterm-constitutional-peace-is-our-obligation.html, accessed 15 June 2015.

One of the main forces behind the Forum Constitutional was a pro-democracy movement – Asociaţia Pro Democraţia (APD). In the past, the APD has consistently contributed an idea of 'grass roots' constitutional politics by, on various occasions, making claims that were intended to lead to a more participatory understanding of constitutional democracy and attempting to raise civic awareness of constitutional matters.[88] In the wake of an earlier presidential and constitutional crisis in 2007, the APD had started a public discussion on constitutional reform by means of various public debates in different Romanian cities. The self-professed aim of the APD was to increase the awareness of citizens concerning the issue of constitutional reform, not least with regard to the choice citizens need to make in the constitutionally arranged-for referendum in case of amendment:

> Since the future reform will influence the consolidation of Romanian democracy for a prolonged period of time, it is necessary that the possible implications of the modifications are understood by the largest possible number of citizens. In contrast to the revision of 2003, which was made under pressure of an external imperative, the debate on a future change of the Constitution needs to take into account both the relations between institutions as well as relations between the state and society, and relations between various groups in society. At the same time, given the fact that every change of the Constitution is to be adopted by referendum, it is necessary to hold a public debate on the Constitutional revision to inform citizens on the issues they will vote on. What is more, the future modification of the Constitution offers a chance to hold an open debate which will help to enrich the political culture of the Romanian citizens, an essential aspect of the consolidation of democracy.[89]

The APD had been one of the driving forces of the organization of both a 2002 and a 2013 Forum Constitutional, which was an 'institutionalised structure of dialogue with civil society regarding the revision of the constitution'.[90] In 2002, as in 2013, the intention was to provide a deliberative public forum to run in parallel with the official Romanian Commission for the Revision of the Constitution.

But while the Constitutional Forum as a civic, inclusive precursor to the parliamentary revision process appeared, procedurally speaking, promising, in retrospect it seems to have been largely inconsequential. Even though the president of the Constitutional Forum, Cristian Pîrvulescu, argued in the wake of the Forum that it would not have been advisable for the bicameral Commission for the

88 G. Andreescu, 'Înstrăinarea de valorile civice prin abuzul drepturilor constituţionale de marjă' in G. Andreescu, M. Bakk, L. Bojin and V. Constantin (eds), *Comentarii la Constituţia României* (Polirom 2011) 33.

89 Asociaţia Pro Democraţia (APD) 'Reforma constitutionala in Romania – Aspecte teoretice şi istorice legate de evoluţia constituţiilor' (2008) 6, http://www.apd.ro/publicatie.php?id=56, accessed 15 June 2015.

90 Forum Constitutional, 'Forumul Constituţional'. Raport final (2002) 11, http:// www.forumconstitutional.ro/raport_final.pdf, accessed 15 June 2015.

Revision of the Constitution to disregard the recommendations of the Forum,[91] the Commission has been criticized for doing exactly that. Nine NGOs accused the Commission for the Revision of the Constitution of a lack of transparency and of being unclear about whether civic propositions were taken into account or not. The organizations asked the Commission to offer clear arguments for the rejection of specific proposals and to engage in debate for a reasonable amount of time.[92] The parliamentary revision process itself was also criticized. Bogdan Dima, who was involved in a civic initiative called the Commission for a New Constitution, expressed strong doubts about what he called the 'anti-revision' of the constitution, which he thought consisted of an 'exclusively political game, generated by personal political relations of some of the key leaders of the last years'.[93] Finally, a constitutional expert, Ioan Stanomir, regarded the current revision process as 'lacking in vision and characterized by amateurism'.[94]

After the initial period of public debate, which included the Constitutional Forum as well as two meetings with the Council of Europe's Venice Commission, the Ponta government produced a draft constitutional revision internally in late 2013, which was submitted to the Constitutional Court[95] and the Venice Commission in February 2014. The Constitutional Court raised several issues of constitutionality in its review of the amendment proposal, finding problems of unconstitutionality with the proposed changes to 26 articles of the 2003 constitution.[96] And according to the Venice Commission, it was regrettable that 'following some initial positive steps indicating an option for an open and transparent approach, the revision process was lead in a less inclusive manner and did not entirely benefit of the timeframe available and the potential input of the various circles having shown interest, in the Romanian society, for the revision of the Constitution'.[97] Since the constitutional review of the Constitutional Court in February 2014, the process of constitutional reform has slowed down considerably (this has also been caused by the National Liberal Party being voted out of the coalition government), being further complicated by the election of a new president, Klaus Iohannis, who belongs to the political opposition, in November 2014. Be that as it may, Iohannis has at various times argued in favour of the

91 See http://www.rri.ro/art.shtml?lang=1&sec=5&art=389435, accessed 15 June 2015.

92 See http://m.romanialibea.ro/stire-304031.html, accessed 15 June 2015.

93 See http://bogdandima.ro/?p=1123, accessed 15 June 2015.

94 See http://www.ziare.com/politica/constitutie/stanomir-amatorismul-defineste-revizuirea-constitutiei-1239834, accessed 15 June 2015.

95 As indicated by Art. 146a of the constitution, the Constitutional Court is to review the constitutionality of the amendments proposed.

96 See http://www.mediafax.ro/politic/analiza-comisia-de-revizuire-a-constitutiei-isi-reia-activitatea-la-un-an-dupa-respingerea-legii-la-curtea-constitutionala-13947715, accessed 15 June 2015.

97 Venice Commission, 'Opinion on the draft law on the review of the Constitution of Romania', Opinion no. 731/2013, CDL-AD (2014) 010, (2014), 32.

necessity of modernizing the constitution. In March 2015, a new parliamentary constitutional reform commission was installed.[98]

The Romanian experience of constitutional politics seems to be one that could be defined as a problematic variant of political constitutionalism, that is, populist-majoritarian constitution-making. Key characteristics are a process that is government-driven, non-consensual and has populist overtones.[99] A process of constitutional revision that was initiated in a promising and inclusive way (as appreciated by the Venice Commission) subsequently turned into a non-transparent, elite-driven exercise in an attempt to impose a partial, non-consensual view onto society by means of a supermajority. This majoritarian avenue seemed to be blocked by April 2014, however, in that the supermajority had turned into a reduced majority.

Concluding remarks

All three cases discussed include significant citizen input and innovative forms of constitutional politics. But none of the cases fully embraces the radical inclusiveness of democratic constitutionalism. The Icelandic case comes closest, but the design of the process ultimately appears detached from the main political institutions and therefore runs into forms of filibustering and outright rejection. The Romanian case includes a promising attempt at widespread and open public debate, but it does not have a significant impact on actual constitutional revision and there is a complete abandonment of publicity and inclusiveness later on in the process. The more moderate experience of Ireland seems the most successful in that structural citizen inclusion has been realized in an innovative way, while the process can boast relatively significant results. The ad hoc Irish experience lacks, however, a robust, institutionalized form of civic influence on constitution-making.

98 See http://www.mediafax.ro/politic/parlamentul-a-modificat-comisia-de-revizuire-a-constitutiei-hasotti-l-a-inlocuit-pe-crin-antonescu-13919315, accessed 15 June 2015.

99 cf. A. Arato and E. Tombuş, 'Learning from Success, Learning from Failure South Africa, Hungary, Turkey and Egypt' (2013) 39(4–5) *Philosophy & Social Criticism* 427.

3 A future for referendums in the fifth French republic?

Jan-Herman Reestman

Introduction

It may come as a surprise, but there is no French tradition that constitutions have to be adopted by the people, at least not until 1945. Although between 1791 and 1945 France wore out nine, ten, eleven or even more constitutions, depending on how one counts, only four of these were adopted by referendum: the constitutions of 1793, 1795 and 1799, and the *acte additionnel* of 1815. If one looks at the period after 1945, however, the picture changes and a tradition may be said to have developed, or at least to be developing. Since then all French constitutions have been adopted by referendum: the Constitutional Act for the Provisional Government on 21 October 1945, the constitution of the fourth republic on 13 October 1946 and that of the fifth republic on 28 September 1958. In view of this sequence, it is hardly conceivable that if ever a sixth French republic sees the light, its constitution will not also be adopted by referendum.

It is *le plus illustre des Français,* Charles de Gaulle, who was personally responsible for the revival of constitutional referendums after the World War I. On 21 October 1945, he and his provisional government organized a referendum, simultaneously with elections for parliament. In the referendum, the electorate was asked to answer two successive questions, the first being whether the Assemblée elected that day was to be '*constituante*'. An affirmative answer to this question implied that the three Constitutional Acts of 1875 on which the third republic was built, were (to be) abolished and that a new constitution had to be elaborated. If so, the next question was whether the government of France should be organized along the lines of an adjoined constitutional bill until the new constitution was adopted. This bill, in turn, stipulated that the new constitution had to be approved by referendum (Art. 3). The French voters answered both questions in the affirmative, with an overwhelming majority of 96 per cent of the expressed votes.

In addition to breathing new life into the practice of having constitutions adopted by referendum, De Gaulle and his political comrade in arms Michel Debré gave national referendums a prominent place in the constitution of 1958 itself. Referendums have served the fifth republic well. They have not only helped to introduce and to root the new constitution, but they have also given France's system of government what seems to be its definite shape. However, the question is whether by doing so referendums have made themselves obsolete. That is the question that is the subject of this contribution. The structure is as follows. In the first part, the constitutional provisions providing avenues for national referendums in the constitution of 1958 are introduced, including a short account of their practical use so far. This part also deals with the effects of the introduction, in 1962, of the direct election of the president of the republic on France's government system. In the second part, the question of whether there is a future for national referendums under the 1958 constitution will be discussed, first by means of a discussion of the motives De Gaulle had for cherishing and organizing referendums, and secondly by means of an analysis of the potential of a new, recently introduced referendum device, the so-called *référendum d'initiative partagée*.

Four avenues for nationwide referendums in the 1958 constitution

The constitution of 1958 provides four different avenues for nationwide referendums.

The first paragraph of Art. 11 gives the president of the republic the prerogative to submit certain categories of government bills to a referendum, on request of the government or of both houses of parliament (Assemblée nationale and Sénat) jointly. The scope of Art. 11(1) has been broadened over the years. Beside bills approving a 'Community agreement',[1] originally only bills regarding the functioning of the institutions and the approval of international treaties that, without being contrary to the constitution, affected the functioning of the (French) institutions fell within it. Later, in 1995, bills regarding socio-economic matters and the public services contributing thereto were added, and in 2005 bills regarding the environment.

The third paragraph of Art. 11 gives one fifth of the members of parliament, supported by one tenth of the voters enrolled on the electoral lists, the right to initiate a referendum; this is the *référendum d'initiative partagée.* Article 11(3), which was inserted in the constitution by the constitutional act of 23 July 2008 and entered into force on 1 January 2015, is far less generous than it seems to be at first sight. We will come back to it later.

Article 88–5 is to a certain extent a *lex specialis* to Art. 11(1). Article 88–5 was introduced on 1 March 2005, under the presidency of Jacques Chirac, at the occasion of the constitutional amendment that enabled the approval of the

1 Initially, referendums were also possible for government bills approving 'un accord de Communauté' i.e. an agreement between the member states (France and former colonies) of the French, a federal-type Commonwealth which the 1958 Constitution installed (Arts 77–87), but which only lasted less than two years. The relevant provisions were deleted by the constitutional amendment of 1995.

European Constitutional Treaty. The adoption of the provision was an attempt to save that treaty by disconnecting the discussion on its approval from the discussion of the accession of Turkey to the EU – it could not save the treaty, as we know now. The provision was amended in 2008 and now holds that a bill approving the accession of a new state to the EU, Croatia excepted, has to be submitted to a referendum unless the two houses of parliament, by passing a motion in identical terms with a three-fifths majority, decide that the bill may be approved by the Congrès, i.e. the joint assembly of both houses. In that instance, Congrès has to approve the accession treaty with a three-fifths majority of the votes cast. The procedure approving the accession of a new EU member state thus mirrors the constitutional amendment procedure in Art. 89 of the constitution.

Article 89 is the sole provision of Title XVI of the constitution, which is named *De la révision*, 'On amendment'. The president of the republic, 'on the basis of a proposal of the prime minister', and members of parliament have the right to initiate constitutional amendments. The procedure consists of two stages. Amendments first have to be adopted by the houses of parliament in identical terms.[2] In the second stage, the amendments have to be approved by the people in a referendum, unless they have a prime-ministerial origin. If that is the case, the president of the republic has a choice and may have the amendments approved by Congrès instead, with a three-fifths majority of the votes cast. It should be noted that in the first stage of this procedure, both houses of parliament have the power to veto proposed constitutional amendments – this prompted De Gaulle to bypass parliament in 1962 and to submit his proposal for the direct election of the president of the Republic directly to the people, as we will see later.

On the basis of Arts 11(1) and 89 of the constitution, nine referendums have been called so far, four by Charles de Gaulle (8 January 1961, 8 April 1962, 28 October 1962 and 27 April 1969), one by Georges Pompidou (23 April 1972), and two each by François Mitterrand (6 November 1988 and 20 September 1992) and Jacques Chirac (24 September 2000 and 29 May 2005). Not all of these referendums concern constitutional amendments in the strict sense, i.e. proposals to change the text of the document that is called the 'Constitution' with a capital C. Although the text of the constitution of 1958 has been amended 24 times,[3] only two of these were approved directly by the people: one under De Gaulle, on 28 October 1962 (introducing the direct election of the president), and one under Chirac, on 24 September 2000 (introducing a five-year term of office for the president). In addition, one constitutional referendum in this sense misfired: the one on 27 April 1969, on the reform of the Sénat and

2 Since 23 July 2008 at least six weeks have to expire between the moment of introduction and the plenary discussion in the house in which the draft is (first) introduced; in the subsequent house at least four weeks must expire, counted from the date of transmission.

3 See the list on the website of the Conseil constitutionnel, www.conseil-constitutionnel.fr/conseil-constitutionnel/francais/la-constitution/les-revisions-constitutionnelles/les-revisions-constitutionnelles.5075.html, accessed 2 June 2015.

regionalization, also called by De Gaulle.[4] However, if we take the term 'constitution' in a broader sense and spell it with a small c, all the national referendums held so far in the fifth French republic may in fact qualify as constitutional. No one will object to this qualification of the referendums on the accession of the UK, Ireland and Denmark to the EU (23 April 1972), on the Treaty of Maastricht (20 September 1992) and on the European Constitutional Treaty (29 May 2005). Undoubtedly also of constitutional importance were the two referendums on Algeria, on 8 January 1961 (on the right of self-determination of Algeria) and 8 April 1962 (approval of the Evian Agreements), and the one of 6 November 1988 on New Caledonia, which has given this former colony the status, more or less, of a self-governing state in the otherwise unitary French republic.

Of these nine 'constitutional' referendums, only one was based on Art. 89 of the constitution: that of 24 September 2000. The resulting amendment of Art. 6 of the constitution reduced the term of office of the president of the republic from seven to five years and thereby introduced the so called *quinquennat*. This amendment rounded off what De Gaulle, 38 years earlier in 1962, had started with a referendum on the introduction of the direct election of the president of the republic. For this constitutional amendment, De Gaulle chose the route of Art. 11, not that of Art. 89, simply because one of the houses of parliament, and perhaps even both, almost certainly would have vetoed the proposal which De Gaulle thought essential for the survival of 'his' fifth republic. De Gaulle's expedient was to bypass parliament and to put the bill directly before the people. The Assemblée nationale countered with the adoption of a motion of no confidence against the government, the only motion of that kind adopted in the fifth republic so far, but it could not stop the organization of the referendum.

Almost the entire political and juridical elite united against the presumed *détournement de pouvoir*. Indeed, although it must be admitted that interpretations in favour of the constitutionality of the procedure are not entirely devoid of persuasiveness, the textual and contextual arguments for the position that Art. 89 provides the one and only procedure for amending the constitution are very strong. Not only was the Conseil d'Etat, whose advice on government bills is mandatory (Art. 39[2] Constitution), opposed to De Gaulle's manoeuvre, but the Conseil constitutionnel, the Constitutional Council introduced by the new constitution with the task of *inter alia* testing the constitutionality of Acts of Parliament (Art. 61 Constitution), was too. In a secret note transmitted to De Gaulle prior to the referendum, it condemned the recourse to Art. 11.[5] However, when asked by the president of the Sénat to declare the act adopted by the people on 28 October 1962 unconstitutional for procedural reasons, the Conseil

4 Like the October 1962 referendum, that of 1969 was called on the basis of Art. 11.

5 For the text of the note and the minutes of the deliberations leading up to it, see B. Mathieu, J.-P. Machelon, F. Melin-Soucramanien, D. Rousseau and X. Philippe, *Les Grandes Délibérations du Conseil Constitutionnel. 1958–1983* (Dalloz 2009) 99–112. In a nutshell, the fascinating minutes give the arguments pro and contra the use of Art. 11 for amending the constitution.

constitutionnel denied competence. It stated that it lacked the power to rule on acts adopted by referendums, because they 'are the direct expression of national sovereignty'.[6] This has become standard case law,[7] and the immunity attributed to acts adopted by referendum has later been extended to constitutional amendments approved by Congrès: the Conseil constitutionnel apparently does not discriminate between the exercise of the constituent power by the people in a referendum and the representative institutions on the basis of Art. 89.[8]

For the assessment of the constitutionality of the recourse to the first paragraph of Art. 11 for a constitutional amendment at the present time, it is crucial to note that Art. 11 has been revised twice, in 1995 and 2008, and that the constituent power has not seized these opportunities to explicitly rule out the recourse to Art. 11(1) for constitutional amendments. On the contrary, while referendum bills ex Art. 11(3) are subjected to a mandatory prior review by the Conseil constitutionnel as to their compatibility with the constitution,[9] which excludes a constitutional amendment via a *référendum d' initiative partagée*, the first paragraph of Art. 11 was deliberately left untouched by the executive in its proposals and by parliament in its examination of the proposals.[10] The ruling majority did not

6 CC decision 62–20 DC of 6 November 1962.

7 CC Decision 92–313 DC of 23 September 1992. Recently, this case law was transposed to the context of 'preliminary constitutionality questions', the procedure, introduced in 2008 and effective since 2010, in which the Council decides on questions regarding the compatibility of enacted acts of parliament with constitutional rights and liberties on referral by the highest non-constitutional courts (Cour de cassation and Conseil d'Etat); see also CC decision 2014–392 QPC of 25 April 2014: 'qu'aucune disposition de la Constitution ou d'une loi organique prise sur son fondement ne donne compétence au Conseil constitutionnel pour se prononcer sur une question prioritaire de constitutionnalité aux fins d'apprécier la conformité aux droits et libertés que la Constitution garantit d'une disposition législative adoptée para. le Peuple français para. la voie du référendum; que, para. suite, il n'y a pas lieu, pour le Conseil constitutionnel, de connaître des dispositions de la loi adoptée para. le Peuple français para. voie de référendum le 6 novembre 1988.' [None of the provisions of the Constitution or of an organic act taken on its basis gives the Constitutional Council the competence to rule on a preliminary question of constitutionality regarding the conformity with the rights and liberties protected by the Constitution of a legislative provision adopted by the people in a referendum; therefore, the Constitutional Council will not take cognizance of the provisions of the law adopted by the French people by a referendum on 6 November 1988.]

8 CC decision 2003–469 DC of 26 March 2003.

9 Article 11(3) and (4) Constitution. Article 45–2 (3) of the organic act on the Conseil constitutionnel.

10 The Comité Vedel, the constitutional experts committee which paved the way for the 1995 constitutional reform, had proposed the introduction of a constitutional review of Art. 11(1) referendum bills, but at the same time proposed an amendment of Art. 89, to the effect that if the houses of parliament could not agree on a constitutional amendment proposal after two readings, the president of the republic could submit to a referendum the text adopted by one of the houses with a three-fifths majority; www.ladocumentationfrancaise.fr/var/storage/rapports-publics/084000091/0000.pdf, accessed 20.5.2015. In the report of the Comité Baladur, a committee filled with constitutional experts and politicians which prepared the constitutional revision of 2008, a reference to the issue is conspicuous for its absence;

want to exclude a return to De Gaulle's practice, if need be.[11] Indeed, as Marthe Fatin-Rouge Stéfanini has observed, the constitutional ideas of De Gaulle are very much still alive today.[12] These developments have not made it easier to hold on to the position that recourse to the first paragraph of Art. 11 for amending the constitution is (still) unconstitutional.[13]

France's semi-presidentialist government system

There is a second reason to linger for a few moments over the referendum of 28 October 1962. In De Gaulle's eyes, the big flaw of the constitutions of the third and fourth republics was that they had enabled parliament to act as the incarnation of national sovereignty: in his view, this was the source of the irresponsibility and impotence of French politics, and of the instability and short life expectancy of French governments. The constitution of 1958 intended to break this 'sovereignty' of parliament by two means. The first was by strengthening the position of the government *vis-à-vis* parliament, as much as is possible in a regime which may be called parliamentary (*parlementarisme rationalisé*). To this end, the government was entrusted with all kinds of prerogatives to influence and guide parliamentary proceedings and was vested with a rule-making power of its own, which the Conseil constitutionnel would have to guard against intrusions by parliament. The second means was the introduction of a president of the republic who, according to Art. 5 of the constitution, guarantees respect for the constitution and who ensures the proper functioning of the public authorities and the continuity of the state by his/her arbitration.

The text of Art. 5 evokes the image of an impartial, non-political power who only takes control of the rudder of the ship of state in cases of national or international political crises. However, De Gaulle, the first president of the fifth republic, elected by an electoral college consisting of parliamentarians and representatives of local and departmental councils, was far more than that from the beginning. His character, his role in World War II, the Algerian war of independence, which had he promised to bring to an end, his role in the transition from the fourth to the fifth republic, his vision of France's mission in the world: all these elements conspired to make him, and not the prime minister, as the constitution foresees

---

www.ladocumentationfrancaise.fr/var/storage/rapports-publics/074000697/0000.pdf, accessed 20 May 2015.

11 M. Fatin-Rouge Stéfanini, 'Vingt-cinq ans de débats et de réformes sur les référendums en France: entre apparences et réalités' (2014) 4 *Revue Française de Droit Constitutionnel* 907, 912–913.

12 Ibid. 913.

13 As the Conseil d'Etat has done in an *obiter dictum* in its judgment of 30 October 1998 (Sarran): 'le peuple français exerce sa souveraineté (. . .) en matière législative dans les cas prévus para. l'article 11 de la Constitution.' [The French people exercises its sovereignty in legislative matters in the cases foreseen in Art. 11 of the constitution.] However, cf. also Fatin-Rouge Stéfanini (n. 11) 915–916.

(Art. 21), the actual leader of the French government. In order to give his successors the democratic legitimacy to play the same prominent political role as he did, he thought it indispensable that they should be elected by universal suffrage.[14] He was undoubtedly right.

The constitutional amendment of 1962 has shaped the political system of the fifth republic decisively. It laid the basis for, or perhaps it is more accurate to say that it enabled, the continuation of the so-called semi-presidential system of government,[15] in which the government is accountable to the Assemblée nationale, but the president, who is not merely a figurehead but the actual government leader, is not. It made the election of the president of the republic the major event in French political life and the president the most important French politician. It led to a sort of polarization of French politics, not only on the occasion of the presidential elections, but also during the elections of the *Assemblée nationale*, in which usually a comfortable majority rallying behind the president is (and was) elected. It was (and is) this bond between the majority in the *Assemblée* and the president which made the president, whose formal competences remain rather limited, the actual government leader. Except of course in times of *cohabitation*.

France has known three such periods of *cohabitation*, that is, periods in which the president was confronted with a 'hostile' majority in the Assemblée and had to share executive power with a government of a different affiliation than his own: from 1986 to 1988, from 1993 to 1995, and, the latest and the longest, from 1997 to 2002. To rule *cohabitations* out for the future and to ensure the political unity of France's bicephalous executive as much as possible, two measures were taken in the year 2000. The *quinquennat* was introduced and the order of the elections for the presidency and the Assemblée was reversed. Since then, first a president is elected, for five years, and thereafter the Assemblée nationale, also for five years. The idea behind the two measures is simple: to guarantee as much as is factually possible that the president for his/her whole term of office is backed by a solid parliamentary majority and thus also controls the government. So far, so good.

The topicality of De Gaulle's motives

The heyday of the referendum in the fifth French republic was under the presidency of Charles de Gaulle, for several reasons. Of all the presidents of the fifth

14 See De Gaulle's message of 2 October 1962 to both houses of Parliament, http://www.droitpolitique.com/spip.php?article161, accessed 20 May 2015: 'je suis convaincu que l'investiture populaire sera nécessaire pour donner, quoi qu'il arrive, à ceux qui me succéderont, la possibilité et l'obligation de porter la charge suprême quel qu'en puisse être le poids.' [I am convinced that, whatever happens, popular investiture will be necessary to give to my successors the possibility and the obligation to carry the weight of the supreme burden, however heavy it may be.]

15 In view of the dominance of the French president, it would be better to qualify the system as '*présidentialiste*'; O. Duhamel, 'Une démocratie à part' (2008) 126 *Pouvoirs* 17.

republic so far, De Gaulle was undoubtedly the one who was ideologically the most attached to referendums. Moreover, he organized four referendums in nearly 11 years, which averages out at one per two-and-a-half years. Since then, referendums have become rarer. Georges Pompidou organized one referendum in four years, François Mitterrand two in 14 years (an average of 1 in 7) and Jacques Chirac two in 12 years (1 in 6); Valéry Giscard d'Estaing and Nicolas Sarkozy did not organize any, and François Hollande, so far, has organized none.

It is surprising that Chirac only organized two referendums and Sarkozy organized none, as they, in an apparent attempt to normalize referendums by making them possible outside the institutional domain, had the scope of bills eligible for referendums under Art. 11(1) extended at the beginning of their (first) presidency, in 1995 (socio-economic matters) and 2008 (environmental matters) respectively. However, they did not wish to use and did not venture to use the opportunities they had created themselves – and neither has Hollande. That brings us back to the question of whether there is a future for referendums under the constitution of 1958. Let us deal with this question first by means of a discussion of the topicality of the motives that inspired De Gaulle to favour referendums and secondly by analyzing the potential of the *referendum d'initiative partagée*.

De Gaulle favoured referendums for several reasons. He saw in them an instrument with which the president of the republic could let the people arbitrate in conflicts between the president and parliament or between the government and parliament. He also considered referendums, more or less in the Rousseauian tradition, as a way to involve the French people in the most important decisions of the French nation. In addition, he considered referendums to be a means by which the president of the republic could render an account to the French people and test his democratic credentials.[16]

It may be clear that the people arbitrating a conflict between the president or the government on the one hand and parliament on the other, has become redundant. The current French republic is a paragon of institutional stability: president, government and the *Assembleé nationale* operate as the proverbial 'one bloc'. Of course, if one looks closer, reality is more nuanced, but that is always the case: the absolute monarchies of the *ancien régime*, for instance, were also less absolute than their appellation indicates, although probably least in France.[17]

Also, the argument in favour of involving the people by way of referendums in the most important decisions of the French nation is very different to the arguments put forward in the 1960s. The French are already involved in the most important event of French political life every five years: the election of the president, who is able to execute *his/her* government programme with the help of *his/her* government and *his/her* parliamentary majority. It should be added that the

16 J.-L. Debré, *Les Idées Constitutionnelles du Général de Gaulle* (LGDJ 1974) 96, 203–204, 286–287.

17 E.H. Kossmann, 'The Singularity of Absolutism' in E.H. Kossmann (ed.), *Politieke theorie en geschiedenis* [*Political Theory and History*] (Bert Bakker 1987) 127–138.

election of the president can even replace a referendum directly. During his campaign for the presidency in 2006 and 2007, Nicolas Sarkozy promised to fight for the replacement of the European Constitutional Treaty by a *mini-traité*.[18] Due to its more limited impact, that *mini-traité* would not have to be submitted to a referendum. And Sarkozy kept his word: he negotiated a *mini-traité*, at least according to his own definition, and he subsequently had the Treaty of Lisbon approved by parliament. Exit the referendum.

Moreover, the perspective of involving the people in the most important decisions of the French nation has undoubtedly lost its appeal due to the temperament of the French people. For one thing, sometimes only a small proportion of them are interested in being involved. For instance, only 30.9 per cent of the electorate participated in the referendum on the *quinquennat* in the year 2000. The proposal was nevertheless approved, because 73.21 per cent of the voters voted in favour of it and French national referendums do not have a turnout threshold.[19]

Some may be of the opinion that the French people are also a capricious master, and perhaps increasingly so, because the outcome of a referendum cannot be taken for granted. The Treaty of Maastricht was approved by a very narrow margin and the European Constitutional Treaty was rejected, although the vast majority of the political elite was in favour of both treaties. Why run the risk of having a bill or a treaty that you think is necessary for France rejected by the people if you have the certainty that parliament will approve the act or treaty almost effortlessly?

The idiosyncrasy of the French people also explains why no president after De Gaulle has ventured to turn a referendum into a matter of personal confidence. None of them has dared to do this. Mitterrand would probably have lost the referendum on the Treaty of Maastricht if he had put his presidency in the balance,[20] and Chirac would have had to retire in 2005 if he had made his fate as president dependent on the outcome of the referendum on the European Constitutional Treaty. In contrast, De Gaulle always made clear that he would consider a vote for or against the act submitted to referendum as a vote for or against De Gaulle. In other words, he always made clear that he would consider the rejection of that act as a motion of no confidence and that he would consequently resign. And he kept his word: when his proposal to reform the Sénat was defeated in 1969, he resigned.

18 http://tempsreel.nouvelobs.com/politique/20060908.OBS1132/europe-sarkozy-veut-un-mini-traite.html, accessed 20 May 2015.

19 http://www.ladocumentationfrancaise.fr/dossiers/d000137-le-quinquennat-presidentiel-referendum-du-24-septembre-2000/resultats-du-referendum-du-24-septembre-2000, accessed 20 May 2015.

20 In the run-up to the referendum and when speaking about the chance of losing it, Mitterrand is reported to have said: 'Il faut savoir prendre des risques. En plus, tomber là-dessus, cela ne serait pas si mal' [You must be able to take risks. Moreover, it would not be that bad to fall because of this.]: M. Winock, *François Mitterrand* (NRF Gallimard 2014) 345. Mitterrand probably did not mean to say that he intended to resign if there was a negative outcome.

Scholars have often chastised De Gaulle for his inclination to make referendums into a matter of confidence, just as uncle and nephew Napoleon had done in earlier times. This turns his referendums into plebiscites, i.e. into procedures in which professional and personal issues are blended in an improper way. I have never understood this critique. In a parliamentary system it is perfectly accepted that a government turns the passing of a legislative proposal by parliament into a vote of confidence. Why, then, is this not acceptable in referendum proceedings?

In addition, there were good reasons why De Gaulle considered it to be necessary to render an account to the people via referendums. The French president is extremely powerful, a lot more powerful than the American president and, in addition, originally the term of office of the French president was almost twice as long as that of his American counterpart. In relation to the use of his enormous power, the French president was accountable to no one, except to God and possibly, after seven years, to the French people, if he/she sought re-election. Of course, he could be impeached for high treason, a term with a criminal law connotation that no one knew the precise meaning of and which was never meant to be applied in practice. Today all this is different. The term of office has been reduced, and nowadays the French president can be impeached by parliament, acting as a high court, if there is a 'breach of his duties patently incompatible with his continuing in office' (Art. 68 Constitution). This seems a far more feasible reason for impeachment, and perhaps one is even allowed to see in the new construction a touch of 'parliamentarization' of the relationship between parliament and president, although of course officially this was not the intention.[21]

The (limited) potential of the *référendum d'initiative partagée*

In 2008, 50 years after its coming into being, Nicolas Sarkozy put his imprint on the 1958 constitution, right beside that of Charles de Gaulle. With the aim of recalibrating the relationships between the institutions, which were thrown off balance by the 'absolutism' of the ruling majority induced by the semi-presidential system of government, Sarkozy initiated an extensive overhaul of the constitution, which affected approximately one-third of its provisions.[22] However, although it fits perfectly in the general picture of the revision, the *référendum d' initative partagée* was not part of Sarkozy's proposals. The amendment is rooted in a proposition of the Comité Balladur, which prepared the constitutional reform of 2008, but the executive refused to inscribe that proposal in its constitutional

21 Rapport de la Commission de réflexion sur le statut pénal du Président de la République, 45–46, http://www.ladocumentationfrancaise.fr/var/storage/rapports-publics/024000635.pdf, accessed 2 June 2015.

22 For a short overview and an analysis, see M. Rosaria Donnarumma, 'Le régime semi présidentiel. Une anomalie française' (2013) *Revue française de droit constitutionnel* 37 (47 ff).

bill. This probably explains why this new referendum device is, in the final analysis, rather disappointing, at least for those who are in favour of referendums.[23]

On the basis of Art. 11(3) of the constitution, one-fifth of the members of parliament, i.e. at least 185 deputies and/or senators out of 925, supported by one-tenth of the voters enrolled on the electoral lists, i.e. approximately 4.5 million voters, have the right to initiate a legislative referendum. The device has become effective as of 1 January 2015, when the required organic act 'regarding the application of Art. 11' entered into force.[24]

The scope of Art. 11(3) is the same as that of Art. 11(1), with three exceptions. The first exception is contained in Art. 11(3): a *référendum d' initative partagée* may not concern the abolition of an act of parliament which has been promulgated within the previous year. The second exception, contained in Art. 11(6), is that a private member's referendum bill may not have the same object as a private member's referendum bill defeated in a referendum in the previous two years. The third exception has already been mentioned: the new referendum device cannot serve to amend the constitution. This is ruled out by the mandatory prior review of the relevant private member's bill by the Conseil constitutionnel. The Constitutional Council is instructed to check not only whether the bill has indeed been proposed by one-fifth of the MPs, whether it falls within the scope of Art. 11(1), and whether the temporal restrictions in Art. 11(3) and (6) have been respected, but also whether '*aucune disposition de la proposition de loi n'est contraire à la Constitution*' (none of the provisions of the private members bill is contrary to the constitution).[25] Only after this check has been performed does the period of nine months start, within which the electorate has the possibility of supporting the private member's bill.[26] At the end of that period, it is once more the Conseil constitutionnel that has to control and state whether the required number of (electronic) signatures has been registered.[27] At first sight, this *referendum d'initiative partagée* seems to give combined parliamentary and societal opposition unprecedented opportunities to rout the ruling majority and to shape the legislative agenda.[28] However, there is an unexpected and problematic conclusion. The private member's bill will only be, and then must be, submitted to a

23 See F. Hamon, 'Le referendum d'initiative partagée' (2014) *Revue française de droit constitutionnel* 253; M. Haulbert, 'Le référendum d'initiative "partagée": représentants versus représentés?' (2014) 6 *Revue de droit public* 1637.

24 Loi organique n° 2013–1114 of 6 December 2013 'portant application de l'article 11 de la Constitution'.

25 Article 45–2 of Ordonnance n° 58–1067 of 7 November 1958 'portant loi organique sur le Conseil constitutionnel'.

26 Article 4 of Loi organique n° 2013–1114 of 6 December 2013 'portant application de l'article 11 de la Constitution'.

27 Article 45–6 of Ordonnance n° 58–1067 of 7 November 1958 'portant loi organique sur le Conseil constitutionnel'.

28 Nevertheless, owing to its fragmentation, it will be not easy for the parliamentary opposition to muster the required number of parliamentarians, according to Haulbert (n. 23) 1650–1651.

referendum by the president of the republic if it has not been 'examined' by each house of parliament at least once within the six months counting from the date on which the *Conseil constitutionnel's* decision has been published confirming that a sufficient number of voters have supported the bill.[29] This makes is extremely easy for the majority in parliament to defuse explosive material in a private member's referendum bill by simply discussing and rejecting the bill.[30] And if the bill is not put on the agenda of the houses of their own motion, the government may do so, as a priority, making use of one of the prerogatives the constitution bestows on it to steer parliamentary proceedings (Art. 48[2]). Indeed, as Francis Hamon has remarked, a *referendum d'initiative partagée* can only take place if none of the important political actors wants to avoid it.[31] In the end, therefore, the *référendum d' intiative partagée*, according to Art. 11(3), 'resembles more with some kind of right of petition which forces parliament to discuss a text, than with a new referendum procedure', as senator Jean-Pierre Sueur has concluded.[32]

Concluding remarks

In contrast to the ideas of Charles de Gaulle, there is no longer any need for presidents of the fifth republic to have recourse to referendums. Conflicts between the president or the government and parliament have practically died out. Certainly, during periods of *cohabitation* conflicts may arise between the president on the one hand and government and parliament on the other. But the chances of the recurrence of such periods have been minimalized, as we have seen. Moreover, the organization of any referendum on the basis of Art. 11(1) and Art. 89 of the constitution requires some kind of consensus about its desirability between two of the three actors involved: president and government, or president and parliamentary majority. So, as is the case in general with the *référendum d'initiative partagée,* in times of *cohabitation* too, a referendum can only take place if opposing political actors agree on it. This will not happen often. The need for referendums has also decreased because the French people these days are already involved every five years in the most important event of French political life: the election of the president of the Republic. Moreover, the need for that president to put his democratic legitimacy to the test in a referendum has diminished thanks to his reduced term of office and the rearrangement of his 'political' accountability.

In addition, referendums are a dangerous instrument for the president, except of course when the outcome is more or less assured beforehand. But the more the outcome of referendums is assured beforehand, the less their added value is (and

29 Article 11(5) Constitution jo. Article 9 of Loi organique n° 2013–1114 of 6 December 2013 'portant application de l'article 11 de la Constitution'. However, neither the Constitution nor the implementing organic act has set a period within which the president has to submit the bill to a referendum.

30 Cf. Haulbert (n. 23) 1652–1653.

31 Hamon (n. 23) 259.

32 Fatin-Rouge Stéfanini (n. 11) 910.

the electorate probably has less desire to participate in them, as the referendum on the *quinquennat* in 2000 witnessed). If the outcome is not assured beforehand, a referendum may come back to the president like a boomerang, even if he/she has not turned the referendum into a matter of confidence: losing a referendum is never good for the president's legitimacy. Of course, Jacques Chirac got away with it in 2005, and some might think he got away with almost everything thanks to his irresistible charm. It takes a very courageous president to exchange the manageable and to a certain extent predictable procedures of representative democracy for the uncontrollable and unpredictable dynamics of referendums. In this analysis, therefore, the chances that referendums will be organized in the upcoming years seem rather slim. From this perspective, the heydays of national referendums in France are over. And certainly the introduction of the *référendum d'initiative partagée* will not bring back them back in bloom.

Part III

Lessons from long direct-democratic experience

The equilibrium between democracy and constitutionalism in Switzerland and California

4 Participation of citizens in constitution-making

Assets and challenges – the Swiss experience

Thomas Fleiner

Introduction. The role of the people in Switzerland

The citizens of Switzerland have several opportunities to participate in the constitution-making process. Since 1848, any constitutional provision can only enter into force if the 'sovereign', which is the simple majority of the voters (at that time, male Swiss citizens) and of the cantons (majority of the voters) approve the new constitutional provision. According to the new constitution of 1848,[1] although 50,000 citizens were given the opportunity to require a revision of the constitution, there was no mention of the content of the revision. For this and probably other reasons, Swiss citizens seldom used these new political rights of direct democracy.[2]

In 1891, the sovereign adopted two important additional possibilities for amending the constitution. The most important object of this revision was the possibility of changing the constitution using a specific text submitted via a popular initiative. If adopted by the sovereign, the proposed text automatically became, and would still become today, part of the constitution. The other possibility was proposing general guidelines as a 'motion' to parliament to edit a new constitutional amendment to correspond with the guidelines of the popular initiative. As a consequence of this proposal, parliament was only competent to elaborate a final text for the approval of the sovereign. If parliament agreed with these guidelines, it had to propose the specific text for the amendment to the sovereign. If it refused to do so, the majority of the people had to decide on the proposal. If the majority of the people agreed with the guidelines formulated by the popular initiative, parliament had to establish a specific constitutional bill and propose it as an amendment for final approval by the sovereign.[3]

1 See the German text of this Constitution http://www.verfassungen.de/ch/verf48-i.htm, accessed 24 April 2015.

2 All votes since 1848 to 1879 in BBl 1879 I 417 in German: http://www.amtsdruckschriften.bar.admin.ch/viewOrigDoc.do?i d=10010243, accessed 24 April 2015.

3 Article 139 para. 4 of the actual Constitution for an unofficial English translation of the Swiss Constitution see also http://www.admin.ch/ch/e/rs/1/101.en.pdf, accessed 24 April 2015.

Opposed to the initial project proposed by the federal council (the executive of Switzerland), the second chamber, that is, the state councillors of parliament, proposed giving citizens a new and very important political right. In fact, the majority of the cantonal councillors wanted to introduce a specific democratic right for citizens to be able to amend the constitution by using a particular text. As a consequence, the second chamber required the federal council to submit to parliament an additional constitutional proposal for the real improvement of direct democracy.

The second chamber opposed the original proposal of the federal council[4] and of the first chamber for the following reasons. The cantonal councillors argued that the right discussed in the original project was in fact not a real democratic right but only the introduction of a petition, because parliament remains the real editor of constitutional amendments. The chamber of the cantons introduced this new democratic right because its majority was convinced that the sovereign (majority of people and cantons) would adopt constitutional decisions in a much more thoughtful way than parliament, although this would depend on the parties' attitudes.[5] As the first chamber followed the proposal of the second chamber, the final result was a text for a constitutional amendment elaborated by parliament that went against the original proposal of the federal council.[6]

This democratic right of the people introduced into the constitution in 1891 (which was very important for the political future of Switzerland) allowed for the possibility of 50,000 (in reality 100,000[7]) signatures of voters being needed for the submission of a written draft of a constitutional amendment for final approval by the sovereign. This new amendment required the constitution to distinguish between a partial and a total revision of the constitution and, consequently, to have different procedures with regard to the different types of revision. Only the constitution of Austria of 1920[8] followed, in its Art. 44, the Swiss example and distinguished, in a similar way to the Swiss constitution, between a partial and a total revision.

Some scholars have criticized the Swiss sovereign, because since the year 2000 the sovereign has adopted some proposals that cause significant problems with regard to human rights and membership of the Council of Europe, including violations of the Human Rights Convention. In addition, with regard to

4 For the original proposal of the federal council see http://www.amtsdruckschriften.bar.admin.ch/viewOrigDoc.do?id=10014845, accessed 24 April 2015.

5 See the report of the committee of the second chamber of 17 December 1890 at http://www.amtsdruckschriften.bar.admin.ch/viewOrigDoc.do?id=10015098, accessed 24 April 2015.

6 See the text of this final result in http://www.amtsdruckschriften.bar.admin.ch/viewOrigDoc.do?id=10015232, accessed 24 April 2015.

7 Article 138 of the constitution see the English text at http://www.admin.ch/ch/e/rs/1/101.en.pdf, accessed 24 April 2015.

8 See the text of this constitution in English at http://www.servat.unibe.ch/icl/au00000_.html, accessed 24 April 2015.

Switzerland's relationship with the European Union, some constitutional amendments contradict some provisions of the bilateral treaties that Switzerland has entered into with the EU.

Recently, the right-wing party the Democratic Union of the Center (UDC) has formulated a popular initiative with the provocative title 'Swiss Law instead of Foreign Judges'. It started to collect the required 100,000 signatures on 10 March 2015; the deadline is 10 September 2016.[9] This initiative will give constitutional provisions absolute priority over international treaty law, the only exception allowed being violation of peremptory rules of international law (*ius cogens*). According to this new popular initiative, the people could propose a provision that contradicts an international treaty. The federal parliament would, accordingly, have either to renegotiate this treaty or to withdraw from it. Such an initiative would of course cause international treaty negotiators to believe that in any international negotiation the judgement of Swiss negotiators would be considered highly questionable and unreliable, because constitutional initiatives could annul any international treaty negotiated by the Swiss.[10]

Before dealing with the concrete popular initiative, one should bear in mind that even by 1848, any amendment of the constitution could only enter into force after approval by the sovereign. According to the constitution of 1848, some 50,000 citizens could propose a revision of the constitution. However, although these citizens could require a constitutional revision, they did not know the content of this revision in advance. As already mentioned, the sovereign introduced this important democratic right only some 43 years later in 1891.

Since 1848, the Swiss constitution has continually expanded popular voting rights and empowered people to participate in important decisions. In the complete revision of the constitution in 1874 that resulted in a new constitution that year,[11] an optional referendum was introduced for citizens opposing legislative acts of parliament. In 1891, the previously mentioned right of the people to a popular initiative to change the constitution was introduced, and in 1921, the optional referendum with regard to international treaties was introduced. Twenty-eight years later, the sovereign adopted a proposal decided on by popular initiative to enlarge popular rights with regard to parliamentary decisions concerning emergencies. It was only in 1971, which was very late, that Switzerland introduced voting rights for women.[12] In 1994, the legislature introduced the right to vote by post. On the basis of a popular initiative, the sovereign changed the constitution in 1921 in order to introduce a new system for the election of the national council. At that time, the sovereign replaced the majority system with

9 See http://www.admin.ch/ch/d/pore/vi/vis460.html, accessed 24 April 2015.

10 The only exception are treaties, which the Swiss voters did accept in a referendum.

11 See the text of the constitution of 1874 at http://www.verfassungen.de/ch/verf74-i.htm, accessed 24 April 2015.

12 See http://www.admin.ch/ch/d/pore/va/19710207/det224.html, accessed 24 April 2015.

a proportional system of election in order to ensure that the parliament that was elected was not the opposite to what the people wanted.

The new constitution, adopted in 1999,[13] requires that popular initiatives have to respect mandatory international law. The political debate on voting rights still continues, in particular with regard to electronic voting. In fact, the federal council and the cantons are preparing for the possibility of people using the internet to vote electronically. Some cantons have already started to introduce this right. In this context, it is essential to mention that the sovereign has rejected some important popular initiatives to enlarge the citizens' democratic opportunities. In 1961, the sovereign rejected an initiative to enshrine the possibility of an initiative to introduce legislation.[14] In 1952 and 1987, the sovereign rejected an initiative to provide democratic rights in relation to expenditure issues concerning military equipment.[15] Although the sovereign expanded some limited political rights with regard to international treaties in 1921, since 1891 it has also rejected some initiatives that aimed to expand the political right of the citizens to participate in the treaty-making power of the federal government and parliament. Three times, in 1900, 1942 and 2013, the sovereign has rejected the adoption of an initiative that proposes a right to a popular election in relation to the election of the federal council.[16] In 1956, the sovereign (composed only of male citizens) rejected the possibility of giving female citizens the right to vote. It took another 25 years until male citizens granted this, with 66 per cent voting for and 34 per cent against the right of women to vote.[17]

The enormous number of popular initiatives containing some quite provocative constitutional proposals has substantially worsened the political climate in Switzerland. Namely, the right-wing party UDC uses this right to propose new constitutional provisions by popular initiative to oppose measures relating to asylum seekers, criminal foreigners and mass immigration. In general, political parties use this popular right to launch constitutional initiatives. These parties use this instrument of direct democracy not only to incorporate new ideas into the constitution but to use political rights as an instrument to gain popularity and better support in the elections from their voters. For this reason, Switzerland has continued to face an increasing number of new initiatives. During the first 50 years of enabling popular initiatives, the people had to vote fewer than 100 times, but during the 50 years between 1961 and 2011, the people voted 464 times. Currently, some 36 popular initiatives are pending, waiting for signatures. For some of these initiatives, the federal council has to prepare its proposal to parliament confirming that the sovereign either recommends or rejects the

13 See the official texts of the Constitution in German, French, Italian and Romansch at http://www.admin.ch/org/polit/00083/index.html?lang=de, accessed 24 April 2015.

14 See http://www.admin.ch/ch/d/pore/va/19611022/index.html, accessed 24 April 2015.

15 See http://www.admin.ch/ch/d/pore/va/19520518/index.html, and http://www.admin.ch/ch/d/pore/rf/cr/1986/19860355.html, accessed 24 April 2015.

16 See http://www.admin.ch/ch/d/pore/va/20130609/det570.html, accessed 24 April 2015.

17 See http://www.admin.ch/ch/d/pore/va/19710207/det224.html, accessed 24 April 2015.

constitutional initiative. Some initiatives have to wait for the final decision of parliament before there is a recommendation to the sovereign either to approve or to reject what is proposed in the initiative. However, parliament can also abstain from any recommendation to the sovereign if there is disagreement between the two chambers.

Several proposals to limit this important democratic right are pending. However, it will be very difficult in a constitutional debate to convince the sovereign to limit its proper democratic right and accordingly to amend the constitution. The main political discussion with regard to popular initiatives focuses on the issue of the acceptability of popular constitutional initiatives. Nobody dares to limit the right of the citizens to launch and to decide on initiatives. There is probably no realistic chance of introducing a constitutional review of popular initiatives and some kind of eternity law into the Swiss constitution, apart from limitations deriving from mandatory international law. Thus, I will analyze in this chapter the constitutional regulations with regard to popular initiatives and determine some possible solutions.

Development of the right of citizens to participate in voting

The majority of the people in all of Switzerland and the majority of the people of the cantons adopted the first constitution of Switzerland in 1848 with a majority of 72 per cent of the voters and 15½ cantons. The constitution of 1848 provided in Art. 1 of the transitory provisions that the new constitution would enter into force in Switzerland after the majority of the voters of all Switzerland and the majority of the voters in the cantons had adopted it. Where a cantonal constitution did not provide a provision for the procedure for its adoption, the cantonal authorities had to decide on the procedure for adopting the new federal constitution. In most cantons, citizens with the right to vote did decide to adopt the new federal constitution; in some cantons, the open assembly (Landsgemeinde) decided; in the canton of Lucerne, abstentions counted as approval; and in the canton of Fribourg, parliament was the competent authority to decide on constitutional revisions, and it adopted the new federal constitution.[18] According to Art. 1 of the transitory provisions of the new constitution, the new constitution would enter into force when the majority of the voters and the majority of the cantons adopted it. This was a revolutionary act. The original treaty of the union of Switzerland of 1815[19] was an international treaty, which only the sovereign cantons could dissolve by unanimity and not by majority.

The constitution of 1848 provided in Art. 112 that the procedure for the revision of the constitution should be similar to the procedure for passing

18 For a table of the cantonal votes, see the historic lexicon of Switzerland at http://www.hls-dhs-dss.ch/textes/d/D9811.php, accessed 24 April 2015.

19 See http://www.verfassungen.de/ch/, accessed 24 April 2015.

legislation.[20] However, unlike in relation to legislation, any constitutional amendment could only enter into force following a mandatory referendum after the majority of the voters and the majority of the voters of the cantons had adopted any amendment. From 1848 until today, the constitution has only once changed the sovereign as constitution maker. In 1971, it granted women the right to vote and doubled the number of citizens with voting rights from one and a half million to more than three million.[21] From 1848 to 2015, the sovereign has not changed because the majority of Swiss citizens with voting rights and the majority of Swiss citizens in the cantons with voting rights are the competent sovereign to change the constitution.

Since 1848, the sovereign has adopted a total revision of the constitution only twice, in 1874 and 1999. In 1872, it rejected a proposal for a complete revision of the constitution. However, although Switzerland is already on its third constitution since 1848, the sovereign has never radically changed the governmental system, nor its federalism. With regard to direct democracy, it has usually expanded rather than diminished the democratic rights of the citizens. With regard to the voting rights of the people, the only relevant provision introduced by the 1874 constitution was the provision for an optional referendum that could be used to vote against legislation adopted by the two-chamber parliament. According to this provision, after the adoption of legislation by parliament, 30,000 (in reality 50,000[22]) people had the right to require a popular referendum in order to make a final decision on the proposed legislation. The legislation proposed by parliament could only enter into force after approval by a majority.

This new provision of the constitution, which the constitutional legislature had proposed after the council of the states (cantons) intervened, gave the people substantial new direct democratic rights. Sixty per cent of voters adopted these new amendments of Arts 118 to 123[23] of the constitution of 1874 (in the constitution of 1999[24] those rights correspond to Arts 139 and 193). With the introduction of the popular initiative into the constitution, the sovereign also adopted the possibility of citizens initiating a constitutional amendment by way of a general proposal instead of via a concrete constitutional draft.

In 1891, this popular right gave almost 7.5 per cent of citizens with voting rights the possibility of requiring a popular vote on their specific proposal and, correspondingly, changing the constitution. Since 1977, the required number of signatures for a popular initiative rose to 100,000. This required number of

20 See the German version of the Constitution of 1848 at http://www.verfassungen.de/ch/verf48-i.htm, accessed 24 April 2015.

21 See citizens with voting rights in February 1971 at http://www.admin.ch/ch/d/pore/va/19710207/det224.html, and in June 1971 at http://www.admin.ch/ch/d/pore/va/19710606/det225.html, accessed 24 April 2015.

22 Article 141 of the constitution.

23 See http://www.amtsdruckschriften.bar.admin.ch/viewOrigDoc.do?id=10015386, accessed 24 April 2015.

24 See http://www.admin.ch/ch/e/rs/c101.html, accessed 24 April 2015.

signatures corresponds to only some 2 per cent of the citizens with voting rights. In 1891, 50,000 signatures corresponded to 7.5 per cent of the citizens with voting rights, because only 650,000 citizens had voting rights in Switzerland at that time. Since 1891, the number of citizens with a right to vote has risen to 5 million, which is roughly eight times more than the number in 1891. Nevertheless, the new constitution requires only 100,000 signatures for a popular initiative. If a proposal for an amendment to the constitution required a particular number of signatures that corresponded to 7.5 per cent of voters (which was the relevant percentage in 1891), the number of signatures required would be 375,000.

Since the introduction of this right to require amendments in the constitution to be carried out via a popular initiative, the people have handed in 429 such proposals. Of those initiatives that proceeded to amend the constitution, the sovereign has only adopted 21 of them. In relation to 16 current initiatives, a committee has collected signatures; some 13 popular initiatives are pending for final recommendation by parliament. In relation to three initiatives, the federal council still has to decide on the different options for its proposal to parliament. So in total, 13 popular initiatives are currently waiting for a final decision from the sovereign.

Procedure with regard to the popular initiative

The legislation on the voting rights of citizens regulates in detail the procedure for the collection of signatures and how the corresponding decisions of the federal council and parliament are to be made. The legislation on political rights guarantees the right for every citizen to use his/her voting rights. Every citizen can use his/her voting rights, in addition to cantonal and municipal democratic rights, in relation to federal decisions, including electing national councillors, voting on initiatives, voting on referendums, signing initiatives and signing requests for referendums at his/her municipality of residence. Unlike municipalities in other states, each municipality of residence in Switzerland registers citizens automatically when they reach the voting age of 20. Unlike many other countries, Switzerland does not require voters to register formally in order to use their voting rights. Each citizen can also formulate a specific proposal for a constitutional amendment. To do this, he/she has to convene a committee for the initiative of at least seven but not more than 27 citizens. The members of this committee have the right to withdraw from the initiative, the latest time for this being when the federal council has decided on the date for the final vote of the citizens.[25]

After the text has been finalized, the committee has to submit it for formal examination to the federal chancellery. The federal chancellery also has to provide translations from the original language of the text into the two other official languages if the committee has not already provided them. The official languages are German, French and Italian. However, the committee can also require

25 See Arts 68 to 76 of the federal law on political rights.

translations of the text of the proposal for the initiative into the fourth national language (though it is not one of the official languages), Romansh, which is, according to Art. 4 of the constitution, a national language, and in particular is also one of the official cantonal languages of the canton of Grison.[26]

Following the only formal examination by the federal chancellery, the committee for the initiative can start to collect the required 100,000 signatures of Swiss citizens. The committee has to gather these signatures within 18 months. After the signatures have been collected, the committee deposits them at the federal chancellery. The federal chancellery examines and counts these signatures. If the committee has collected the required number of signatures, the federal council has to decide whether it will propose that parliament should approve or reject the proposal that will be voted on in the initiative. It can also propose a constitutional counterproposal to parliament. After considering the proposal of the federal council, the two chambers decide whether they recommend to approve or to reject the initiative. Parliament can also develop the original proposal and propose that the sovereign adopts a constitutional counterproposal. After agreement of the two chambers is reached, the federal council determines the date for the final voting. If the two chambers do not reach agreement, the federal council decides on the date of the final vote of the citizens without an official recommendation to approve or reject the proposal of the initiative. The chambers can also propose a counterproposal to the one put forward by the initiative. If they do this, they also propose that the citizens vote at the same time on the proposal of initiative and on the counterproposal.

Once the two chambers have come to a final decision, the federal council determines, at least four months before the vote of the citizens takes place, the themes on which the voters will have to vote. It also has to inform citizens of the pros and cons of the proposal of the initiative, according to the discussion that took place in parliament. As set out in the leaflet distributed to every voter, the federal council has to follow the recommendations of parliament and has no option of supporting an opinion that deviates from that of the majority of parliament.[27]

The impact of direct democracy in Switzerland

Direct democracy has had a substantial impact on the nation building of the nation of Switzerland. It has also strengthened the stability of society and the governmental system. Moreover, it has influenced the mutual understanding of regions and cantons that use a different language and has influenced, via the proportional system, several national institutions and authorities. This unquestioned

26 According to Art. 3 of the constitution of the canton of Grison, the equality of Italian, Romansh and German is guaranteed; see also http://www.gr-lex.gr.ch/frontend/versions/2489?locale=de, accessed 24 April 2015.

27 See Arts 10 and 11 of the federal law on political rights.

legitimacy of the constitutional system has even influenced political parties, lobbyists and NGOs.

In 1848, institutions in Switzerland, including the governmental system and a society that was divided between Protestants and Catholics, were extremely weak and fragile. Economically, Switzerland was in 1848 one of the poorest countries in Europe.[28] However, according to the Sustainable Development Solutions Network (SDSN), in 2015 Switzerland became the happiest country in the world.[29] Moreover, the important rift that divided political and civil society happened 167 years ago, not so much in relation to language, but religion. In fact, the outbreak of the civil war in 1847 divided Catholics and Protestants. The new constitution was mainly a compromise between the liberal and Protestant cantons that were influenced by the French revolution and the conservative cantons that were ruled by Catholic parties dreaming of restoring the lost times of the 'ancient regime'. After losing the constitutional vote in 1872, the winners of the constitution of 1874 gained additional support for discriminating against the order of Jesuits as well as against monasteries. Nevertheless, the constitution of 1874 was a big step towards the building of one nation. Although it discriminated against Catholics, it established one market economy, one army and a united legal system.

The most important factor that impacted on the unification of Switzerland was certainly direct democracy. From 1848 to the time of the new constitution of 1874, the Swiss people had already experienced nine different votes. It is also important to mention that with regard to direct democracy, the cantonal constitutions and even the municipalities were often the pioneers that influenced direct democracy on the federal level. Following the introduction of the right of the people to initiate a constitutional amendment in 1891, the number of annual votes almost doubled each year. It was only during World War I and World War II that there were fewer popular initiatives. Although in most cases the people refused to adopt the proposals put forward, the direct democratic debate all over Switzerland enabled a social cohesion of society. People became aware that common interests did not depend on religion but on different opportunities based on the economy, education and the region in which one resides. The results of the votes became a common, very interesting and influential element in Swiss politics. In many cases, even the losing party accepted a result as legitimate. In the later nineteenth century, the turnout of voters was usually some 50 to 60 per cent of male citizens with voting rights. Today, the turnout is often even lower than 50 per cent.

Direct democracy has also influenced Switzerland's governmental and federal system. At the end of the nineteenth century, some European states developed

28 See the historic lexicon of Switzerland at http://www.hls-dhs-dss.ch/textes/d/D16090.php, accessed 24 April 2015.

29 See http://www.google.ch/url?sa=t&rct=j&q=&esrc=s&source=web&cd=6&ved=0CDEQFjAF&url=http%3A%2F%2Fworldhappiness.report%2F&ei=nCQ6Vey4BobTaKKgNgK&usg=AFQjCNFFloP-jnR5eOqdfMlAkl09tFz9XQ, accessed 24 April 2015.

their governmental system and turned it into a new, democratic, parliamentary democracy. Switzerland has a unique governmental system that is influenced by direct democracy. Every four years, parliament elects seven members as equal partners of the executive, which the constitution, in Art. 174, labels 'the federal council'. The body of the federal council (which is not a coalition government), decides in most cases by consensus and exceptionally by its majority. In Switzerland, there is no agreement between the leading parties to form a government supported by the majority of parliament.

Switzerland has no prime minister, who controls and sometimes nominates the members of the executive based on the prime minister's majority in parliament. The prime minister controls his/her cabinet but such control depends on whether the prime minister has a majority in parliament. In Switzerland, the majority in parliament only has the power to elect the members of the federal council every four years. Once elected, the members of the federal council remain in power for four years unless they voluntarily resign from office. During these four years, parliament has no power to withdraw all or some members of the federal council. The constitution even ignores any impeachment procedure. According to political tradition, parliament, apart from some exceptions, has usually re-elected former members of the federal council when they have agreed to apply as candidates for election. In addition, all members of the federal council are equal partners. The only function of the president of the federal council is to prepare and moderate the meetings of the council. However, he/she has no power to impose his/her opinion on the body of the federal council, which can always decide by majority, even if this decision goes against its president's wishes. Thus, at the end of the nineteenth century the governmental system of Switzerland was able to develop because the constitution guaranteed the legitimacy of the balance between the three branches of government.

According to the constitution, parliament is the most powerful institution compared to the other two governmental branches. As parliament has the constitutional power to elect members of the federal council, it could easily have developed into a parliamentary government, depending on the respective majority of the two chambers. However, federalism and direct democracy impeded such development, because parliament needed an executive that could integrate the different political tendencies of the country and that could propose statutes and constitutional provisions to the legislature that had high chances of gaining the approval of the people, who were and still are the real opposition to the political establishment.

Foreign scholars also consider Switzerland to be one of the leading countries of compromise. Indeed, direct democracy forces the political elite to accept a compromise that has high chances of being accepted via a direct democratic decision of the people. In the governmental system of Switzerland, the real opposition is not an opposition party or a shadow prime minister, but the people. Often the votes of the people contradict the majority opinion of parliament and the legislature. Getting approval from the people requires the political elite to compromise in order to get the final support of the voters.

Problems of direct democracy

Switzerland may be famous for its direct democracy, but in a new democracy survey of 30 countries, it only managed to gain 14th place.[30] The Democracy barometer, co-authored by researchers at Zurich University and the Social Science Research Center Berlin (WZB), concludes that Denmark, Finland and Belgium, between 1995 and 2005, had the world's best functioning democracies. Britain and France were among the worst performers. The barometer shows the development of the 30 top democracies around the world during the period 1995–2005. It uses 100 empirical indicators to measure how well a country complies with the three democratic principles of freedom, quality and control, as well as the nine basic functions of democracy, such as the rule of law, transparency and participation.With regard to the impact of direct democracy, one can focus on the following major problems: lack of financial transparency, exclusion of foreign taxpayers with a Swiss domicile, the idea that the will of the sovereign is the will of God, lack of international credibility and efficiency, problems regarding the participation of citizens, and the lack of eternity clauses combined with a constitutional court.

Financial transparency

Recently (June 2014), the group of states that are against corruption in the Council of Europe (GRECO) published a report alleging that Switzerland does not comply with the recommendations of the group.[31] With regard to transparency, GRECO criticized Switzerland for the fact that there is no transparency with regard to party funding. In fact, there is no federal legislation that would require parties to make their financial support transparent. In addition, there is no legislation that would require groups initiating a popular initiative to make their financial supply transparent either. Thus, GRECO recommended introducing accounting rules for political parties and election campaigns. Switzerland should ensure that income, expenditure and the various elements of assets and liabilities are accounted for in detail and in full and are presented in a coherent format. Only the Socialist Party, as one of the leading Swiss parties, supports this criticism of Switzerland's direct democracy.[32]

The practical argument against more transparency refers to the reality of the system of direct democracy. On the federal, cantonal and municipal level, Switzerland has so many different votes that it is almost impossible to regulate the financing of each of those campaigns. In addition, the federal council always insists that transparency should include party financing as well as voting campaigns.

30 See http://www.mediadesk.uzh.ch/articles/2011/schweizer-demokratie.html, accessed 24 April 2015.

31 See http://www.ejpd.admin.ch/content/dam/data/bj/sicherheit/kriminalitaet/korruption/grecoberichte/ber-iii-2014–14-e.pdf, accessed 21 September 2014.

32 See the website of the socialist party at http://www.sp-ps.ch/de/publikationen/medienmitteilungen/parteienfinanzierung-liegt-weiterhin-im-dunkeln, accessed 24 April 2015.

However, for the last 20 years to the time of writing, the federal council has not made any concrete proposals for improvement.

There is also an ideological argument against transparency. The request for transparency suggests the idea that one might be able to buy the vote of the people. The citizenry, however, is mature. Voters are well aware of the different issues relating to a decision. Thus, requiring transparency is often considered to be an argument that negates the idea of the maturity of the citizen. However, one has to be aware that in many cases the losing minority insists on the fact that there was an imbalance in the financial support of the campaign. In a recent case of a vote on the secession of the district of Laufen from the canton of Berne to a neighbouring canton, the federal court quashed the democratic decision of the citizens who voted to join the other canton. It argued that there was an enormous amount of secrecy and a lack of transparent financial support on one side and therefore it annulled the vote because, the court stated, it did not respect the freedom of the citizen to form an opinion and to give a genuine expression of his or her will.[33] Article 34 par 2 of the Swiss constitution guarantees the right to vote as a fundamental human right. Accordingly, each citizen must have the 'freedom to form an opinion and to give a genuine expression of his or her will' in any federal, cantonal or municipal vote. It seems obvious that the lack of transparency is in contradiction to this basic principle.

Exclusion of foreign taxpayers and foreigners with a Swiss domicile

Every fourth worker in Switzerland has a foreign nationality. Some of them are border crossers but most of them have a Swiss domicile. However, Switzerland excludes them from having any citizens' rights. In some cantons, although these are rare, foreigners with residency rights in a municipality of the canton have voting rights on local and cantonal levels. Nevertheless, on the national level they do not have any voting rights. The previous exclusion of women from having voting rights has demonstrated that people accept such exclusion often because foreigners, who, although they are equal citizens, are often unaware of political decisions, although as taxpayers they often have to pay for the consequences of such decisions. Nevertheless, some cantons have recently introduced the right to vote on a cantonal level and some have introduced it on a municipal level.[34] Although some cantons have tried to include foreigners in the democratic system, voters rejected such proposals. For this reason, I doubt whether in the near future there will be any chance to change this system. If citizens during the nineteenth century had not been discriminated against by not being allowed to vote and if women had not been denied voting rights until 1971, I am sure that many of the negative results of recent votes in Switzerland would not have happened.

33 Decision of the federal tribunal of 20 December 1988 (BGE 114 Ia 427).

34 For a survey of the different cantons, see https://www.ekm.admin.ch/ekm/de/home/buergerrecht-citoyennete/Citoy/stimmrecht.html, accessed 24 April 2015.

The will of the sovereign is the will of God

The argument *vox populi, vox dei*, the voice of the people is the voice of God, has a long tradition in democratic development. In early times, voters were armed, and in order have a peaceful end to a fight, people accepted that the most powerful party would win in relation to the relevant decision. In political debate in Switzerland, the right-wing party, the Union Democrats, regularly insists that popular rights need to be respected and therefore the people and all authorities need to oppose any attempt to limit popular rights because this is antidemocratic. Based on this absolute right of the people, the sovereign has recently adopted some proposals voted for in popular initiatives which contradict human rights, the rule of law, international treaties and obligations that Switzerland has with the EU.

With regard to the issues concerning these popular initiatives, some chambers are not willing to follow strictly the will of the people. Therefore, the Union Democrats intend to launch a popular initiative that focuses on the relationship between the constitution and international law. According to this party, the constitutional articles must have priority over international law with the only exception being mandatory international law. In a new Art. 156a of the constitution, this proposal requires the authorities to either renegotiate the treaty or to cancel it, in case a proposal of an initiative contradicts international law or treaties.[35]

International credibility and efficiency

It is easy to understand the kind of arguments that consider that only the people of Switzerland are able to make the final decisions, even if such decisions go against international agreements and conventions and what is politically, economically and morally good. However, such arguments undermine the international efficiency and credibility of Switzerland and its negotiators. Of course, the supporters of such opinions argue that the position of Switzerland's federal council is even stronger when the negotiation team can count on the majority of the people and of the cantons. This argument is only valid if Switzerland remains a partner to count on internationally. If Switzerland's partners fear that popular initiatives may always question the result of an international treaty or agreement, none of them will negotiate with a country that in the end can always contradict, via a popular initiative, any international agreement.

Participation of citizens

The average percentage of participation of Swiss citizens is often less than 50 per cent. Swiss voters have many opportunities to participate in votes and elections each year. At the federal level, voters vote in general on eight to twelve issues. However, they also vote at the level of the cantons and at the level of the

35 See http://www.admin.ch/ch/d/pore/vi/vis460t.html, accessed 24 April 2015.

municipalities. Thus, many citizens have to participate in and to elect people in relation to the affairs of their municipality, of their canton and of the federation several times per year.

Several surveys show that more educated people with a high income, more men than women and more older than younger people participate in voting and elections.[36] According to a new survey, some 25 per cent of citizens do not participate because they have no interest at all in politics. They seem to be content with political institutions and prefer to participate in issues of direct democracy rather than in elections. Of the abstentionists, only 16 per cent do not participate because they are annoyed by politics or because they mistrust the institutions and the status of democracy. Besides the frequency of voting procedures, there are other reasons for their abstention. Often, those who do not take part in political processes do not feel well informed enough. Switzerland should therefore focus more on political education in schools. Some experts argue that this abstention can help minorities to achieve voting results that are in their interests. More than other voters, voters belonging to minorities will use their voting possibilities in order to achieve a voting result that is in favour of the interests of minorities.

The lack of eternity clauses combined with a constitutional court

Many constitutions of countries with a civil law tradition have eternity clauses in their constitution. Some of those eternity clauses guarantee human rights. With regard to popular initiatives that require a partial revision of the constitution, there are some eternity clauses in the constitution. Principally, these initiatives have to comply with those clauses. However, parliament, which has the final say on deciding whether the initiative complies with the constitution, is very generous with regard to those initiatives. In principle, it decides in cases of doubt in favour of the right of the citizens to vote on the proposal of the initiative. Therefore, parliament, based on a proposal of the federal council, decided recently that even the proposal banning minarets conforms with mandatory international law, although it clearly discriminates against a religious minority.

The other constitutional limit with regard to popular initiatives requiring a partial revision of the constitution is that they must comply with the principle of consistency. Recently, parliament accepted the result of a popular initiative that would mean that it would be legal to limit the growth of the population in Switzerland to 0.2 per cent per year, and at the same time it required that the federal government invest 10 per cent of the fund for cooperation in countries that agree to family planning. This is completely contradictory to the intention of the constitution in terms of enabling citizens to vote on one subject and not on two different issues. Family planning in developing countries and a reduction in the extent of immigration into Switzerland are different issues, and citizens may have

36 See Sonntagszeitung of Neue Zürcher Zeitung from 19 April 2015.

different opinions on each of these issues. However, parliament decided again, because this was a case in doubt, in favour of democracy. In the long run, Switzerland will need some eternity clauses in the constitution and a constitutional court with the power to review and control popular initiatives that are requesting partial revision. However, such ideas are marginal because the Swiss population is rather reluctant to give powers to a small number of judges.

Recently, the constitutional court in Austria annulled a constitutional provision in the legislation. It mainly argued that the Austrian constitution of 1920 distinguishes in Art. 44 between a total and a partial revision. While the legislature can decide on partial revisions with a qualified majority, only the people can decide on a total revision. The usual legislature cannot change the main constitutional principles.[37] Switzerland could and should learn from this decision.

Conclusions

The system of direct democracy in Switzerland has many defects. However, it will be extremely difficult to convince the sovereign of these deficiencies and to improve the system. Despite this, it is necessary to evaluate the impact of direct democracy on the political stability of Switzerland. Considering the positive impact that this system has on the peaceful harmony of the political and social society of a country with great potential for conflict, it would be wrong to abolish the system as a whole. It would be wrong to change the entire system just because it has some faults. The history of direct democracy in Switzerland has already demonstrated that any improvement of the system, such as the acceptance of gender equality in voting, takes a long time and therefore requires some patience. Only a long period of misuse of voting rights can convince the majority of the voters and the cantons to accept a constitutional provision that will limit their possibilities to intervene in the constitution.

37 See http://www.ris.bka.gv.at/Dokumente/Vfgh/JFR_09988989_00G00012_01/JFR_09988989_00G00012_01.pdf, accessed 24 April 2015.

5 Direct democracy vs fundamental rights? A comparative analysis of the mechanisms that limit the 'will of the people' in Switzerland and California

Claudia Josi

Introduction

The term 'direct democracy' is used to describe a type of political system that is characterized by its emphasis on providing mechanisms for political participation and decision-making in which citizens get to vote and decide on matters of public concern without the interference of any intermediaries that represent their interests. In this sense, it entails: 1) a political system in which the will of the people is expressed directly by the citizens and not by elected representatives and 2) certain mechanisms that allow the people to express their will directly concerning certain questions or political decisions. Direct democracy can thus be differentiated from a representative democracy, but both can coexist as different mechanisms through which domestic decisions can be made.

Referendums and popular initiatives (also known as ballot initiatives) are two of the most common direct democracy mechanisms. Despite differences in the way that different countries outline these two types of direct democracy mechanisms, they all share certain common core elements. Both referendums and popular (or ballot) initiatives are proposed by groups of organized citizens (such as interest groups or political parties). In referendums, citizens vote on whether a law (approved by the legislature) should be rejected. This effectively grants citizens a veto power. In popular (or ballot) initiatives, however, citizens have the power to propose new laws.

This chapter will focus on the mechanism of popular initiatives, as they are a powerful vehicle that citizens can use to actively propose new legislation. Popular initiatives can be launched without the consent of the legislature, or even in spite of congressional or parliamentarian opposition. Also, because they have their own procedure and special legitimation, they may serve as a means to circumvent limitations that 'ordinary' legislation enacted by parliament or the legislature might face, and thus are particularly prone to create conflicts with minority rights, fundamental rights of other affected groups and other constitutional safeguards.

However, just like in any other law-making process, there can be legal restrictions on the content, subject matter and purpose of this direct democracy mechanism. For example, possible restrictions regarding the subject matter may limit the possibility of proposing certain initiatives, such as respecting fundamental human rights, or there may be other considerations, such as the constitutional setup or international law obligations.

From a comparative analysis perspective, this article explores whether and to what extent legislation in Switzerland and California provides for substantive and procedural restrictions on this direct democracy mechanism, placing special emphasis on whether the scope and enjoyment of fundamental rights may be subjected to popular (or ballot) initiatives. After laying this groundwork, this article will analyze two recent examples – one from Switzerland and one from California – in which a conflict between popular initiatives and fundamental rights arose. From a critical perspective this article then makes certain recommendations aimed at improving the legal restrictions of popular initiatives and the mechanisms of control, such as administrative pre-election control or post-election judicial review, to ensure that the scope and enjoyment of fundamental rights is not liable to modifications by popular initiatives.

Direct democracy mechanisms in Switzerland and California

In order to frame the issues addressed in this article, it is necessary to understand how direct democracy mechanisms fit into the general political framework and cultures in Switzerland and California.

Direct democracy in Switzerland

The Swiss political system is generally described as a federal semi-direct parliamentary system, due to the high degree to which direct democracy mechanisms are used, particularly popular initiatives and referendums. The political culture in Switzerland is deeply influenced and characterized by these direct democracy mechanisms that exist on both a federal and a cantonal level.[1]

In Switzerland, popular initiatives are allowed at federal and cantonal levels. In federal popular initiatives, Swiss citizens may propose an amendment (or 'partial revision') to the constitution,[2] but they may not propose new federal laws or amendments of those laws. The scope of popular initiatives at the cantonal level varies from canton to canton. Generally, in cantonal popular initiatives, citizens of a canton can propose new cantonal laws or amendments to cantonal law, as

1 For an overview of the political system, see, for example, Th. Fleiner, 'Switzerland: Constitution of the Federal State and the Cantons' in L. Basta Fleiner and Th. Fleiner (eds), *Allgemeine Staatslehre: Über Die Konstitutionelle Demokratie in Einer Multikulturellen Globalisierten Welt* (Springer 2004) 103–144.

2 Federal Constitution of the Swiss Confederation [Swiss Federal Constitution], Art. 139, http://www.admin.ch/ch/e/rs/1/101.en.pdf, accessed 26 May 2015.

well as amendments to the cantonal constitution. In this paper, we will focus on federal popular initiatives.

Initiatives aimed at modifying the federal constitution require the collection of 100,000 signatures of people who are eligible to vote.[3] These signatures must be collected within a period of 18 months.[4] Once there are enough valid signatures, the initiative is put to a popular vote. A popular initiative may be formulated as a general proposal or – as is more often the case – as a precisely formulated text. If it is formulated using specific language, parliament or the government can no longer alter the wording of the initiative. The government may (and often does) respond to an initiative with a direct counterproposal (generally less far-reaching) in the hope that a majority of the people and cantons will support that counterproposal instead of the original initiative.[5]

In Switzerland, popular initiatives never originate from parliament or government, but always from the people. They are regarded as the driving force behind direct democracy.[6] The acceptance of such proposals needs what is known as the double majority – the proposal must be accepted both by the popular majority (i.e. the majority of the valid votes cast in the whole country) and by the cantonal majority (i.e. voters in a majority of the cantons must accept the proposal).[7]

Direct democracy in California

In the US, the political framework regarding direct democracy is different. While no direct democratic mechanisms are allowed at the federal level, almost half the states allow citizen-sponsored ballot initiatives. The vast majority of the states provide either initiatives and/or referendums.[8] Of the 24 American states that have some type of direct democracy mechanism, 18 have provisions that allow state constitutional amendments.[9] Twenty-two states allow citizens to propose new state statutes via initiative.[10] As California has one of the richest experiences in direct democracy, and especially in popular initiatives (here called ballot initiatives), this paper will focus on this particular state.

California allows citizens to use the initiative process to create laws or statutes and to amend the state constitution. As in Switzerland, popular initiatives can be

3 Swiss Federal Constitution, Art. 139(1).

4 Ibid.

5 Swiss Federal Constitution, Art. 139(4).

6 The Federal Authorities of the Swiss Confederation, The Swiss Confederation–A Brief Guide 2011, at 16, http://www.admin.ch/ch/e/pore/index3.html, accessed 26 May 2015.

7 Ibid.

8 D.F. Damore, Sh. Bowler and S.P. Nicholson, 'Agenda Setting by Direct Democracy: Comparing the Initiative and the Referendum' (2012) 12(4) *State Politics & Policy Quarterly* 367, 368.

9 National Conference of State Legislatures, 'Initiative and Referendum in the 21st Century', Final Report and Recommendations of the NCSL I&R Task Force (2002), http://www.iandrinstitute.org/New%20IRI%20Website%20Info/I&R%20Research%20and%20History/I&R%20Studies/NCSL%20-%20Final%20Task%20Force%20Report%20on%20I&R%20IRI.pdf, accessed 26 May 2015.

10 Ibid.

drafted either as general (or indirect) initiatives, putting forward a general idea, or as precisely formulated initiatives, proposing specific wording of the proposal. The most common form of initiative is the formulated initiative. A less common form is the general initiative. Contrary to the requirements that apply in Switzerland, initiatives in California need only a simple majority of the vote to pass, and they usually pass only by narrow margins. Since 1978, Californian citizens have approved hundreds of initiatives on a vast range of issues.[11]

The California constitution describes the available mechanisms of direct democracy in Art. 2 under the heading 'voting, initiative and referendum, and recall'.[12] Article 2, Section 8(a) of the constitution outlines the mechanism of the initiative as 'the power of the electors to propose statutes and amendments to the constitution and to adopt or reject them'.[13]

In California, a popular initiative may be proposed by electors equal in number to 5 per cent in the case of a statute and 8 per cent in the case of an amendment to the constitution of the votes for all candidates for governor at the last gubernatorial election.[14] The secretary of state then submits the measure at the next general election that is held at least 131 days after it qualifies or at any special statewide election held prior to that general election. The governor may call a special statewide election for the measure.[15]

Restrictions on the content and scope of popular initiatives

Direct democratic mechanisms, such as popular initiatives, can be subjected to restrictions on the basis of form and subject matter. The most important ones in relation to this analysis are so-called subject restrictions. These are laws that limit the scope or content of ballot measures. Typically, these restrictions prevent laws from addressing certain subjects, such as fundamental freedoms and rights, religious institutions, or other politically complex issues, such as taxes and spending power. In the following chapter, we will analyze the restrictions that Switzerland and California place on the subject matter of initiatives.

Subject matter restrictions in Switzerland

In Switzerland, the conditions for and limits on federal popular initiatives are defined in Art. 139, Section 3 of the Federal Constitution as follows:

> If the initiative fails to comply with the requirements of consistency of form, and of subject matter, or if it infringes mandatory provisions of international law, the Federal Assembly shall declare it to be invalid in whole or in part.

11 'Lessons from California: The Perils of Extreme Democracy: California Offers a Warning to Voters all over the World', *The Economist* (20 April 2011), http://www.economist.com/node/18586520, accessed 26 May 2015.
12 Further references see, Cal. Const. Art. 2, sec. 10 and 11.
13 Cal. Const. Art. 2, sec. 8(a).
14 Cal. Const. Art. 2, sec. 8(b).
15 Cal. Const. Art. 2, sec. 8(c).

In this sense, the constitution defines three criteria for the admissibility of a popular initiative. First, the initiative must be consistent in its form. This criterion requires an initiative to be either formulated as a concrete legislative project or as a general proposition. Second, the initiative must be consistent in its subject matter. This criterion requires that each initiative address only those issues that are closely interrelated. The linking of different subjects that are not connected into one initiative is not allowed as this would possibly confuse the voters and impede the clear expression of their will. This limitation is aimed at guaranteeing that the citizens can clearly express their opinion in the vote.[16] Third, the initiative must be in accordance with 'mandatory provisions of international law', the so-called international *ius cogens.* If an initiative conflicts with international *ius cogens*, the federal parliament can declare a popular initiative invalid and refuse a vote on the said initiative. However, this material restriction on the possibility of the proponents defining the initiative is itself limited; it only refers to 'mandatory provisions of international law', not international law in general. This means that if an initiative is opposed to international agreements or norms that are not part of the *ius cogens*, the parliament has no authority to declare this proposal invalid and is obliged to present the initiative to the people and the cantons for a vote.[17] It is also important to note that the Swiss constitution does not exclude certain subject matters, such as tax law, from the possibility of being subjected to popular vote, nor does it prescribe any other material limits, such as constitutional provisions, to the legality of a popular initiative.

Subject matter restrictions in California

In the US, several states that allow citizens to initiate legislation through ballot initiatives have adopted restrictions and regulations that limit the scope and content of proposed initiatives. In California, Art. 2, Section 8 of the state constitution establishes the following limitations:

> (e) An initiative measure may not include or exclude any political subdivision of the State from the application or effect of its provisions based upon approval or disapproval of the initiative measure, or based upon the casting of a specified percentage of votes in favour of the measure, by the electors of that political subdivision.

16 Th. Fleiner, P. Forster, A. Misic and U. Thalmann (eds), *BV 2000: Die neue schweizerische Bundesverfassung: Föderalismus, Grundrechte, Wirtschaftsrecht und Staatsstruktur* (Helbing & Lichtenhahn 2000) 65.

17 In the case of an acceptance, its text will be interpreted as being as consistent with international law obligations as possible in order to conflict with as few international law obligations as possible. However, if this is not possible, the approval of the initiative by popular vote has to be understood as an implicit mandate for the Federal Council (the Executive branch) to terminate said international treaty.

> (f) An initiative measure may not contain alternative or cumulative provisions wherein one or more of those provisions would become law depending upon the casting of a specified percentage of votes for or against the measure.[18]

Also, similar to the Swiss criterion of the consistency in the subject matter, California establishes the 'single-subject rule'. This rule states that each proposed measure must address only one subject.[19]

Finally, Section 12 of the California state constitution refers to the only material limit on the subject matter of initiatives:

> No amendment to the Constitution, and no statute proposed to the electors by the Legislature or by initiative, that names any individual to hold any office, or names or identifies any private corporation to perform any function or to have any power or duty, may be submitted to the electors or have any effect.

Consequently, besides the exclusion of 'personalized' initiatives, California does not establish any material restriction concerning the subject matter of an initiative. Also, unlike Switzerland, California's legislation does not require any formal review of the wording, substance, legality or constitutionality of ballot initiatives before signature collection begins.[20] This means that no previous administrative control will affect the proponent's freedom of speech to put forward their initiative in any way.

Recent examples in which the subject matter of proposed initiatives has conflicted with individual fundamental rights

Switzerland's 'minaret initiative'

In recent years, Switzerland has experienced a series of popular initiatives, which have challenged the balance between the will of the people and respect for the fundamental rights of minorities. Among these, the 2009 'minaret initiative' was one of the darkest moments of Swiss direct democracy. In this paper, we will use this initiative as an example for our analysis.

On 29 November 2009, Swiss citizens accepted a popular initiative that established a constitutional ban on the construction of minarets in the country. There are several factors that motivated the launching of this initiative.

18 The same provision is repeated in Cal. Const. Art. 2, sec. 11 concerning city and county initiatives.

19 Cal. Const. Art. 2, sec. 8(d).

20 Center for Governmental Studies, 'Executive Summary–Democracy by Initiative: Shaping California's Fourth Branch of Government' (2008) 9, http://www.policyarchive.org/handle/10207/bitstreams/5800.pdf, accessed 26 May 2015.

The population of Muslims in the country had grown from about 50,000 in 1980 to over 300,000 in 2010.[21] This meant that more than 4.3 per cent of all residents in Switzerland were Muslims, so Islam became the second-largest religion in the country. Although by now 12 per cent of Muslims in Switzerland have a Swiss passport, the religion is still perceived as 'foreign'. But it is not only the increasing population that has been a trigger for anti-Islamic tendencies. In addition, the perceived threat of Islamic terrorism and the global 'war on terror' has provoked an increased hostility and resentment towards the Muslim population.

Catalysts for the popular initiative were several requests for the construction of minarets, in the cities of Langenthal, Wil and Wangen,[22] that led to popular protests and heated debates at the local level. In the eyes of the critics, the construction of mosques and minarets symbolized the growing threat of Islam to so-called traditional Swiss values. Supporters of the initiative argued that minarets do not in fact have any religious purpose, but instead serve as a religious–political symbol of power and dominance.[23] Opponents of the initiative warned that it violated the freedom of religion, granted in the Swiss federal constitution (Art. 15) and in the European Convention of Human Rights (Art. 9), to which Switzerland is a party. They also argued that the prohibition on building minarets would infringe the prohibition on discrimination granted in the Swiss federal constitution (Art. 8), as it targeted in a discriminatory way only the Muslim population of Switzerland.[24] Several international bodies also expressed their concern about their opposition to this initiative and warned that it would violate international law that was recognized by Switzerland.[25]

21 Swiss Federal Statistical Office, http://www.bfs.admin.ch/bfs/portal/en/index/themen/01/05/blank/key/religionen.html, accessed 26 May 2015.

22 In particular, the request to build a minaret on top of the Turkish cultural association building in Wangen provoked the fiercest opposition of the local population. After popular protests, the collection of signatures against the plans to build a minaret and a series of legal battles, the Muslim association won the case and was able to build the minaret. However, the case became emblematic for the growing conflict between parts of the Swiss local population and the Muslim community, with arguments similar to those used in the discussions regarding the plans to build a mosque near Ground Zero in New York.

23 Website of the Initiative-committee, http://www.minarette.ch/darum-geht-es/index.html, accessed 26 May 2015.

24 See, among others, the statement of the platform of Swiss Human Rights institutions, http://www.humanrights.ch/en/Switzerland/Internal-Affairs/Groups/cultural/idart_7358-content.html, accessed 26 May 2015.

25 See, among others, the statement of the High Commissioner on Human Rights, Ms. Navi Pillay (1 December 2009), http://www.ohchr.org/EN/NewsEvents/Pages/DisplayNews.aspx?NewsID=9651&LangID=E); S, accessed 26 May 2015, the statement of the Special Rapporteur on freedom of religion or belief, Ms. Asma Jahangir (30 November 2009), http://www.ohchr.org/en/NewsEvents/Pages/DisplayNews.aspx?NewsID=9649&LangID=e), accessed 26 May 2015, or the statement of the director of the OSCE Office for Democratic Institutions and Human Rights (ODIHR), Ambassador Janez Lenarcic (30 November 2009), http://www.osce.org/odihr/51680, accessed 26 May 2015.

The question of the legality of this initiative

The proposed constitutional ban on building minarets raised the question of the legality of this particular popular initiative. The Swiss government, as well as the vast majority of the Swiss Federal Parliament, was strongly against the ban. However, according to the conditions set out in Art. 139(3) of the federal constitution, the parliament can only reject an initiative if it violates 'mandatory provisions of international law'. It is generally accepted that these norms of *ius cogens* include the prohibition of crimes against humanity, genocide, slavery and torture. However, in the case of the minaret initiative, whether the affected right to religious liberty had already emerged as *ius cogens* was disputed. Despite the strong opposition of the Swiss government,[26] the parliament, human rights groups,[27] churches,[28] and liberal parties,[29] the initiative won, gaining 57.5 per cent of the votes.[30]

Owing to the way in which the judiciary is set up in Switzerland, the result of this vote was binding and barred from judicial review. In 2009, the Federal Court rejected two cases against the new constitutional provision as the claimants had failed to demonstrate a concrete affectation of their constitutional rights, and they therefore lacked legal standing. In addition, the European Court of Human Rights rejected two petitions against the minaret ban on the same procedural

26 See, among others, statements by the Swiss Federal Council, http://www.news.admin.ch/message/index.html?lang=en&msg-id=20878, accessed 26 May 2015; http://www.ejpd.admin.ch/ejpd/en/home/dokumentation/mi/2008/2008-08-27.html, accessed 26 May 2015.

27 See, among others, statements of the Association Humanrights.ch / MERS, http://www.humanrights.ch/en/Switzerland/Internal-Affairs/Groups/cultural/idart_7358-content.html, accessed 26 May 2015; Amnesty International Swiss Section, http://www.humanrights.ch/upload/pdf/091026_amnesty_minarettinitiative.pdf, accessed 26 May 2015; Terres des Femmes, http://www.humanrights.ch/upload/pdf/091106_Offener_Brief_Minarettinitiative2.pdf, accessed 26 May 2015 and the Swiss Society for Minorities, http://www.gms-minderheiten.ch/attachments/098_Minarettverbot%20-%20diskriminierend%20und%20unnötig.pdf, accessed 26 May 2015.

28 See, among others, statements of the Swiss Federation of Protestant Churches, http://www.sek-feps.ch/de/themen/minarettinitiative, and http://www.sek-feps.ch/de/themen/minarettinitiative/stellungnahmen-des-sek, accessed 26 May 2015.

29 See, among others, statements of the Swiss Green Party, http://www.gruene.ch/web/gruene/de/positionen/soziales/integration/medienmitteilungen/nein_zur_minarett_initiative_20-10-09.html, accessed 26 May 2015; the Swiss Democratic Socialist Party, http://www.sp-ps.ch/ger/Medien/Pressedienst/2009/Nein-zur-Anti-Minarett-Initiative, and the Swiss Green Liberal Party, http://www.grunliberale.ch/abstimmungen.htm, accessed 26 May 2015.

30 Official results of the vote from the Swiss Federal Statistical Office, http://www.bfs.admin.ch/bfs/portal/de/index/themen/17/03/blank/key/2009/01.html, accessed 26 May 2015; for more information also see the official webpage of the Swiss Federal Assembly, http://www.parlament.ch/d/wahlen-abstimmungen/volksabstimmungen/volksabstimmungen-2009/abstimmung-2009-11-29/seiten/default.aspx, accessed 26 May 2015.

grounds in 2011.[31] Therefore, following the popular vote, a new constitutional provision was included in the Swiss federal constitution prohibiting the construction of minarets.[32]

California's 'Proposition 8'

Several popular initiatives in California have also raised tensions between the expressed will of the people and the state's obligation to respect, protect, and guarantee fundamental rights. One of the most emblematic was the November 2008 vote on Proposition 8 (also called Prop 8). Prop 8 was a ballot initiative proposing a constitutional amendment of the state constitution defining marriage as exclusively applicable to opposite-sex couples. The approval of this proposition added a new provision to California's state constitution, which provides that 'only marriage between a man and a woman is valid or recognized in California'.[33] This restrictive definition of marriage that referred only to opposite-sex couples targeted California's Supreme Court's ruling in *In re Marriage Cases*[34] that established that same-sex couples have a constitutional right to marry. In this case, the Supreme Court concluded that 'permitting opposite-sex couples to marry while affording same-sex couples access only to the novel and less-recognized status of domestic partnership improperly infringes a same-sex couple's constitutional rights to marry and to the equal protection of the laws as guaranteed by the California State Constitution'.[35] Proposition 8 aimed at overturning this judgment by means of a constitutional amendment to the California state constitution.

> Prop 8 was approved by a 52 per cent majority.[36] Its full text was as follows:
> Section I. Title
> This measure shall be known and may be cited as the 'California Marriage Protection Act'.
> Section 2. Article I.
> Section 7.5 is added to the California Constitution, to read: Sec. 7.5. Only marriage between a man and a woman is valid or recognized in California.

31 See, among others, 'Minarettinitiative: Muslime blitzen in Strassburg ab' *Tagesanzeiger* (8 July 2011), http://www.tagesanzeiger.ch/schweiz/standard/Minarettinitiative-Muslime-blitzen-in-Strassburg-ab/story/25570382, accessed 26 May 2015.

32 Swiss Federal Constitution, Art. 72(3).

33 Cal. Const. Art. 1, sec. 7.5.

34 *In re Marriage Cases,* 43 Cal.4th 757 (Cal. 2008).

35 Ibid. See also Judicial Council of California, News release No 26 (15 May 2008), http://www.courts.ca.gov/documents/NR26–08.PDF, accessed 26 May 2015.

36 'Secretary of State Debra Bowen Certifies Eighth Measure for November 4' (2 June 2008) *Secretary of State of California*, http://admin.cdn.sos.ca.gov/press-releases/2008/DB08–068.pdf, accessed 26 May 2015.

The question concerning the constitutionality of Proposition 8

The supporters of Prop 8 argued that the initiative was not an attack on the gay 'lifestyle', but rather an effort to preserve what they held as core values surrounding a vision of traditional marriage. They also claimed that it intended to overturn the decision of four activist Supreme Court judges in ruling Proposition 22 unconstitutional in the *In re Marriage Cases*.[37] On the other side, opponents of Prop 8 argued that the initiative was unconstitutional on due process and equal protection grounds, as it codified discrimination against same-sex couples and failed to provide for marriage on an equal basis. They also warned that popular initiatives amending the constitution should not be taken lightly; using them to take away rights from one particular group could open a Pandora's Box of other ballot initiatives that might eliminate other rights, including religious freedom and civil rights.

The question of the constitutionality of Proposition 8 has gone a long way through California's judicial system since its approval by popular vote in 2008. On 4 August 2010, in the case of *Perry v Schwarzenegger*, US District Court Judge Vaughn Walker declared this ban unconstitutional as it violated the due process and equal protection clauses.[38] This decision was upheld by the United States Court of Appeals for the Ninth Circuit on 7 February 2012 in the case of *Perry v Brown*.[39] According to the court, what made Proposition 8 unconstitutional was that these couples already had the right to marry in the state, a right that was taken away by the initiative. 'Withdrawing from a disfavored group the right to obtain a designation with significant social consequences is different from declining to extend that designation in the first place', wrote Justice Stephen Reinhardt.[40]

In 2013, the case of *Hollingsworth v Perry* was considered by the US Supreme Court after it accepted to review the petition for certiorari filed on 31 July 2012 by the proponents of Prop 8.[41] However, in its decision the Court avoided deciding whether the ballot initiative violated the US constitution's due process

37 Prop 22 was a law enacted by Californian voters in March 2000, adding Section 308.5 of the Family Code and restricting marriages to only those between opposite-sex couples. Being a simple act, it was struck down as inconsistent with the state constitution. The goal of Prop 8 was to establish the same restriction, but as a constitutional provision. In the eyes of the proponents this would 'protect' it from judicial review. Actually, the wording of Prop 8 was exactly the same as that of Prop 22.

38 *Perry v Schwarzenegger*, 704 F. Supp. 2d 921, 927 (N.D. Cal. 2010).

39 *Perry v Brown*, 681 F.3d 1065 (9th Cir. 2012).

40 Ibid. 1080 (9th Cir. 2012).

41 See, among others, S. Thomaston, J. Combs and A. Bink, 'Supreme Court Will Hear Challenges to Prop 8, DOMA' *The Huffington Post* (7 December 2012), http://www.huffingtonpost.com/scottie-thomaston/supreme-court-will-hear-challenges-to-prop-8-doma_b_2260539.html, accessed 26 May 2015. The full decision is available at http://www.scribd.com/doc/114792870/Supreme-Court-Order, accessed 26 May 2015.

and equal protection clauses and should therefore be declared unconstitutional. Rather, it decided to dismiss the appeal on jurisdictional grounds, ruling that private parties did not have 'standing' to defend California's voter-approved ballot measure barring gay and lesbian couples from state-sanctioned wedlock. Although this ruling was somewhat disappointing for the supporters of same-sex marriage, by dismissing the case, the court left in place the lower court decision that allowed same-sex marriage to be reinstated. Within hours of the ruling, California's Gov. Jerry Brown directed the California Department of Public Health to advise the state's counties that they must begin issuing marriage licences to same-sex couples in California as soon as the Ninth Circuit had confirmed that the stay was lifted. Brown said he interpreted the high court opinion as making Prop 8 unconstitutional and unenforceable.[42]

However, dissenting Justice Anthony Kennedy criticized the court's majority that ignored the initiative process that led to the passage of Proposition 8.

> What the court fails to grasp or accept is the basic premise of the initiative process. And it is this. The essence of democracy is that the right to make law rests in the people and flows to the government, not the other way around. Freedom resides first in the people without need of a grant from government . . . The California initiative process embodies these principles and has done so for over a century . . . In California and the 26 other states that permit initiatives and popular referendums, the people have exercised their own inherent sovereign right to govern themselves. The court today frustrates that choice.[43]

In this statement, Justice Kennedy expressed the tension between respect for fundamental human rights and respect for the democratically expressed will of the majority.

Critical analysis of the status quo and proposals for improvement

The question of the constitutionality of Prop 8, as well as the dilemma concerning the legality of the 'minaret initiative', have led to important debates regarding the legal restrictions on the subject matter of popular initiatives as well as on the mechanisms of control of the 'will of the people'. In the following chapter, we will attempt to analyze the status quo concerning the legal restrictions on popular initiatives and the mechanisms of control and will develop proposals for an improvement of the current legal set up. The mechanisms of control in Switzerland are obviously hardly comparable to those in California. Switzerland is a state and therefore we are dealing with the last 'level' of control, whereas California still

42 See, among others, B. Mears, 'Supreme Court Dismisses California's Proposition 8 Appeal' *CNN* (27 June 2013), http://www.cnn.com/2013/06/26/politics/scotus-prop-8/, accessed 26 May 2015.

43 Ibid.

has Federal courts that can exercise control over state decisions. However, both case studies provide interesting experiences that might be useful when discussing the issue at the heart of this chapter, the limits of the 'will of the people' when it comes to making decisions about fundamental rights and the mechanisms available to balance possibly clashing interests.

Critical analysis of the legal setup of popular initiatives in Switzerland

In the last 10 years, popular initiatives, such as the minaret initiative, have increasingly conflicted with fundamental rights and other international law obligations. Even though initiatives that were to some extent incompatible with fundamental rights have also been put forward in the past, the fact that they are actually accepted by popular vote is a recent trend.[44] These conflicts are even more critical because of the structure of Switzerland's judicial branch. As a result of the lack of a constitutional court in which legislation can be challenged, the result of a popular referendum is binding and is barred from (abstract) judicial review. The Swiss federal constitution states in Art. 190 that federal administration and federal courts are bound to apply federal laws and international law.[45] This mandate of obligatory application of federal law also applies to the Swiss Federal Court (the highest court in the Swiss judiciary, similar to the US Supreme Court) and denies the court the competence to annul, derogate or reject its application even in a case in which it finds that a federal law is incompatible with the constitution.[46] While the court is able to determine that a federal law is incompatible with the federal constitution, it does not have the competence to annul or derogate the said law. This therefore prevents a judicial review of the federal legislation (including the federal constitution) by the federal court. As a consequence, in Switzerland only a concrete administrative act (e.g. a specific decision of an administrative entity) applying the relevant law can be challenged as unconstitutional. If the federal court establishes a violation of constitutional rights, the concrete act can be challenged and eventually annulled. This, however, does not affect the validity of the law in question and Swiss courts continue to be required to apply it.

Andreas Gross, a member of the centre-left Social Democratic party in the Swiss House of Representatives, maintains that the results from the minaret vote will contribute to a rethinking of Swiss democracy. 'The Swiss have learned now that there is a problem [with direct democracy] and you can't vote on basic human rights', he said in 2010.[47]

44 A. Ritter, 'Kalifornien als Vorbild', *University of Zurich* (23 August 2012), http://www.uzh.ch/news/articles/2012/kalifornien-als-vorbild.html, accessed 26 May 2015.

45 Swiss Federal Constitution, Art. 190.

46 Swiss Federal Constitution, Art. 189.

47 J. Slater, 'The Swiss Vote More Than Any Other Country' *Swissinfo* (29 March 2010), http://www.swissinfo.ch/eng/specials/switzerland_for_the_record/world_records/The_Swiss_vote_more_than_any_other_country.html?cid=8483932, accessed 26 May 2015.

In reaction to several popular initiatives that have conflicted with fundamental rights in recent years, the Swiss government is considering different means to strengthen the restrictions on popular initiatives as well as the control of the content of such initiatives. One proposal, presented by Federal Chancellor Simonetta Sommaruga, Head of the Federal Justice and Police Department, suggests an initial check of the content of an initiative by the federal administration, similar to an advisory opinion. The federal administration would only provide an assessment on the compatibility of the initiative with international law, but would not be able to declare it invalid. This assessment would allow the proponents to modify the original text of the initiative if they wished to do so or to maintain the original proposal. In any case, the findings of the assessment would be made public and would have to be published on the forms used for the collection of signatures.[48]

Another proposal focuses on strengthening parliament's ability to declare an initiative invalid when it conflicts with core fundamental rights. Until the time of writing (October 2015), parliament's power to declare a popular initiative invalid has been limited to initiatives that violate international *ius cogens*. This parliamentary motion was presented two years ago by Daniel Vischer, a member of the commission on political institutions of the House of Representatives.[49] It aims to broaden the scope of the subject-matter restrictions of popular initiatives to include fundamental rights. Andreas Auer, Professor of Constitutional Law at the University of Zurich and Director of the Centre for Democracy in Aarau, agrees that Switzerland has to develop ways to 'prevent people from launching initiatives that directly violate internationally guaranteed human rights'.[50] However, he considers that although the government and parliament could examine proposals that are put forward, they should not have the final say on whether a vote can be submitted to the people or not. His view is, 'It must end up in a court. This is my conviction. These questions cannot be decided by political bodies like parliament or the government, but by judges. Human rights questions are delicate questions.'[51]

A recent PhD thesis in political science at the University of Zurich has analyzed the effectiveness of the initial control mechanism of Swiss popular initiatives.[52] The outcome is surprising and frustrating at the same time. It establishes that

48 Federal Justice and Police Department (EJPD), 'Zusatzbericht des Bundesrats über das Verhältnis von Völkerrecht und Landesrecht: Bessere Vereinbarkeit von Volksinitiativen mit dem Völkerrecht', *Public Statement by Federal Chancellor Simonetta Sommaruga, Head of the Federal Justice and Police Department to the Media* (31 March 2011), http://www.ejpd.admin.ch/content/ejpd/de/home/dokumentation/red/2011/2011-03-31.html, accessed 26 May 2015.

49 J. Slater, 'Defending Popular Rights–By Limiting Them?' *Swissinfo* (1 December 2009), http://www.swissinfo.ch/eng/politics/internal_affairs/Defending_popular_rights_by_limiting_them.html?cid=7813618, accessed 26 May 2015.

50 Ibid.

51 Ibid.

52 A. Christmann, *Die Grenzen direkter Demokratie. Volksentscheide im Spannungsverhältnis von Demokratie und Rechtsstaat* (Nomos 2012).

for most Swiss members of parliament the question of the validity of a particular initiative was an assessment based more on political than on legal considerations, as declaring invalid a popular initiative is an unpopular decision for a member of parliament that could have an effect on his or her reelection. However, this dominance of political considerations in this decision renders the Swiss control mechanism ineffective.[53] The possibility of a directly affected person challenging in court an initiative that has been adopted by popular vote would be a possible remedy to this situation. Seventy per cent of the Swiss population would welcome true judicial control based on legal instead of political considerations. A solution would be to extend the competence of the Swiss Federal Court to allow for judicial review of popular initiatives.[54]

Another important question is the scope of fundamental rights or internationally recognized human rights that has to be protected. Unfortunately, an analysis of the question of where exactly the limits should be established would exceed the scope of this chapter. However, if the desired outcome is to ensure that fundamental rights may not be subjected to the will of the people, then the current restriction of the subject matter to one that respects international *ius cogens* is insufficient. The redefinition of the subject-matter limitation could be done by the legislature or by the judiciary, for example based on the definition of the 'core of fundamental rights' of the jurisprudence of the European Court of Human Rights.

Critical analysis of the legal setup of ballot initiatives in California

Proposition 8 has demonstrated that popular initiatives in California have created conflicts between the will of the people and fundamental rights. Even though California's legislation does not provide much regulation concerning the material limits of ballot initiatives, the judiciary has developed important conditions for the validity of a ballot initiative. Over the years, courts in California have consistently interpreted that ballot initiatives have to comply with the constitutionality requirement in the same way as any other piece of legislation enacted by the legislative.[55] This practice of judicial review has resulted in a rich jurisprudence concerning the constitutionality of ballot initiatives. The courts will consider invalidating initiatives, particularly where the substance of the initiative conflicts with an existing provision of either the state or the US constitution.[56]

The leading case that has developed this principle of the constitutionality requirement limiting the legislative power of the people is *Legislature v*

53 Ibid.

54 Ritter (n. 44).

55 *Legislature v Deukmejian*, 669 P.2d 17, 27 (Cal. 1983).

56 T. Westen, *Democracy by Initiative: Shaping California's Fourth Branch of Government* (Center for Governmental Studies 2008) 108, http://www.policyarchive.org/handle/10207/bitstreams/5800.pdf, accessed 26 May 2015.

Deukmejian.[57] In this case, the proponents of a ballot initiative tried to argue that initiatives should be exempted from a certain constitutional rule applying to the legislative process of law-making. The Supreme Court of California rejected this argument and stated that the initiative power to propose and enact statutes is a form of legislative power 'which otherwise would reside in the Legislature' and therefore was subject to the same rules and limitations.[58]

In the case of *Wallace v Zinman*,[59] the court unambiguously confirmed that initiative statutes have to comply with the same constitutional limits and rules as ordinary laws:

> We do not recognize an initiative measure as having any greater strength or dignity than attaches to any other legislation . . . It is only another system added to our plan of state government by a permissive amendment to the constitution, but it was at no time intended that such permissive legislation by direct vote should override the other safeguards of the constitution . . . We have a state government with three departments, each to check upon the others, and it would be subversive of the very foundation purposes of our government to permit an initiative act of any type to throw out of gear our entire legal mechanism. Our common sense makes us rebel at the suggestion.[60]

As a result, in California their legality can be challenged in court even after they have been accepted by popular vote. Opponents of various popular initiatives in California have challenged almost two-thirds of the ballot initiatives accepted by popular vote in court. From 1964 to 2007 at least a third of the accepted popular initiatives (21 out of 65) have been completely or at least partially overturned by the courts.[61] Initiatives have been challenged on a wide variety of grounds. Often, state and federal courts have invalidated initiatives for violating some constitutional principle.[62] Consequently, judicial review – and following on from this the protection of individual fundamental rights – is much better developed in California than in Switzerland, where the parliament has the last say concerning the validity of a ballot initiative.

However, the question is whether this strong post-election judicial review – that does not have any initial control that prevents clearly unconstitutional initiatives

57 *Legislature v Deukmejian*, 669 P.2d 17, 27 (Cal. 1983).

58 Ibid.

59 *Wallace v Zinman*, 254 P. 946 (Cal. 1927).

60 Ibid. 949 (Cal. 1927).

61 Westen (n. 56).

62 C.B. Holman and R. Stern, 'Judicial Review of Ballot Initiatives: The Changing Role of State and Federal Courts', Center for Governmental Studies, http://www.iandrinstitute.org/New%20IRI%20Website%20Info/I&R%20Research%20and%20History/I&R%20Studies/Holman%20-%20Judicial%20Review%20of%20Ballot%20Initiatives%20IRI.pdf, accessed 26 May 2015.

being put to a vote – is the best solution. Post-election judicial review has led to frustration among California's citizens, as initiatives are presented to the people, campaigns are fought that cost millions of dollars, the people are asked to make up their minds and vote – and after all this the courts strike down the legislative or constitutional amendment that has already been accepted by popular vote.

A solution to this would be a pre-election judicial review of ballot initiatives. Nevertheless, even though the principle of judicial review of ballot initiatives appears well-established in the US, studies have shown that courts in some states, including California, express considerable deference to initiatives and have shown a reluctance to remove an initiative from the ballot prior to an election.[63] Most state and federal courts exercise judicial restraint when it comes to pre-election review of ballot initiatives, especially on substantive rather than procedural grounds.[64] The exercise of such restraint in pre-election review is based on the principle that an initiative is not yet within the purview of either the executive, legislative, or judicial branches before it goes from a mere proposal to an actual law.[65] The California Supreme Court has stated that 'it is usually more appropriate to review constitutional and other challenges to ballot propositions or initiative measures after an election rather than to disrupt the electoral process by preventing the exercise of the people's franchise, in the absence of some clear showing of invalidity'.[66]

Consequently, in California, only six initiatives have been subjected to pre-election judicial review. Of these, only three initiatives have been removed from the ballot. More commonly, initiatives in California are challenged after voters have approved them.[67] However, a systematic initial check of the legality and constitutionality of an initiative would help to prevent people's frustration regarding voting on something that might later be struck down by a court.

An administrative control, for example, similar to an advisory opinion or a mandatory pre-election judicial review, would be a possible solution. A similar system has been established in Florida, where the constitution requires substantive pre-election review of initiative proposals. This review is concluded by the state supreme court of all initiatives that collect 10 per cent of the requisite signatures. The 10 per cent threshold prevents burdening the court with proposals that might not go to vote anyway, but guarantees a judicial pre-election review for those that are heading towards being voted on.[68] Of course, the question of a pre-election review of ballot initiatives would have to be balanced with the right

63 Ibid.

64 Ibid.

65 See J.D. Gordon III and D.B. Magieby, 'Pre-Election Judicial Review of Initiatives and Referendums' (1989) 64 *Notre Dame Law Review* 298, 311.

66 *Brosnahan v Eu*, (Brosnahan I) 31 Cal.3d 1, 4 (Cal. 1982).

67 Holman and Stern (n. 62).

68 California Commission on Campaign Financing, *Democracy by Initiative: Shaping California's Fourth Branch of Government* (Center for Governmental Studies 1992) 108–109, http://policyarchive.org/handle/10207/bitstreams/215.pdf, accessed 26 May 2015.

to freedom of expression. Much more than in Switzerland, this right is very much entrenched in US constitutional values. Some scholars argue that pre-election judicial review of initiatives would violate the first amendment of the US constitution.[69] Also, the US Supreme Court stated in *Meyer v Grant* that political speech in an initiative process must be free from content-based interference by the state.[70] Unfortunately, a deeper analysis of this question would exceed the scope of this paper, but Florida's experience has shown that pre-election judicial review would not necessarily conflict with the right to freedom of expression.[71]

Conclusion: The need for an improved judicial review of popular initiatives

Since the early democratic experiences in Rome and Athens, direct democracy mechanisms have strengthened the participation of civil society and citizen engagement with the political decision-making process. However, there are good reasons for proceeding with caution, especially when it comes to enabling a majority to decide on fundamental rights or minority rights. As the experience of the 'minaret initiative' (and other critical initiatives) in Switzerland has shown, 'mandatory provisions of international law' has proven to be an insufficient subject-matter limitation for popular initiatives. Therefore, Switzerland needs to develop new conditions for the exercise of direct democracy in order to guarantee better protection of the fundamental rights of individuals. As is the case in California, Switzerland should consider as a subject-matter restriction on popular initiatives constitutionally recognized fundamental rights or human rights, as they are established in the main international human rights instruments.

The mechanisms of control also require some improvements. The Swiss experience has revealed that a mechanism of judicial review (pre-election or post-election) is necessary and preferable to the current parliamentary control mechanism. Even though an administrative control is a very convenient and efficient means for the state to regulate certain aspects of the initiative process, the potential for failure or abuse is great. As members of parliament are under pressure in relation to their possible re-election, they are susceptible to basing their decision concerning the legality of a ballot initiative on political rather than legal considerations. Thanks to their judicial independence, judges are less likely to be affected by these considerations. In order to guarantee the rule of law and equal protection of all citizens (pre-election or post-election), judicial review by strong, independent courts is needed. This is even more necessary when it comes to the

69 S. Radcliffe, 'Pre-Election Judicial Review of Initiative Petitions: An Unreasonable Limitation on Political Speech' (1994) 30 *Tulsa Law Review* 425, 430–431.

70 *Meyer v Grant*, 486 US 414 (1988). For a detailed analysis of this case see Radcliffe, Ibid. 425, at. 438.

71 See the example of Florida; for a detailed analysis see California Commission on Campaign Financing (n. 68).

protection of minority rights and potentially 'unpopular' social groups, such as criminals and foreigners.

In California, pre-electoral judicial review might also be a solution in order to prevent the frustration that ballot initiatives provoke when they are declared unconstitutional only after their acceptance by the citizens. A system of initial administrative control similar to an advisory opinion (such as the proposal put forward for Switzerland) or a systematic pre-election judicial review similar to the one in Florida would help to better guarantee fundamental and constitutional rights while at the same time prevent voter frustration in California.

Despite the strong arguments for an improved pre-election judicial review of popular initiatives put forward in this chapter, direct democracy mechanisms are an important tool in today's democratic setup. However, democracy is more than just citizen participation in the decision-making process. It is also about minority protection and respect for the rule of law. As we have seen throughout this analysis, direct democracy mechanisms must respect certain established limits on the extent to which the will of the people may become the law of the land.

Part IV

New trends in popular involvement

Best practices and fatal mistakes in the Icelandic and Irish cases

Part IV

6 The people's contribution to constitutional changes

Writing, advising or approving? – Lessons from Iceland

Björg Thorarensen

Introduction

The process of constitutional rewriting in Iceland between 2010 and 2013 reflects the growing trend in European states to provide an opening for a constituent power to be manifested and to find the means to implement the idea of democratic constitutionalism. This idea requires that citizens should be enabled to initiate, deliberate and decide on constitutional changes through the most participatory methods possible. These trends can be seen not only in new democracies in the making but also in established European democratic states with stable institutions guaranteeing democracy, the rule of law and human rights. However, even the most liberal constitutions are not characterized by heightened opportunities for popular participation in the initiation of changes, participation in the constitutional process or in further development of the constitutional system.[1] Accordingly, the concept of legal constitutionalism presupposes that democratic politics abides by the constitutional limitations set around it.[2] It is therefore worth studying why and how the people can be involved in such tasks and can contribute to constitutional changes within the constitutional boundaries deriving from the amendment procedures stipulated in the constitution itself.

Examples of constitutional revision that has taken place in the last decade and that has been entrusted to specially established constitutional conventions, such as in Austria (2003), Ireland (2012) and Iceland (2010), illustrate the different methods chosen in order to reach the objective of involving the people in the

1 J.I. Colón-Ríos, *Weak Constitutionalism: Democratic Legitimacy and the Question of Constituent Power* (Routledge 2012) 21.

2 P. Blokker, 'Constitutional reform in Europe and recourse to the people'. Paper presented at the Roundtable on Constitutional Change and the People, University of Luxembourg, 12 December 2014.

process, although these have been different in scope and scale.[3] The Icelandic exercise, which will be analyzed further in this chapter, was unique in the sense that it aimed at entirely detaching the making of a new constitution from the political forum to a specially elected Constitutional Assembly. However, most steps taken on the way were marked by controversy. Firstly, there were flaws in the election of the Constitutional Assembly, resulting in the annulment of the election by the Supreme Court of Iceland. This cast doubt on the legitimacy of the Constitutional Council appointed by the parliament, the Althingi, to finalise the task. Secondly, after the Council eventually submitted its draft of a new constitution to the Althingi in July 2011, it was not processed further for more than a year. In October 2012 an advisory referendum was held on the question of whether the draft should be used as the basis for a new constitution; five other questions were also asked on certain elements in the draft. Thirdly, the outcome of the referendum raised more controversies, both on how to interpret the answers to open questions and, not least, on whether the draft should be considered binding upon the legislature, as the people had 'decreed' that it be adopted unchanged in substance. Eventually, a bill on a new constitution was blocked by the Althingi in spring 2013.

The Icelandic innovation attracted significant attention worldwide. It was appraised by many and the draft constitution-making process was declared to be 'tremendously innovative and participatory'.[4] It has also been described as the 'most consultative and participatory constitutional drafting to date'.[5] Furthermore, the draft proposals from the Constitutional Council have been recognized as the 'world's first crowdsourced constitution'.[6] A great deal has been written about the process itself, the ideology behind it, the methods applied, the advantages and shortcomings of the exercise and how the precedent Iceland set may provide a model for other countries that seek to involve citizens in democratic processes. Much less has been written and analysed from the viewpoint of constitutional law regarding the material proposals and their content, such as their rationality and their impact on the political and legal system or how they would,

3 For further discussion on the aims and working methods of the Constitutional Convention in Austria see, for example, A. Gamper, 'The Austrian Constitutional Convention: Continuing the Path to Reform the Federal State?' *Revista d'Estudis Autonòmics i Federals*, No 2/2006, 9ss. The analysis of the Irish Constitutional Convention can be seen, for example, in D.M. Farrell, 'The Irish Constitutional Convention: A Bold Step or a Damp Squib?' in G.F. Ferrari and J. O'Dowd (eds), *75 Years of the Constitution of Ireland: An Irish-Italian Dialogue* (Clarus Press 2014) 191.

4 Z. Elkins, T. Ginsburg and J. Melton, 'A Review of Iceland's Draft Constitution' *The Comparative Constitutions Project* (14 October 2012), 11, www.comparativeconstitutionsproject.org/reports-and-other-publications/, accessed 30 June 2015.

5 H. Fillmore-Patrice, 'The Iceland Experiment (2009–2013): A Participatory Approach to Constitutional Reform' 12, www.democratizationpolicy.org/uimages/pdf/dpc%20policy%20note%202_%20the%20iceland%20experiment.pdf, accessed 30 June 2015.

6 S. Suteu, 'Constitutional Conventions in the Digital Era: Lessons from Iceland and Ireland' (2015) 38 *Boston College International & Comparative Law Review* 252; H. Landemore, 'Inclusive Constitution-Making: The Icelandic Experiment' (2015) 23(2) *The Journal of Political Philosophy* 188.

for instance, enhance the protection of human rights through judicial control. Those who scrutinized and commented on the substance of the draft, including many Icelandic scholars of Political Science and Law and the Council of Europe's Venice Commission, expressed scepticism, and many expressed severe criticism of the quality of the draft constitution. The proposed new institutional system was described as complex and marked by a lack of consistency.[7]

In this chapter some assessment will be made from the viewpoint of constitutional law of the objective behind the process, and the material proposals will be evaluated to some extent. The process was strongly inspired by the principle that constituent power derives from the people, which is one of the cornerstones of Icelandic constitutional theory. However, the idea of moving the making of a new constitution from the political forum and elected representatives of the Althingi turned out to be self-contradictory in the context of constitutional democracy, from the standpoint of legal constitutionalism. The question of why the momentum attained following the economic collapse was lost and the aims of the exercise were not achieved will be addressed. In this respect, problems related to advisory referendums will also be addressed, including how and why the constitution itself prevents the circumvention of its own provisions on the procedure for constitutional amendments, even if these were to be effected though democratic processes and with a strong wave of public support.

The background of the request for constitutional revision

There appeared to be a widespread opinion that the constitution of Iceland could be blamed for playing a role in the collapse of the banks in 2008 and the economic crisis in the country. Indeed, the present Icelandic constitution, adopted in 1944, is outdated in many respects. In 1944, Iceland decided to break off the union with Denmark and establish a separate republic. Only minimal amendments were made to the previous constitution for the purpose of giving effect to the transformation from constitutional monarchy to a republican form of government with a directly elected president. A comprehensive revision was postponed to a more favourable time. The Constitution of the Republic of Iceland, No. 33/1944, took effect following a decisive referendum in which it was approved with approximately 95 per cent of the vote. Over 98 per cent of the electorate participated in the referendum.

Some parts of the Icelandic constitution, especially as regards the executive and its relation to the Althingi, and the provisions on the judiciary, have remained more or less unchanged from the time that Iceland, under Danish rule, received its first constitution from the Danish Monarch in 1874, with subsequent

7 Venice Commission (European Commission for Democracy through Law), *Opinion on the Draft New Constitution, Council of Europe* (11 March 2013), para. 182, http://www.venice.coe.int/webforms/documents/?pdf=CDL-AD%282013%29010-e, accessed 30 June 2015.

additions made in the second constitution of 1920.[8] Thus, important provisions of the Icelandic constitution that have been unaltered since 1874 do not reflect the current reality regarding the executive and the work of the government, or the role of the Althingi in supervising the executive. The constitution does not mention key concepts, such as 'democracy', 'nation', 'parliamentary rule' or even 'government'. Furthermore, the present constitution has in a way kept the flavour of an 'imposed constitution', imposed initially by the Danish monarch, and the Icelandic people have never written or adopted autonomously a new and comprehensive document that matches the nature of the independent republic.[9]

However, some important amendments have been made to the constitution, for example regarding the organization of the Althingi in 1991 and the electoral system in 1984 and 1999. Most importantly, extensive revision was made to the human rights chapter in 1995, when a number of new human rights provisions were added to the constitution. Certain constitutional customs and unwritten rules have developed outside the constitutional text, the most important being the parliamentary rule and the principle of judicial review. The new human rights chapter of 1995 is the principal reason that the powers that the courts have to exercise judicial review of legislation have expanded. Part of the reason for the impact of this chapter is that the influence of international agreements on human rights, particularly the European Convention on Human Rights and the main UN treaties, has increased in light of the declared intention in relation to constitutional reform in 1995 that these should be taken into consideration in the interpretation of the human rights provisions of the constitution.

While it is certainly an exaggeration, or at least a great simplification, to say that the causes of the bank collapse can be traced to the flaws of the constitution, there were nevertheless direct links between the economic crisis and the public demand for constitutional reform. Not only was the debate on the need for homogenization and modernization of the constitutional structures revived, but the collapse and the economic crisis also aroused deep public anger towards the government and state institutions for their lack of control and their failure to take action against the banks, which had expanded immensely in only a few years.[10]

8 The Constitution of the Kingdom of Iceland, No. 9/1920, was adopted after Iceland was granted sovereignty in 1918 and achieved recognition of its equal status in a union with Denmark under a joint monarchy.

9 B.Th. Bergsson and P. Blokker, 'The Constitutional Experiment in Iceland' in K. Pocza (ed.), *Verfassunggebung Konsolidierten Demokratien: Neubeginn oder Verfall eines Politischen Systems* (Nomos 2015) 155.

10 This was confirmed in an extensive report issued in April 2008 by the Special Investigation Commission elected by the Althingi at the end of 2008 to investigate the events that led to the collapse of the three main banks in Iceland and to seek to answer what caused their failure. When the banks collapsed in October 2008, the size of Iceland's financial system was nine times the gross domestic product of the country. *Aðdragandi og orsakir falls íslensku bankanna 2008 og tengdir atburðir* [*Events Leading to, and the Causes of, the Collapse of the Icelandic Banks in 2008, and Related Events*], Volume 1, Chapter 1, 31. See also Appendix 8 to the report: M.J. Flannery, 'The Importance of Government Supervision in Producing

Furthermore, the collapse resulted in a call for a certain degree of reassessment of values and a need for some form of reckoning with the past. Undoubtedly, one of the consequences of the crisis was an unprecedented lack of confidence both in the political parties and in the ability of the elected representatives of the nation in the Althingi to make decisions on important public affairs, and finding a way to restore this confidence was in itself a separate matter for concern.

Since politicians had failed to carry out the long-awaited revision of the constitution, there was an opportunity here for the nation to adopt a constitution, a covenant on the organization of the state and the position of its citizens, deriving from the nation itself. The resignation of the government and the general elections of 2009 had paved the way for steps to be taken in a new direction. In summary, these were the underlying reasons why and the circumstances in which the new coalition government, consisting of the Social Democratic Alliance and the Left Green Movement, gave particular priority to the project of revising the constitution of Iceland as one of its main tasks when it came to power following elections in 2009.

The innovative methods – and setbacks

The new approach taken in 2009 was to involve the nation directly in the task of the reform process in a way that was unprecedented in constitutional history. It was inspired by the view that the nation, as the constituent power, should have a direct impact on the constitution's contents and the values it was to reflect, without any involvement of the political parties during the initial stages of drafting the text. On 16 June 2010, the Althingi passed Act No. 90/2010 establishing a consultative Constitutional Assembly that had the task of revising the constitution.[11] The Act provided for election on an individual basis to the Constitutional Assembly in order to select 25 delegates who were given the role of reviewing the Icelandic constitution and submitting a proposal for a new constitution to the Althingi. The task and points of emphasis were further defined in the Act.

The Act also provided for a new means of seeking the principal viewpoints and points of emphasis of the public concerning the structure of the country's government and its constitution. A special body, the Constitutional Committee appointed by the Althingi, prepared a National Forum, which was held and completed in a single day on 6 November 2010. This was attended by

---

Financial Services' (2009); E.G. Gunnarsson, 'The Icelandic Regulatory Responses to the Financial Crisis' (2011) 12 *European Business Organization Law Review* 2.

11 The Act is accessible in English translation at thjodfundur2010.is/other_files/2010/doc/Act-on-a-Constitutional-Assembly.pdf, accessed 30 June 2015. For a more detailed description of the Act and the revision process, see B. Thorarensen, 'The Impact of the Financial Crisis on Icelandic Constitutional Law: Legislative Reforms, Judicial Review and Revision of the Constitution' in X. Contiades (ed.), *Constitutions in the Global Financial Crisis: A Comparative Analysis* (Ashgate 2013) 273–275.

950 people from all over the country, selected at random from the National Register. The main conclusions from the National Forum were divided into broadly-framed themes, grouping together the viewpoints of the participants and reflecting some basic values that they wished to see form the basis of Iceland's new constitution. The Constitutional Committee then processed the information collected at the forum and prepared the work of the assembly by submitting an extensive report that included ideas that were to serve as a basis for the drafting process. The idea of gathering a large group of people for a single day to seek the viewpoints of citizens on a new constitution was both praised and criticized in the public debate. It became subject to criticism because of the tight schedule of the forum as well as the very vague and general statements it produced. Many considered it highly doubtful that the statements could be described as 'the will of the nation'.[12]

In the election of the Constitutional Assembly, which took place on 27 November 2010, 25 individuals were elected from 522 candidates. This unexpectedly large number of candidates caused difficulties with regard to publicity and the execution of the election. It was a cause for disappointment, however, that participation in the election was much less than expected, with only about 37 per cent of the electorate turning up at the polls. This was considerably short of the normal turnout in elections of candidates to the Althingi, which generally exceeds 80 per cent. Among the reasons suggested for the low turnout was that the large number of candidates in the election made it difficult for voters to pick candidates from the great number of mostly unknown people. As the candidates had no connections with political parties and acted solely in their own personal capacity, it seemed to be difficult for voters to assess what policies they advocated. Furthermore, there was a lack of political campaigning and debate, as well as a lack of support from the largest opposition party, the Independent Party.

The election of the Constitutional Assembly was disputed on the grounds of various alleged electoral defects in its execution, among them the violation of the right to vote by secret ballot. Following the invalidation of the election by the Supreme Court of Iceland on 25 January 2011, the Althingi responded on 24 March 2011 by appointing the 25 candidates who had been elected to take a seat in a new body, the Constitutional Council, which was given the same consultative role as the Constitutional Assembly had been intended to perform. This decision by the Althingi was severely criticized, mostly by the opposition parties, on the grounds that it constituted a circumvention of the decision of the Supreme Court. Others pointed out that, on the contrary, the decision of the Supreme Court would be observed by admitting the invalidity of the election, but that this could not prevent the Althingi from appointing the individuals elected to the Assembly as its advisors. It was clear, however, that there was little consensus on the direction that the matter had taken and that this was

12 Bergsson and Blokker (n. 9) 160.

likely to weaken the outcome of the whole project, as the initial idea had been that specially elected representatives of the nation should be given the task of writing a new constitution. The legitimacy of the Council was questionable thereafter; firstly, there was a low turnout and, secondly, the initial objective that representatives should be directly elected was impaired, ending with the Council's political appointment.[13]

The Constitutional Council was finally convened in early April 2011. It faced an extremely difficult task. It was working in an environment of heated political argument; it was completely different in nature from a lawfully elected assembly; and its legitimacy was open to question. However, in the short space of time accorded to the Council, less than four months, it succeeded in organizing its work well. Also, all its proceedings were open and transparent. It gave great priority to maintaining open communication with the public and its work could also be seen on the major communicative media such as Facebook, YouTube and Flickr. Its proposals were unanimously approved by all delegates on the council and submitted to the Althingi as a bill for a new constitution of Iceland at the end of July 2011.

The response of the coalition parties in the Althingi was somewhat vague, and it seemed unclear what the next steps in the procedure should be. As the main opposition party, the Independence Party, which had been against the appointment of the council from the outset, also sharply criticized the substance of the council's proposals, the coalition parties hesitated in relation to what the next steps should be, what stance they should take on the proposals and how they should discuss their substance. Instead of preparing and processing the task further with the aim of introducing a bill on constitutional amendments in the Althingi, as initially planned, it was referred to one of the parliamentary standing committees, the Constitutional and Supervisory Committee. Thus, for more than a year, nothing really happened in the processing of the proposals. This entailed the loss of valuable time, since if the Althingi were to be able to approve the draft constitution, it would have to do so by spring 2013 because a general election had been scheduled for April that year.

In summer 2012, the parliamentary committee handling the matter commissioned a team of four experts to make the necessary technical adjustments to the draft, including clarification of its internal cohesion and the removal of possible inconsistencies, while making minimum changes to its substance. Political disputes continued regarding the continuation of the matter, but eventually the Althingi – that is, a majority of MPs in the governing coalition parties – decided to hold an advisory referendum on the original proposals on 20 October 2012, even though they were still at that time under examination by the team of experts as described above. The referendum included six questions. The most important one was whether the Constitutional Council's proposals should form the basis of

13 Ibid. 161.

a bill for a new constitution. The other five questions concerned particular elements in the proposals.[14]

The turnout in the referendum, 49 per cent, was considerably lower than the usual level in parliamentary elections, but 64 per cent of those who voted on the question indicated that they wanted the Constitutional Council's proposals to form the basis of a new draft constitution. After the team of legal experts submitted its report, with some technical amendments, to the Althingi in the middle of November 2012, the majority of the Constitutional Committee finally introduced a bill to the Althingi, based on the council's proposals, for a new constitution. By this time only four months remained of the Althingi's electoral term.

The mandate of the Council and its material proposals

The issues to be addressed by the Council were defined quite broadly in the mandate and covered both specific items as well as extensive areas. Accordingly, the following eight items were to be addressed specifically:

- The foundations of the Icelandic constitution and its fundamental concepts;
- The organization of the legislative and executive branches and the limits of their powers;
- The role and position of the president of the republic;
- The independence of the judiciary and their supervision of other holders of governmental powers;
- Provisions on elections and electoral districts;
- Public participation in the democratic process, including the timing and organization of a referendum and a referendum on a legislative bill for a constitutional act;
- The transfer of sovereign powers to international organizations and the conduct of foreign affairs;
- Environmental matters, including the ownership and utilization of natural resources.

14 The referendum included five further questions as follows:

- In the new Constitution, do you want natural resources that are not privately owned to be declared national property? (74 per cent voted yes).
- Would you like to see provisions in the new Constitution on a national church in Iceland? (51 per cent voted yes).
- Would you like to see the new Constitution authorize the election of particular individuals to the Althingi more than is the case at present? (69 per cent voted yes).
- Would you like to see a provision in the new Constitution giving equal weight to votes cast in all parts of the country? (58 per cent voted yes).
- Would you like to see a provision in the new Constitution stating that a certain proportion of the electorate is able to demand that issues should be put in referendum? (63 per cent voted yes).

(Source: National Election Commission. Advertisement of the result of 23 October 2012)

The list was not exhaustive since the Council was authorized to address additional matters to those referred to above.[15]

The Constitutional Council's proposals allowed for a number of changes compared with the current constitution.[16] The Council decided to draw up a whole new constitution instead of suggesting amendments to the present constitution. This had been left open in the mandate which stated that the Council should be convened for the 'purpose of reviewing' the Constitution of the Republic, no. 33 of 17 June 1944. As regards the material proposals, among the notable features was the presentation of various fundamental concepts regarding constitutional structure. This aimed at enhancing the image of the constitution as a national covenant and its symbolic value. There were also numerous proposals for improvements in the present system, in particular a strengthening of the role of the Althingi and its supervisory control over the executive, clarification of the duties of ministers towards parliament and new provisions designed to increase the independence of the courts. The proposals included clearer and more detailed rules on the executive and the position of the government and new methods for the formation of governments. New provisions were made on foreign affairs, international cooperation and treaties, including authorizing the legislature to delegate state power to international organizations. This is only possible to a limited extent under the current constitution and has become a hindrance in Iceland's participation in European cooperation, e.g. under the EEA Agreement.[17]

Even though the proposals did not involve fundamental changes to the Icelandic system of governance, they were radical in many respects, for instance with regard to institutional structures in the political system. Furthermore, drawing inspiration from constitutions around the world, they included new provisions on referendums and popular initiatives. The proposals bore the marks of having been prepared in a very short time, not all of them carefully considered, and there was a lack of harmonization. The Council sought unanimity in relation to adopting all of the proposals. This may have resulted in a lack of a critical approach or debate within the Council and encouraged compromises regarding some of the proposals that were harshly criticized later. Great emphasis was placed on human rights provisions, with a completely new human rights chapter drawing inspiration from various constitutions and international human rights instruments. Despite the fact that the revision of the human rights chapter was not included in the main tasks of the revisions as defined in the initial Act on the Constitutional Assembly

15 One can compare the wide mandate of the Constitutional Council to that of the Irish Constitutional Convention established in 2013. The Irish mandate included eight specific issues, such as the voting age, provisions for same-sex marriage and a reduction of the presidential term. See D.M. Farrell, 'Deliberative democracy, Irish-style: Ireland's Constitutional Convention of 2013' (2013) 34 *Inroads* 110.

16 An English translation is accessible at http://stjornlagathing.is/other_files/stjornlagarad/Frumvarp-enska.pdf, accessed 30 June 2015.

17 Thorarensen (n. 11) 280.

and the chapter had only recently been revised and updated, this in fact became the most extensive part of the Council's proposals.

From the outset there was much criticism of the quality of the proposals and the purpose and the possible unforeseeable consequences of suggested changes. When the bill was eventually introduced in the Althingi in November 2012, the formal opinion of a number of experts and stakeholders was sought by the Constitutional Committee. Comments were also invited from anyone interested in the matter. Many comments were received. While many welcomed the proposals, particularly in view of the broad democratic participation in their preparation, most of the more detailed comments were highly critical, both of their substance and of the short time allowed for bringing the matter to a conclusion. In this respect, the opinion of the Venice Commission, which visited Iceland in January 2013 and met representatives of the Constitutional Council, MPs, academics and representatives of NGOs, etc., had a great influence.[18]

The Venice Commission's report expressed grave doubts about the proposals. Among other things, it described the proposed constitutional order as being associated with a complex set of mechanisms aimed at enabling increased direct participation of citizens in decision-making. While drawing on the existing system, it was considered that this introduced a series of changes and innovations, most of which were intended to confirm the option of a strong parliamentary regime that underlined the proposed system. Although in itself such a model might be deemed suited to the specific context in Iceland, its translation into legal and constitutional terms raised a number of issues of concern. Thus, the Venice Commission deemed the proposed institutional system to be rather complex and marked by a lack of consistency. This criticism applied both to the powers granted to each of the main constitutional actors – parliament, government and president, the balance between them and their inter-institutional relations being seen as often too complicated – and to the mechanisms of direct participation introduced by the bill. The many possibilities for the intervention in decision-making by the people through referendums was welcomed in principle, but these decision-making mechanisms as expressed in the constitutional provisions were found to be complicated and would need careful review, from both the legal and the political perspective. Overall, the Venice Commission saw a risk of political obstruction and instability that could seriously undermine the country's good governance.[19] As regards the human rights provisions, the Venice Commission expressed its concern over the lack of clarity in the delineation of rights. Most of the provisions were worded in very general terms, failing to provide sufficient clarity on whether concrete rights and obligations could be derived from them

18 The Venice Commission (the European Commission for Democracy through Law) acts as the Council of Europe's advisory body on constitutional matters and is composed of constitutional and international law experts and members of the judiciary or national parliaments of Member States of the Council of Europe.

19 Venice Commission (n. 7) paras 179–182.

and, if so, what these would be, and there was a substantial risk that the public would take them as promises to ensure high living conditions.[20]

In short, the Venice Commission strongly recommended that the task of continuing the work of constitutional revision should be left to the future parliament, with sufficient time allowed for a consideration of the comments made and questions raised by the various stakeholders so as to make the necessary improvements to the bill.

The Parliamentary Ombudsman of Iceland also submitted a detailed opinion on the bill, expressing concerns regarding its material proposals. The ombudsman considered that there was a serious lack of a comprehensive assessment of the aims and effects of the amendments proposed in the bill. Various innovations seemed to have been modelled on the constitutions of dissimilar states without attention being given to their original contexts, including a consideration of the effectiveness of the judiciary in applying constitutional provisions.[21]

It was evident that the very short time remaining before the dissolution of the Althingi in March 2013 was completely insufficient to allow it to carry out a detailed examination of the extensive amendments involved in the proposals and make the necessary adjustments to take account of the criticisms and comments that had been received. Even if it were possible to force the proposals through with a narrow majority of the MPs of the governing parties, it still remained, under the existing rules applying to constitutional amendments, for the bill to be approved without amendment by the new parliament following the forthcoming elections in order for it to take effect.

In the closing days of the parliamentary session at the end of March 2013, the leader of one of the governing parties, the Social Democratic Alliance, proposed a new bill instead of the former one. This allowed for the addition of an interim provision to the existing constitution allowing for a new mechanism for amendments. It was proposed that, until 30 April 2017, it would be possible to amend the constitution if, after being passed with the support of at least two-thirds of MPs, amendments were then approved by at least 40 per cent of the electorate in a national referendum. This bill was passed and was also approved by the new parliament following the general elections of 2013, and it entered into force as the Constitutional Act, No. 91/2013. Following elections in April, 2013 in which the left-wing parties comprising the last government sustained a resounding defeat, the new centre-right government appointed a new committee with representatives from all the political parties to propose some necessary amendments to the constitution. It remains to be seen what will come out of the work of this committee. It is likely that some amendments will be suggested but it seems clear that the idea of writing a new constitution for the republic of Iceland has been shelved.

20 Ibid. para. 32.
21 Letter of the Parliamentary Ombudsman to the Constitutional Committee of the Althing, 21 January 2013, 4.

Assessment of the referendum and the 'legal value' of the draft constitution

The unique process that the government of Iceland decided to set in motion in order to revise the constitution in 2009 is without parallel and was characterized by extensive consultation with the electorate on the contents of the proposed constitution. This new method of creating a constitution attracted attention and admiration in many parts of the world. Three foreign academics, Elkins, Ginsburg and Melton, frequently cited by those who supported the immediate adoption of the draft constitution, stated that the document proposed by the Constitutional Council reflected significant input from the public and would mark an important symbolic break with the past.[22] However, very few foreign scholars made an attempt to assess the quality of the proposals in the context of the existing political system and practice. Comparing the texts of the present constitution of Iceland and the product of the Constitutional Council will give very little indication of the potential changes if the context and political reality are not taken into account. Judicial practice, such as the interpretation of terms and concepts in the human rights provisions in the context of international human treaties must also be taken into account when assessing their field of application. This cannot be deduced simply from the written text and must also be fully understood before such provisions are rewritten or deleted.

Those who supported the project with the most enthusiasm in public debate, including some who had been representatives of the Constitutional Council, regarded the outcome of the advisory referendum of 20 October 2012 as imposing a binding requirement on parliament. They claimed that it was the Althingi's democratic duty to comply with the will of the electorate and approve the draft constitution. Accordingly, the Althingi had waived its right to discuss the substance of the constitution any further, including as regards its legal and political implications, after the bill was introduced in November 2012. Public discussion of the fate of the bill became very heated at times, and allegations were made, such as 'in spite of popular support, Iceland's new crowd-sourced constitution was killed by politicians'.[23]

In fact, statements of this type contain intrinsic contradictions. One of the cornerstones of Iceland's constitutional structure, ever since democratic processes were introduced and the country received its first constitution, has been the concept of popular sovereignty and even that the people are the constituent power. In other words, the view is that the constitution is granted by the people themselves and that the power to which it refers originates from the people. Thus, a sharp distinction is drawn between the entity that creates the constitution and

22 Elkins, Ginsburg and Melton (n. 4) 11.

23 Th. Gylfason, 'Democracy on Ice: A Post-Mortem of the Icelandic Constitution' (19 June 2013), http://www.opendemocracy.net/can-europe-make-it/thorvaldur-gylfason/democracy-on-ice-post-mortem-of-icelandic-constitution, accessed 30 June 2015.

the ordinary legislature that enacts laws in accordance with the authority it is granted under the constitution.[24]

Iceland's constitution of 1944 reflects this view: it was approved by the people in a referendum following the examination and passing of a bill on a draft constitution by the Althingi. The people's decision was, legally, the final word in accordance with the rules laid down in the constitution itself, and thus the electorate set its seal of approval on the work done by its elected representatives. The purpose of this procedure is to make it likely that the representative decision makers will strive to fulfil the demands of the people, whose approval of the outcome is necessary, and at the same time to give legitimacy to the final document in a decisive referendum. The 1944 constitution contains built-in rules calling for a particularly exacting procedure for making amendments and making them considerably more difficult than amendments to ordinary legislation. As in other states based on constitutional democracy, these principles in Icelandic constitutional law are intended to ensure that the constitution reflects certain fundamental values that underpin society and are unaffected by short-term political trends and the power wielded by a narrow parliamentary majority at any given time. Thus, a barrier is in place to prevent pressure from interest groups in society resulting in constitutional change being forced through via channels other than those prescribed in the constitution itself.

Prevention of opportunistic amendments or revisions can be ensured either by demanding that changes to the existing constitution be supported by a qualified majority of MPs or by accepting the support of an ordinary majority but then demanding that parliament be dissolved and elections held and then that the new parliament approve the measure taken. To accommodate the fundamental view that the nation is the entity that grants the constitution, it is necessary to find a mechanism to ensure that the electorate will be involved, directly or indirectly, in the process of amendment. Some states have adopted a procedure in which all changes made to the constitution by parliament are subject to final approval by the people. Among the Nordic countries, Denmark has the most elaborate arrangement in this respect. There, the approval of two parliaments is required, with a general election in between, after which it must be put to a special referendum in which a majority of those voting, and at least 40 per cent of those entitled to vote, must be in favour of the amendment of the constitution.[25]

24 Iceland's Constitution of 1944 makes no distinction (as is done in some states) between piecemeal amendments and a comprehensive revision or the enactment of a completely new constitution. There are certain arguments in favour of having particular rules on the enactment of a new constitution, on the one hand, and subsequent amendments to it, on the other. See E. Smith, *Konstitutionelt Demokrati. Statsforfatningsretten i Prinsipielt og Komparativt Lys* (2nd edn, Fagbokforlaget 2012) 96.

25 This procedure, which is laid out in Art. 88 of the current Danish constitution of 1953, is unusually difficult, which may have contributed to the fact that the constitution has not been amended since its adoption. See H. Krunke, 'Formal and Informal Methods of Constitutional Change in Denmark' in X. Contiades (ed.), *Engineering Constitutional Change: A Comparative Perspective on Europe, Canada and the USA* (Routledge 2013) 80–82.

The procedure laid down in the second paragraph of Art. 79 of the Icelandic constitution, approval by two parliaments and a general election in between, combines these two aims, i.e. ensuring broad parliamentary support over and above a simple majority in one parliament and also granting the people indirect involvement in the process. The electorate is given a chance to declare its position on the amendment by either supporting or rejecting political parties in the general election following the first approval of the bill.

While provisions on referendums as part of the process of constitutional change differ from one European state to another, they have one feature in common: the people, as the constituent power, have a clear role to play in the process, either by giving their approval to the measure taken by parliament or by rejecting it, in a legally binding manner. The decision by the governing parties to hold an advisory referendum on the proposals of the Constitutional Council on 20 October 2012, before the bill had been examined by the Althingi, was therefore seen by many, including the author of this chapter, as ill-advised. Not only did it arouse false expectations regarding the legal value of the outcome *vis-à-vis* the Althingi, but answers given to the open and general questions presented in the referendum were open to a variety of interpretations and to disputes as to what answers had in fact been given.

The value of advisory referendums has been called into question from the point of view of constitutional legal theory.[26] The phenomenon has been criticized because this particular form of referendum is so loosely regulated and fits so poorly into the constitutional and political system of a country that it may cause various problems, one of the main ones being the question of how advisory referendums are to be reconciled with the principle of the free mandate of members of parliament, which is enshrined in most democratic constitutions. In this respect, both the timing and the choice of issues that are suitable for putting to a referendum are important.[27]

It can be maintained that the advisory referendum on the Constitutional Council's proposals in October 2012 combined all the shortcomings of such referendums: the questions were imprecise, the timing was unfortunate and, most importantly, it gave the impression that the Althingi had been deprived of its competence to discuss and amend the material proposals in the bill. This created a clear clash with the principle of a free mandate as stipulated in Art. 48 of the Icelandic constitution, which states that the members of the Althingi are bound solely by their conviction and not by any instructions from their constituents. Owing to the relatively low turnout in the referendum and the varying

26 Advisory referendums have more frequently been held in the Nordic states, where traditionally national constitutions do not provide for referendums as part of the legally-binding decision-making procedures. Questions on the accession of Sweden (1994), Finland (1994) and Norway (1972 and 1994) to the European Union were put to referendums, and in all instances the political decisions taken on accession were in line with the outcomes.

27 M. Suksi, 'The Advisory Referendum in Finland' (1999) 5(4) *European Public Law* 551.

interpretations of its conclusions, political pressure to continue the exercise was clearly reduced.

In the light of these events, it perhaps came as no surprise, but all the same as a deep disappointment, that no substantive proposals made in the bill on a new constitution were enacted before the end of the parliamentary term in spring 2013. However, it was clear from the outcome of the general election that the electorate was not vastly concerned about the issue, or did not regard it as a priority. A new political party, the Democratic Watch, fielded candidates in the election, including some who had sat as representatives on the Constitutional Council. The party's main election platform was to continue with the revision of the constitution and to respect the outcome of the referendum of October 2012. The party received very little support, earning only about 2.5 per cent of the vote and failing to gain any seats in the Althingi. This was emphasized by the fact that the parties that fared best in the elections, the Independence Party and the Progressive Party, were those that had been most vigorous in their opposition to a new constitution on the basis of the proposals from the Constitutional Council. It should also be noted that revision of the constitution was not among the main election issues, and probably accounted for only a small part of the massive loss of support for the outgoing government parties.

Conclusion

As a method of revising the Icelandic constitution, the creation of the Constitutional Assembly, which later became the Constitutional Council, was a radical innovation with noble aims, including the restoration of public faith in political institutions. The reasons for the failure of the exercise are manifold, and involve a number of factors, both political and legal.

The idea of shifting the task of writing a constitution from the political forum to a consultative body raised questions about whether it is possible, in a constitutional democracy, to bypass the existing constitution's amendment process.[28] Is a specially elected group of 'non-political' individuals more representative and can it be defined as 'the people' as a special source of power in clear contradistinction to political entities? The involvement of the citizens during the initial stages, through the method of crowd-sourcing, so that they could reflect their will in the preparation and drafting of a new constitution, was indeed a positive step, introducing innovative political and democratic processes. It might eventually have strengthened the democratic foundations and legitimacy of a new constitution, as well as being likely to create greater consensus regarding it. However, as the matter developed, and with the emergence of claims that the Council's role was to draft a comprehensive and complete document, it proved to be an unrealistic approach on the part of those who most enthusiastically supported the creation of a new constitution. Accordingly, defining constitution-making as a non-political

28 Colón-Ríos (n. 1) 181.

issue and distancing it entirely from the political forum was bound to end in failure. Political involvement had to come into the picture and the political forces in the country needed to take a stance on the substance of a new constitution before its final adoption. The exercise was never intended to replace the legitimate processes provided for in the constitution, since to do so would be in clear defiance of the principles of constitutional democracy. An advisory referendum, or other evidence of powerful popular support, could not legitimize such a deviation from the constitutional process.

It is important to distinguish between the involvement of the people in *preparing* a constitution and influencing its substance, on the one hand, and *writing* a constitution on the other. The fact that a group of individuals with little or no experience of legislative work (and indeed they had been chosen for the task precisely because of their non-involvement in politics) managed to produce a comprehensive document was a great achievement. But even though the basic frame and main components of their proposals were intended to be the basis for processing by the legislature, the task needed to be continued in the Althingi. The material quality of the document had to be improved. A thorough assessment was needed of the innovative institutional framework suggested, for the sake of harmonization and to avoid having political obstructions and instability undermine good governance.

Most importantly from a practical point of view, the coalition parties in the Althingi failed to react promptly to the proposals when the Council submitted them in July 2011. Surprisingly, they failed to adopt any position on their substance. This resulted in hesitation on how to proceed and how to introduce and handle a bill for a new constitution, a situation which ended a year later in the controversial decision to hold the advisory referendum. A whole year was lost, which should have been used to elaborate the Council's proposals further via the parliamentary process, assess their probable impact and address their material shortcomings. Expecting that four months would be sufficient for the Althingi to discuss a bill of such a fundamental significance and take proper account of all the issues that needed to be addressed was wholly unrealistic.

Finally, from early on in the exercise it became unlikely that the consensus aimed at the initial establishment of the Constitutional Assembly would be achieved. This was partly due to the extremely low turnout in the election of the Constitutional Assembly in 2010, but more importantly it was due to the invalidation of the election by the Supreme Court. The inevitable consequence of this was that the Constitutional Council, which replaced the assembly following the passing of a parliamentary resolution, lost the popular legitimacy that the Assembly could claim in its early days, before the election was annulled. From that time on, the staunch resistance of the largest opposition party in the Althingi to any continuation of the revision process effectively made the Council into a creature of a political nature, exposing it to severe criticism and so dividing voters into two groups in terms of their attitude to the task.

In spite of all this, it is at least safe to assert that following the new paths that were chosen to revise the Icelandic constitution had a powerful impact on public awareness in Iceland regarding the significance of the constitution and its core principles, which in itself is a positive development. The amount of attention that this new experiment in constitutional revision in Iceland attracted outside the country is also likely to make both citizens and governments in other countries think about whether, and if so how, greater consultation of the electorate can be achieved concerning the substance and aims of constitutions. Thus, much can be learned from this experiment regarding means and ends, the advantages and drawbacks of various methods and, not least, the limitations imposed by constitutions themselves on innovations concerning the revision of the foundations on which democratic states are built.

7 Bringing people into the heart of constitutional design

The Irish Constitutional Convention of 2012–14[1]

David M. Farrell, Clodagh Harris and Jane Suiter

In late 2012 the Irish government took the long-anticipated step of establishing the Irish Constitutional Convention (www.constitution.ie), whose first formal session was held during the weekend of 26–27 January 2013. Internationally, there have been plenty of examples over the years of the involvement of citizens in debates on constitutional reform, whether this occurs when they are given a voice in referendums or public initiatives or when they are allowed to run for election as members of a convention (a recent example being Iceland's Constitutional Council of 2011). Ireland's Constitutional Convention also included citizens as members, but it is the nature of how these citizens were selected to participate and how the process was run that are of particular interest. There are a small but growing number of cases in which governments have opted to follow 'deliberative principles', selecting citizens at random rather than by election and managing the discussions along deliberative lines.

Irish policymakers were influenced by the citizens' assemblies on electoral reform in the Canadian provinces of British Columbia (2004) and Ontario (2007) and the Dutch citizen's forum (Bürgerforum) that was set up in 2006.[2] In all these cases, the citizen members were selected at random rather than running for election, and deliberation was the modus operandi. Together with the Irish Constitutional Convention, these cases represent a new type of constitutional convention that is not covered by existing typologies:[3] this new type is a constitutional convention as a 'mini-public'.[4]

1 An earlier version of this chapter was presented to the conference on 'Constitutional Change and People' at the University of Luxembourg, 12 December 2014. We are grateful to the participants for their comments and feedback and to Akisato Suzuki for his research assistance. We were members of the academic and legal team that supported the work of the Convention.

2 P. Fournier, H. van der Kolk, R. Kenneth Carty, A. Blais and J. Rose, *When Citizens Decide: Lessons from Citizen Assemblies on Electoral Reform* (Oxford University Press 2011).

3 On these, see J. Wheatley and F. Mendez (eds), *Patterns of Constitutional Design: The Role of Citizens and Elites in Constitution-Making* (Ashgate 2013).

4 D. Farrell, '"Stripped Down" or Reconfigured Democracy' (2014) 37 *West European Politics* 439.

The origins of the Irish Constitutional Convention

Irish citizens are pretty accustomed to debates over changes to the country's constitution. The 'fixed' nature of the constitution means that it requires a referendum to change, something that has been attempted 39 times since its promulgation in 1937, placing Ireland third in Europe for the number of post-war referendums held.[5] The referendum barrier means that constitutional reform is not something entered into lightly; but inevitably, reform is unavoidable.[6] Various governments – particularly over the past 20 years or so – have established processes to review the constitution with a view to large-scale constitutional reform, including the following: the 1967 review comprising parliamentarians; the 1982 review carried out by legal experts; and the 1995 Whitaker review by (mainly academic) experts from law, political science and social policy, which produced a telephone book-sized analysis of the constitution and recommended extensive revisions to it. However, despite the eminence of the membership no amendments emerged. It became a useful academic resource, but it failed politically. Later reviews were carried out by parliamentarians, but again these have failed to have a significant impact. When a referendum has taken place on an issue that an Oireachtas (Parliament) Committee on the Constitution has made a recommendation about, it is notable that the government ignored the wording recommended by the committee.

The context of the 2012–14 Convention was very different to anything Ireland had witnessed before. This convention emerged out of a compromise between two parties, Fine Gael (a centre-right party) and Labour, that came to power in the 2011 'electoral earthquake', an election that occurred in the midst of the worst economic crisis in the state's history and which was to see the electoral wipe out of Ireland's till then long-dominant Fianna Fáil party.[7] Fine Gael and Labour had included in their election manifesto proposals for establishing citizen-oriented fora to discuss possible constitutional reforms in a number of areas. In Fine Gael's case, the proposal was for a British Columbia style citizens' assembly to consider electoral reform. Labour's plan was for the establishment of a constitutional convention (made up of equal proportions of politicians, experts and ordinary citizens) to consider a root-and-branch review of the Irish constitution. The outcome of the 2011 general election was the formation of a Fine Gael/Labour coalition, whose

5 See http://www.c2d.ch/index.php, accessed 29 June 2015.

6 Many of the referendums to date have been the outcome of international obligations requiring constitutional amendment (principally due to EU Treaty reforms and the Northern Ireland peace process); others have resulted from social and political modernization requiring updates to a constitution that had been written in a different age (e.g. removing a ban on divorce and lowering the voting age to 18; although in some prominent cases – notably the various abortion referendums – the referendums have sought to 'defend against' the march of social reform).

7 M. Gallagher and M. Marsh, *How Ireland Voted 2011: The Full Story of Ireland's Earthquake Election* (Palgrave Macmillan 2011).

'Programme for Government' sought to marry the sometimes quite disparate manifesto promises of both parties. As regards the parties' respective proposals relating to citizens' assemblies and constitutional conventions, the coalition's compromise resulted in the promise to establish a constitutional convention to examine eight specific issues:

- Reduction of the presidential term of office to five years;
- Reduction of the voting age to 17;
- Review of the Dáil's (lower house of parliament) electoral system;
- Irish citizens' right to vote at Irish embassies in presidential elections;
- Provisions for marriage equality;
- Amendment to the existing clause in the Irish constitution on the role of women in the home and the encouragement of greater participation of women in public life;
- Increasing the participation of women in politics; and
- Removal of the offence of blasphemy from the constitution.

The parliamentary resolution that established the convention also permitted it to propose other relevant constitutional amendments after the original eight reports were completed, thereby giving the convention some limited agenda-setting powers. This somewhat eclectic mix of items, from the relatively mundane issue of the length of office of the Irish president (whose role is largely ceremonial) to the potentially explosive issue of marriage equality, merely reflected the decision of the inter-party negotiators to 'park' certain matters that were in their respective election manifestos that were unlikely to be resolved easily during their febrile and intense negotiations. They were up against the (largely media-driven) clock to conclude the negotiations and establish a government, so what better way to deal with these matters than wrap them all together and give them to the Constitutional Convention to consider.

It was to take a further 18 months before the Constitutional Convention was finally established – at the end of 2012 – with its work programme starting in early 2013. It was given a small budget (less than €1 million) when compared with the British Columbian budget of CAN$5.5 million and the Dutch Bürgerforum's €5.1 million, and a deadline of one year to conclude its work (a deadline that was later extended by several months).

Chaired by Tom Arnold (the former chief executive of the leading Irish international charity, Concern), the other 99 members of the convention consisted of 66 citizens and 33 elected legislators (29 of these from the Irish Parliament and four from the Northern Ireland Assembly). Whereas the parties could determine by themselves how to select their members (with the parties' allocations proportionate to their representation in parliament), the citizen members were selected at random by a survey company, which had a brief of ensuring that the membership was a fair reflection of the population in terms of gender, age, region, education and socio-economic status – a tall order with just 66 individuals but one that was achieved.[8] To allow for the possibility of members not being available for all meetings, a list of substitute members was drawn up at the same time.

The work of the convention

The Irish Constitutional Convention completed its work in February 2014 and was formally wound down a month later. In this section we say something about how it operated and what it did.

Meetings took place roughly once a month and lasted for most of a weekend (all day Saturday and all Sunday morning), with members voting at the end of the weekend on what recommendations to make. As mentioned above, the mode of operation was 'deliberation'. What this meant was that the 99 members (the chair being the 100th) were arranged in circular tables of eight (comprising a mix of politician and citizen members). At each table there was a trained facilitator and a note-taker. The role of the facilitator was to ensure that discussions kept to the point and were respectful, and that every member had an equal opportunity to speak. The table allocations were rotated after each weekend so that members had to mix with different members.

The itinerary generally operated as follows (depending on the topic there was some variation from this):

- Short (15 minutes each) presentations by experts in the area (these varied for each topic), followed by questions and answers from the floor. Briefing documents were provided by the experts several days in advance so that the members had an opportunity to inform themselves as much as possible. These 'plenary sessions' were televised and live-streamed (and are available on the website at www.constitution.ie);
- Small group deliberation in closed session (i.e. no cameras);
- A plenary (open) session to hear feedback from the deliberation;
- Presentations by a selection of advocacy groups;
- More deliberation, feedback and plenary discussions (possibly with more expert involvement at this point);
- Agreement on the 'ballot paper' (to determine the convention's recommendations on the topic);
- The vote on the recommendations (decisions were made by majority vote).

The convention members proved quite inventive in stretching their remit beyond the narrow confines set by the government, starting at its January 2013 weekend gathering – its first full meeting. There the convention considered two themes,

8 J. Suiter, D. Farrell, C. Harris and E. O'Malley, 'The Irish Constitutional Convention: A Case of "High Legitimacy"?' in M. Reuchamps and J. Suiter (eds), *Constitutional Deliberative Democracy in Europe* (ECPR Press 2016), Chapter 3.

namely: whether to reduce the voting age to 17 and whether to reduce the president's term of office from seven years to five. Having read the briefing materials, heard from experts and advocacy groups, and deliberated over the relevant arguments, the convention members took decisions that undoubtedly went beyond their brief. Specifically, the convention voted in favour of:

- Reducing the voting age to 16 (the age proposed by many of the advocacy groups promoting a reduced voting age), not 17 (the age they were asked to consider);
- Reducing the age of candidacy for presidential candidates; and
- Giving citizens a direct role in the process of nominating presidential candidates (the convention voted against the proposal to reduce the presidential term).

This willingness to extend the agenda beyond the specific question set by government continued in all the remaining meetings. By the end of its operation, this was to result in no less than 40 specific recommendations, 18 of which would require constitutional change (see appendix).

How successful was the Irish Constitutional Convention?

The launch of the Irish Constitutional Convention (ICC) attracted little by way of positive reaction. Instead, it was met with a mix of indifference from the public, cynicism from the ranks of those members of the media commentariat who bothered to pay any attention to it and howls of derision via social media. The criticisms of the convention fell into three groups: its composition, its agenda and its limited advisory role. How justified are these criticisms?

Composition

Let us start with the issue of how the convention membership was comprised. The main point of contention here was over the mixing of ordinary citizens with elected politicians, the argument being that the latter would be likely to dominate the discussions and intimidate the citizen members. This was very different from the Canadian and Dutch citizens' assemblies, which had followed the principle that politicians should be excluded from the process. In these cases there were no politician members (indeed, politicians were screened out in the randomized process of recruiting members); politicians were not even invited to address the assembly.

The intention behind this was to ensure that the process was independent of party politics and that there would be no dilution of its deliberative element. But questions were raised over the degree of realism in some of the output of the assemblies. As Ratner observes of the British Columbia citizens' assembly (CA): 'the exclusion of political voices from CA deliberations becomes grounds for criticism of their judgment'.[9] It also provided the political parties with a good excuse not to involve themselves with the referendum campaigns that followed in the cases of the British Columbia and the Ontario citizens' assemblies. None of the major parties campaigned in the referendums; they remained 'completely silent' throughout,[10] as a consequence of which the referendum campaigns had great difficulty in drumming up voter interest. In effect, the parties were able to kill off awkward electoral reform proposals by simply ignoring them. Patrick Fournier and his colleagues draw the following conclusion from this experience:

> With respect to the political parties, our findings are absolutely unequivocal. The parties were strikingly absent from the whole process. This itself raises important questions about the consequences of such a situation. The risk, of course, is that assembly members may not have fully appreciated the problems and opportunities that parties face under different electoral systems.[11]

Arguably, the Irish government's decision to include politician members in the ICC reduced this risk of political detachment, but it was hardly designed with this purpose in mind. The outlook was not good: the many critics did not like the inclusion of political members.[12] In the parliamentary debate that established what opposition there was to establishing the ICC politicians raised concerns over how the politician members may 'have an undue bearing on the deliberations'.[13] Another deputy, Stephen Donnelly, made the following, quite telling, observation:

> [A] mistake has been made in including politicians, although it might seem odd for a politician to say that. . . . [B]est international practice does not include elected representatives in constitutional conventions. Two of the best recognised speakers in the world on this matter are Archon Fung from the Harvard Kennedy School, under whom I had the privilege to study, and Ken Carty from the University of British Columbia in Canada. In their work in this field, they acknowledge that the presence of partisan influence can lead to distorted deliberations and outcomes. Professor Fung says that in

9 R.S. Ratner, 'Communicative Rationality in the Citizens' Assembly and Referendum Process' in M. Warren and H. Pearse (eds), *Designing Deliberative Democracy: The British Columbia Citizens' Assembly* (Cambridge University Press 2008) 163.

10 Fournier, van der Kolk, Carty, Blais and Rose (n. 2) 109.

11 Ibid. 111.

12 At a public seminar in the Royal Irish Academy in Dublin that was held on the eve of the establishment of the ICC, Ken Carty, the research director of the British Columbia citizens' assembly speculated on whether including politicians might actually help to politically anchor the ICC. See video coverage here: https://www.youtube.com/watch?v=3E6Z_AW3CRk&feature=youtu.be, accessed 26 June 2015.

13 Catherine Murphy, Dáil debate 10 July 2013.

> deliberative democracy 'powerful participants may seek to improperly and unreasonably exclude issues that threaten their interests from the scope of deliberation'.

There was every reason why such a concern might be raised. At that point, there was no way of knowing how the ICC would operate; it was not inconceivable that the politician members – some of whom turned out to be very senior – might seek to establish rules of procedure more akin to the parliamentary styles of operation rather than deliberative procedures.[14] The government resolution establishing the ICC was silent on the question of its mode of operation, so anything was possible. There was also the fear that the politician members might seek to dominate the proceedings by being the first to the microphone and intimidating the citizen members.

Both sets of concern spoke to the danger of politicians controlling the process – a danger that ultimately did not come to pass. This was for a number of reasons, two of which stand out in particular. First, the secretariat was careful when designing how the ICC should be managed to follow best practice in operating along deliberative lines, including complementing open plenary sessions (that were live-streamed) with private round-table discussions; arranging members in mixed (politicians and citizens) groups at tables of eight (and rotating the memberships of tables from one meeting to the next); and using trained facilitators to ensure that all members had an equal chance to contribute to discussions.

Second, an important decision on rules and procedures was made by the ICC members at their inaugural meeting. A notable feature of these rules was an agreement to take decisions (on the ICC's recommendations) by secret ballot, in effect preventing any attempt by political parties to apply a party whip to their members. Based on these rules and procedures, the Chairman established a set of principles by which the ICC should operate, which he reminded members of on numerous occasions and which were included in his introduction to each of the ICC's reports. The key mantras were openness and transparency, fairness, 'equality of voice' and collegiality.

Survey evidence indicates that the ICC was successful in ensuring that all members had a fair hearing and that no one group dominated the proceedings.

14 This was precisely the situation that occurred in the case of the Australian 1998 constitutional convention – the only other such case (at least in modern times) of a convention whose membership comprised a mix of politicians and ordinary citizens. In that case, the decision was taken to operate along normal parliamentary lines. For more, see *Constitutional Convention 2–13 February 1998, Transcripts of Proceedings*. Parliament of Australia, http://www.aph.gov.au/Parliamentary_Business/Hansard/HANCON, accessed 29 June 2015; J. Warhurst, 'From Constitutional Convention to Republic Referendum: A Guide to the Processes, the Issues and the Participants' (1999) Australian Parliamentary Library Paper, No. 25. Canberra, http://www.aph.gov.au/binaries/library/pubs/rp/1998–99/99rp25.pdf, accessed 29 June 2015; G. Williams, 'The 1998 Constitutional Convention: First Impressions, Parliament of Australia' (1998) Current Issues Brief, http://www.aph.gov.au/About_Parliament/Parliamentary_Departments/Parliamentary_Library/Publications_Archive/CIB/CIB9798/98cib11, accessed 29 June 2015.

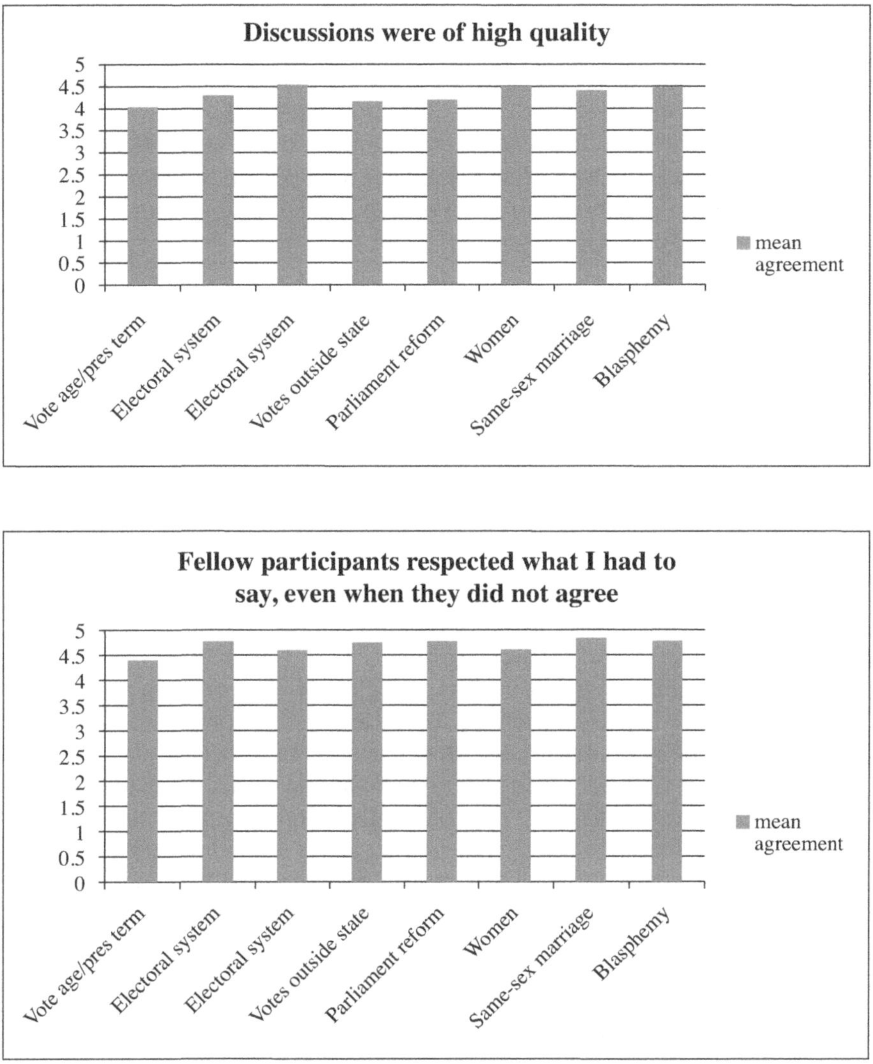

Figure 7.1 Attitudes of members to participation in the convention

Source: Weekend surveys of convention members (response rate generally about 60 per cent)

The members were surveyed before and after each meeting and the evidence throughout was that the bulk of members were satisfied with how things operated. Figure 7.1 provides some sample survey evidence showing consistently strong agreement across all weekends that discussions were of a high quality and that members felt that they received a fair hearing.

A further advantage of having politicians among the ranks of the members is that it helped to dissipate the sense of disconnect between the convention and the political class that was so apparent in the cases of the Canadian and Dutch citizens' assemblies, where the political class quite deliberately did not join in with the work of the citizens, making it difficult for these assemblies to gain much political purchase. In the Irish case, on the contrary, there was a coterie of members of the political class who, if anything, became cheerleaders of the process – as witnessed during the parliamentary debates about convention reports.

Agenda

The second area of criticism was the agenda of the Constitutional Convention, which was seen as too limited and yet overly crowded at the same time. The first point relates to the fact that the list of eight matters was too restrictive and did not deal with the fundamental issues of constitutional reform that many called for. More to the point, specific matters of constitutional reform that were also on the coalition government's political reform agenda (e.g. children's rights or the abolition of the upper house of parliament) were not included on the list of items. The criticism of the crowded nature of the agenda relates specifically to the fact that the convention was given just 12 months to conclude its work, with space and resources for just nine weekends of meetings. (In the end a further two months was added to the schedule.)

Soon after its launch, an editorial in Ireland's best-selling daily newspaper, the *Irish Independent*, dismissed the ICC as 'unelected and powerless'.[15] The more cerebral *Irish Times* was even more condemnatory, accusing the government of 'a political sleight of hand'. According to the editorial writer, the convention was 'all form and little substance'.[16] One of the *Irish Times* regular opinion writers, Noel Whelan, referred to it as 'one part Oireachtas [parliamentary] committee and two parts focus group'.[17] A fellow opinion writer for the same newspaper, Fintan O'Toole, referred to it (deliberatively) vaguely as 'the phantom Citizens' Union – the citizens' assembly or people's convention'. For O'Toole this was 'not a comprehensive redesign of the Republic but a public chat about subjects selected in advance by the government'.[18]

The media were not alone in reacting negatively to the ICC. In the parliamentary debate on 10 July 2012 on the government's announcement of its establishment, opposition deputies were highly critical. The leader of Sinn Féin, Gerry Adams, was unequivocal in seeing it as 'minimalist, disjointed and piecemeal'.[19] The party's deputy leader, Mary Lou McDonald, was equally forthright:

15 'Fine Words Don't Do Collins Justice' (editorial) *Irish Independent* (20 August 2012).

16 Both quotes from 'The Way Politics is Done' (editorial) *Irish Times* (12 July 2012).

17 N. Whelan, 'Constitutional Convention Will Have Its Remit Severely Pruned' *Irish Times* (25 February 2012).

18 Both quotes from F. O'Toole, 'Tammany Hall lives on in feeble reforms' *Irish Times* (28 June 2012).

19 This and the next quote are from Dáil debates, 10 July 2012.

> This convention could and should be a significant platform for constitutional reform. There should be a myriad of issues to be debated, including long awaited and fundamental political reform. Instead the convention is in real danger of becoming, as one commentator put it over the weekend, 'a purgatory into which a selection of constitutional issues will be parked before being further delayed or diverted when they return to the parliamentary process.

There is no disputing the point that the original agenda was far from comprehensive and was certainly eclectic. But, as we have seen above, the members were very adept at finding ways to extend the remit of the Convention, resulting in no less than 40 separate recommendations for reform (see appendix), and some quite significant proposals were included in the mix. Furthermore, in the parliamentary resolution that established the convention, it was explicitly stated that its work need not be limited to the eight themes it was organized to consider. The resolution stated that following completion of its deliberations on the eight themes, it could consider other possible areas for amendment. To that end, the convention held nine regional meetings across the country (attended by almost 1,000 people) and encouraged submissions for 'any other amendments' from civil society and the public more generally, and in late 2013 arranged a series of meetings around the country to allow members of the public to make a pitch for issues to be considered by the convention. In the end, there were 800 public submissions covering a range of 30 possible topics. Having sought government approval for time for an additional meeting, the convention was then in a position to allocate its final two weekends to discussing 'any other amendments'. The 800 submissions were grouped into topic areas, which the members then voted on, resulting in a decision that the final two topics were Dáil reform (i.e. reform of the lower house of parliament) and whether to enshrine economic, social and cultural rights in the constitution.

Limited role

The convention members may have been inventive in stretching their list of agenda items, but ultimately the question that mattered was how the political elite would react, which takes us to the third area of criticism, the fact that the convention could only make recommendations, that is, that its role was advisory rather than declaratory. The recommendations of the convention were sent back to government to consider rather than going directly to the people as referendum proposals – very different from what happened in British Columbia and Ontario, where the proposals were put directly to the citizens in referendums.[20] This leaves the final power with government to determine whether or not its recommendations will ever see the light of day in the form of referendum questions.

20 On the implications, see M. Saward, 'Making Democratic Connection: Political Equality, Deliberation and Direct Democracy' (2001) 36 *Acta Politica* 361.

But it seemed that it was not that easy for the government to sweep the recommendations under the carpet. The government had given a specific undertaking to respond, and in timely fashion too, by way of a formal ministerial statement to the parliament within four months of receipt of a report by the convention. Based on the government's response to the first three reports – which were all debated on schedule – there was some reason for optimism that the government was taking this process seriously. These were the reports of the first three weekends of meetings that discussed the voting age, the length of the presidential term of office (both of these items were dealt with in Report No. 1), the role of women in the home and women in politics (both of these were dealt with in Report No. 2), and marriage equality (Report No. 3). The reaction to these reports was as follows:

- The government agreed to hold three referendums (that it said would be scheduled for early 2015) on reducing the voting age to 16, on reducing the age of presidential candidates, and – of greatest significance – on marriage equality.
- The other recommendations contained in these reports were referred either to the relevant parliamentary committee or to a relevant government department task force for further consideration.

But this early flutter of government interest was to dissipate over time: the delays in government response grew ever longer; some reports are still awaiting a response, and (at the time of writing) as the date of the next election draws near there is now a real prospect that no response will be forthcoming to these. There was also a subsequent government reversal on its commitment to holding a referendum on the voting age; this has since been deferred indefinitely.

The table in the appendix in this chapter provides details on the current state of play relating to the government's responses to the ICC's 40 recommendations. In summary, to date, of the 40 recommendations of the convention:

- Five have been accepted (two of these resulted in referendums in May 2015);
- Eight have been 'parked' by being sent for further consideration (which means that many will probably never see the light of day);
- Four have been ignored (in the sense that the ministerial response to the relevant ICC report simply said nothing about these items);
- Two have been given what can, at best, be described as an ambiguous response (these relate to the proposals for referendums on voting age and blasphemy, which the government appears to have accepted but has not set a date for the related referendum);
- Five have been rejected; and
- 16 have yet to be responded to (mostly relating to the final two reports of the convention that have been awaiting – for a very long time indeed – any kind of government reaction).

This summary presents a pretty mixed picture: the most charitable way of looking at this is that the government has given a relatively positive reaction to about a third of the ICC's recommendations (that is, if we add together those that have been accepted, parked or given an ambiguous response); but perhaps a more realistic assessment is that only five of the 40 recommendations have actually been accepted and have been followed by action (representing 12.5 per cent of the total).

Conclusion

As a process, the Irish Constitutional Convention was a great success,[21] but in terms of its outcomes it is still too soon to provide a definitive judgement. The government's responses to date have undoubtedly been mixed, but it did at least proceed to hold the two promised referendums – on marriage equality and the age of presidential candidates – on the same day (22 May 2015). As might have been expected, the former item completely overshadowed the latter both in terms of media coverage and campaign interest by political parties and wider civil society. As a consequence, unsurprisingly, the presidential age referendum was heavily defeated. But the marriage equality referendum passed successfully and by an equally resounding margin – thus marking the first case in the world of a successful policy outcome resulting from a process of deliberation.[22] In this sense at least, we can judge the Irish Constitutional Convention to have been successful in terms of outcomes.

Across the world's established democracies, the trend in recent years has been towards engaging with citizens and increasing the scope for ordinary citizens to have a say. Initiatives like the British Columbia, Ontario and Dutch citizens' assemblies and the Irish Constitutional Convention can be seen as illustrative of this 'democratic transformation'.[23] Processes such as this form a potential part of the 'ecology' of democratic institutions, as a complement to our representative institutions.[24] They are, of course, not without their weaknesses, but what cannot be denied is that at their heart they represent a serious intention by the political elite to re-engage with society, and they are a step towards a form of democracy that seeks to place the citizen centre stage.

21 Suiter, Farrell, Harris and O'Malley (n. 8).

22 J. Elkink, D. Farrell, Th. Reidy and J. Suiter, 'The 2015 marriage referendum: Conservative Ireland is dead and gone', 2015 (Draft paper).

23 B. Cain, R. Dalton and S. Scarrow (eds), *Democracy Transformed? Expanding Political Opportunities in Advanced Industrial Democracies* (Oxford University Press 2003); Farrell (n. 4).

24 M. Warren, 'A Second Transformation of Democracy?', in B. Cain, R. Dalton and S. Scarrow (eds), *Democracy Transformed? Expanding Political Opportunities in Advanced Industrial Democracies* (Oxford University Press 2003) 223–249.

Appendix

Outcome of the Irish Constitutional Convention (as of May 2015)

Topics	*Convention's recommendations*	*Outcome*
1. Reduction of the presidential term of office to five years and alignment with local and European elections	1. No change to length of the presidential term of office	Government accepted
	2. *Reduce the age of candidacy for presidential candidates	Government accepted. Referendum held on 22 May 2015 (rejected)
	3. *Give citizens a say in the nomination process for presidential candidates	Government rejected
2. Reduction of the voting age to 17	4. *Voting age should be reduced to 16	Government accepted, then rescinded. Position ambiguous
3. Clause on role of women in home and encouraging greater participation of women in public life	5. *Article 41.2 (on the role of women) should be made gender-neutral to include other carers both 'in the home' and 'beyond the home'	Government established task force. Still awaiting its report
	6. Re Art. 41.2.2 (the state's support for carers) the state should provide 'a reasonable level of support'	Government established task force. Still awaiting its report
4. Increasing the participation of women in politics	7. *The constitution should be amended to include an explicit provision on gender equality	Government established task force. Still awaiting its report
	8. There should be more government action to encourage greater participation of women in politics	Government established task force. Still awaiting its report
	9. *The constitution should be amended to include 'gender-inclusive' language	Government established task force. Still awaiting its report

Topics	*Convention's recommendations*	*Outcome*
5. Provisions for same-sex marriage	10. *The constitution should be amended to allow for same-sex marriage	Government accepted. Referendum held on 22 May 2015 (passed)
	11. The state should enact laws incorporating necessary changed arrangements in regard to the parentage, guardianship and upbringing of children	Government accepted; legislation on adoption passed
6. Review of the Dáil electoral system	12. The electoral system should be amended to ensure that the smallest constituency size is a five-seater	Government rejected
	13. The electoral system should be amended to remove the alphabetical order of candidates on the ballot paper	Electoral Commission should look into this
	14. The state should establish an Electoral Commission	Government accepted; public consultation in progress
	15. Polling hours/days should be extended	Electoral Commission should look into this
	16. There should be greater access to postal voting	Government ignored this
	17. Accuracy of the electoral register should be improved	Government 'agreed', but committed to nothing new
	18. Introduce measures to increase electoral turnout	Government 'agreed', but committed to nothing new
	19. Education programmes should be introduced in schools	Government 'agreed', but committed to nothing new
	20. *There should be non-parliamentary ministers in government	Government rejected
	21. *Members of the Dáil should be required to resign their seats on being appointed to ministerial office	Government rejected this proposal
	22. *Citizen-initiatives should be introduced (for influencing parliamentary agenda and for calling of referendums)	Government rejected this proposal

(*Continued*)

Topics	*Convention's recommendations*	*Outcome*
7. Irish citizens' right to vote at Irish embassies in presidential elections	23. *Rights for citizens abroad and citizens in Northern Ireland to vote in presidential elections	Government response expected imminently
8. Removal of the offence of blasphemy from the constitution	24. *The offence of blasphemy should be replaced by a new general provision to include incitement to religious hatred	Government accepted; referendum promised but no date set
	25. Section 36 of the Defamation Act should be replaced by detailed legislative provisions to include religious hatred	Government to give this 'more consideration'
9. Dáil reform	26. *Constitutional reform to enhance the status of the office of Ceann Comhairle (CC)	No response so far
	27. *Constitutional reform to elect the CC by secret ballot	No response so far
	28. *Include references to Dáil committees in the constitution	No response so far
	29. *Amend Art. 17.2 (re government prior approval for expenditure proposals)	No response so far
	30. The existing Dáil Reform Committee (DRC) should include external members and former TDs	No response so far
	31. The DRC should bring forward proposals for genuine Dáil reform	No response so far
	32. Introduction of family-friendly hours	No response so far
	33. CC to chair a forum to set the Dáil agenda	No response so far
	34. Proportional allocation of committee chairs and secret ballot for their election	No response so far
	35. More technical and professional resources to the committees	No response so far

Topics	*Convention's recommendations*	*Outcome*
	36. The Working Group of Committee Chairs should be given the power to call the Taoiseach	No response so far
	37. Introduce committee weeks	No response so far
	38. More 'free votes' on Dáil and committee business	No response so far
10. Economic, social and cultural rights	39. *Constitutional amendment to strengthen the protection of ESC rights; that this be realized progressively, subject to maximum available resources and that this be justiciable	No response so far
	40. *In amending the constitution, specific additional rights should be enumerated (housing, social security, etc.)	No response so far

* Indicates those recommendations that should require a referendum to implement (18 by our estimation).

Part V

The dilemma of introducing constitutional referendums

Luxembourg and Greece

8 The 'sudden eagerness' to consult the Luxembourgish people on constitutional change

Jörg Gerkrath

The Grand Duchy of Luxembourg is certainly not renowned for making frequent use of direct popular consultations in the field of constitutional change. Its current constitution, dating back to 1868, was amended some 37 times between 1919 and 2009. None of these amendments has ever been submitted to direct popular consent. If one were looking for characteristic elements of the country's constitutional culture, one would think in particular of 'constitutional stability', 'search for cross-party political consensus', 'legal pragmatism', 'attachment to monarchy' and 'strong commitment to the model of representative democracy'.

Referendums as instruments for consulting the people on legislative, international or constitutional issues, however, are not completely unknown to the Luxembourgish constitutional landscape. First introduced in 1919 to allow consultations of the voters in cases determined by legislative acts, and then in 2003 to give the people the final say on constitutional amendments, they have so far remained exceptional. Only three referendums have been organized, on different matters and in different circumstances, in 1919, 1937 and 2005.

For the very first time in the country's constitutional history, the current coalition government, with its slim majority in the Chambre des députés (hereafter 'the Chambre'), now intends to hold two further referendums in order to accomplish far-reaching constitutional revisions initiated in 2009. The first one, meant to be merely consultative, was scheduled to take place on 7 June 2015. Voters had to answer three questions regarding specific constitutional issues, which remained disputed after the general amendment procedure. The outcome will have to be transformed into fully-fledged articles of the draft constitution. The second referendum is currently planned for October 2017. Intended to take place after an obligatory first reading of the draft constitution in the Chambre, it will allow the people to ratify – or to reject – the complete final document.

The question a propos the role of the people in constitutional change is thus extremely topical regarding present-day constitutional practice in the Grand Duchy. In order to allow a proper study of the state of affairs in Luxembourg and to facilitate the comparative analysis, the present contribution is structured in five sections. The first section explores the double legal basis of referendums. Section two recalls the three historic precedents of popular consultations in Luxembourg. By contrast, section three then explains how the current constitutional revision draft can be submitted to popular consultations twice, and section four will deal with the significance of this 'sudden eagerness'. Finally, section five will discuss the merits of popular consent to constitutional amendments in a traditional parliamentary system like the Luxembourgish one, that is based on the principle of representative democracy.

The constitution allows a call for two different types of referendums

The initial text of the 1868 constitution did not contain any element of direct democracy. Moreover, it did not even make a clear choice between the democratic and the monarchical form of government. The formal democratization of Luxembourg's political system was realized by three subsequent constitutional amendments that took place in 1919, 1948 and 1998. Since 15 May 1919, Art. 32 has indicated that 'the sovereign power resides in the Nation', and the Amendment Act of 21 May 1948 added in Art. 51 that 'the Grand Duchy of Luxembourg is ruled by a system of parliamentary democracy'. Since the Amendment of 12 January 1998, the first article of the constitution specifies, furthermore, that the Grand Duchy of Luxembourg is 'a democratic state'.

In addition to this democratization process, which in fact mainly strengthened the position of the Chambre, two distinct amendments, of 15 May 1919 and 19 December 2003, introduced the possibility of consulting the people through referendums.[1] As will be shown, both amendments reserve, however, a predominant place in the Chambre, notably with regard to the launching of any popular consultation. Nevertheless, the two procedures differ very broadly when it comes to their scope and effects.

The amendment of 1919 did indeed establish a procedure, which can be described as a 'consultation-referendum', whereas the amendment of 2003 introduced the possibility of the people voting on constitutional amendments previously adopted by the Chambre, which can be understood as a 'ratification-referendum'. Regarding the settlement of further organizational questions, both procedures rely quite extensively on ordinary legislation.

The 'consultation-referendum'

After the First World War, the Chambre, which had been elected, in accordance with Art. 114 of the constitution, with the power to revise a small number of

1 Furthermore, by virtue of Art. 35 of the 'Municipalities Act' of 13 December 1988, referendum can be held within the municipalities (cf. Memorial A n° 64, 13.12.1988, 1222).

constitutional provisions,[2] decided to further democratize the organs of the state. This led, on 15 May 1919, to the very first constitutional amendment.[3] Sovereignty was explicitly conferred on the nation, and the grand duke retained no powers other than those explicitly conferred on him by the constitution itself – or by legislative acts implementing the constitution (Art. 32). Secret treaties were abolished. Article 52 of the constitution conferred the right to a direct, single vote. Women, like men, were entitled to vote; restricted suffrage, based on a property or income qualification, was ruled out. The electoral system was based on proportional representation. The minimum voting age was reduced from 25 to 21 years, and to qualify for election a person had to be 25 on the day of the elections. Four articles were amended: Art. 32 (sovereignty of the nation and constitutional powers of the grand duke), Art. 37 (treaty-making power), Art. 52 (elections of members of the Chambre) and Art. 75 (allowances of members of the Chambre).

As in 1918, the grand duchy experienced turbulent political circumstances which appeared to threaten the monarchy and the government, and the Grand Duchesse Marie-Adelaide agreed in November 1918 to hold a referendum in order 'to decide on the form of the Luxembourgish state according to the peoples' right of self-determination'.[4] This decision and the following legislative Act of 3 April 1919 'instituting a referendum on the dynastic question and the form of the state' were adopted in the absence of any constitutional basis. During the same period, the Chambre was, however, discussing the above-mentioned constitutional amendments. It decided to introduce a brief reference to the possibility of holding referendums. This mention was added as a final subsection to Art. 52 that dealt with, among other things, the election of the members of the Chambre. The decision in favour of Art. 52, one of the few provisions declared amendable by the previous Chambre, was motivated by a member of the Chambre arguing that a referendum was merely an extension of the electors' voting rights.[5] A further amendment, adopted in 1948, transferred the content of Art. 52 to Art. 51, where it has since remained unchanged.

2 The revision procedure of Art. 114 required at that time the adoption of a 'declaration of revision' by the Chambre and the grand duchesse in order to designate the provisions of the Constitution, which should be amended. Such a declaration was followed by the dissolution of the Chambre and the election of a new Chambre that was entitled to make the amendments.

3 Constitutional Amendment Act (loi de révision constitutionnelle) of 15 May 1919, Mém. 33, 16 May 1919, 529.

4 See B. Fayot, *Les Quatre Référendums du Grand-Duché de Luxembourg, Essai* (Editions De La Petite Amérique 2006) 7.

5 cf. the thorough study of Luc Heuschling, 'Le Discours sur la valeur consultative du référendum (Art. 51 § 7 Const.), Une déconstruction historique' 1 *Pasicrisie luxembourgeoise* 1, quoting Auguste Thorn. Manuscript available at http://orbilu.uni.lu/handle/10993/20296, accessed 27 May 2015.

Consequently, Art. 51 (7) states:

> The electors may be requested to pronounce themselves by way of a referendum in cases and under conditions to be determined by law.[6]

The provision is part of chapter IV of the constitution 'On the *Chambre des Députés*', and is situated as a seventh and last subsection of a provision that mainly deals with the composition and election of the Chambre.

For these reasons it has to be read in conjunction with the provisions that require the assent of the Chambre to each legislative act (Art. 46), reserve the initiative for these acts to the Chambre and the Grand Duke (Art. 47) and prohibit any imperative mandate given to the members of the Chambre (Art. 50). Placed 'under the regime of parliamentary democracy' (Art. 51 [1]), the grand duchy conferred in truth a rather marginal place to the referendum in its political system. It is the Chambre that decides whether or not a referendum will be held. It decides when it will be held and what questions will be put to the electors. Nonetheless, the constitution does not specify the matters that will be considered by the referendum.

Electors cannot request a referendum. Moreover, referendums organized under Art. 51(7) are considered to have only consultative force. Although Art. 51(7) does not explicitly say so, the predominant opinion in Luxembourg is indeed that the electorate does not decide the matter in question but only gives its opinion, leaving the final decision to the legislature, which is only bound in political and not legal terms.[7] The Conseil d'Etat, the main advisory organ, which understands its proper role as 'guardian of the Constitution' and exercises within the parliamentary procedure a moderating function similar to that of a second chamber, has strongly contributed to this reading of Art. 51(7) through its various opinions.[8] In a recent study, Luc Heuschling shows, however, that this predominant interpretation, born in a specific historical context and confirmed by the Chambre's practice, suffers from a number of inconsistencies.[9] We will see in the next section that the Luxembourgish practice of holding referendums does indeed lead to a more nuanced discussion.

The 'ratification-referendum' on constitutional amendment

In 2003, more than 80 years after the first introduction of the referendum, the Chambre adopted an amendment of the amendment procedure established by Art. 114 of the constitution.[10]

6 Original French text: 'Les électeurs pourront être appelés à se prononcer para. la voie du référendum dans les cas et sous les conditions à déterminer para. la loi.'

7 cf. P. Schmit and E. Servais, *Précis de Droit Constitutionnel, Commentaire de la Constitution Luxembourgeoise* (Saint-Paul 2009) 43; P. Majerus, *L'Etat Luxembourgeois* (6th edn, Editpress 1990) 135; and Conseil d'Etat, *Le Conseil d'Etat Gardien de la Constitution et de Droits et Libertés Fondamentaux* (Conseil d'Etat 2006) 213.

8 See V. Gillen, 'Le Conseil d'Etat et le Référendum', in Conseil d' Etat, *Le Conseil d'Etat face à l'évolution de la société luxembourgeoise* (Conseil d' Etat 2006) 223ff.

9 cf. Heuschling (n. 5).

10 Constitutional Amendment Act of 19 December 2003, Mémorial A-185, 31 December 2003, 3969.

Article 114 as modified in 2003 states at present:

> Any revision of the Constitution must be adopted in identical terms by the Chamber of Deputies in two successive votes, separated by an interval of at least three months.
>
> No revision will be adopted, if it doesn't meet at least a two-thirds vote of the members of the Chamber; proxy votes not being admitted.
>
> The text adopted on first reading by the Chamber of Deputies is put to a referendum, which replaces the second vote of the House, if within two months following the first vote request is made either by over a quarter of the members of the Chamber or by twenty-five thousand registered voters on the electoral lists for elections. The revision is adopted, if it receives a majority of valid votes. The law shall regulate the details of the referendum.

In addition to the 'consultation-referendum' of Art. 51(7), the new amendment procedure of the constitution creates the possibility of holding a true decision-making referendum on constitutional amendment. The option to bring about a referendum concerning the text of the revision draft as adopted on first reading by the Chambre is definitely the most important innovation of this amendment. It requires that at least 16 members of the Chambre or 25,000 voters registered on the electoral lists for the parliamentary elections ask for it. The right to initiate the organization of a referendum on constitutional revision has thus been assigned to two different groups: a parliamentary minority and a relatively large group of citizens.

Given the high number of signatures that must be collected, the success of a popular claim for a constitutional referendum seems quite unlikely. After the amendment of December 2003, 13 further amendments took place in accordance with the new procedure but none of them was put to a referendum. The future will show whether parliament made the conditions too restrictive. In January 2009, a claim for a referendum procedure was launched for the first time by a citizens' committee: 25,000 of about 230,000 listed voters were asked to sign, in their local town halls, the petition calling for a referendum. As only around 500 signatures were gathered, the necessary quorum was not met by a long way and the referendum did not take place.

With regard to the outcome of a hypothetical referendum allowed by constitutional amendment, Art. 114 states: 'the revision is adopted if it receives a majority of valid votes cast'. This is clearly a legal basis for a decision-making referendum, and not just an advisory one. The choice of the citizens will replace the vote of the Chambre as to whether to ratify the text adopted on first reading or whether to reject it.

Organizational questions are settled by legislative Acts

Both Art. 51(7) and Art. 114 refer to ordinary legislative Acts in order to determine, respectively, the 'cases and conditions' or 'the details' of a referendum. These rules have been fixed by the 'Act of 4 February 2005 on the national referendum', which applies to both types of referendums.[11] Whereas the organization of a consultative referendum (Art. 51[7]) requires the adoption of a specific legislative Act containing the question and fixing the date of the consultation, ratification-referendums falling under Art. 114 are already fully organized by the legislative Act of 4 February 2005.

This Act notably establishes the conditions for the collection of the 25,000 signatures required by Art. 114. The date when the signatures can begin to be collected is decided by the prime minister on the request of 'an initiative committee consisting of five voters at least, no later than the fourteenth day following the adoption of the text of the constitutional revision in the first reading by the Chamber of Deputies'. The maximum period of two months to collect signatures that is allowed by the constitution is partly consumed by several preparatory operations, for each of which the Act sets specific deadlines.

In addition, the Act of 4 February 2005 contains many mostly technical details on the organization of referendums, namely on the presentation of the voting papers, the voting modalities and the counting of the votes. No quorum of participation is required. Article 37 declares the vote compulsory in accordance with the relevant provisions of the electoral Act.[12] Voting has been compulsory in the grand duchy since 1924 for all registered voters. Exceptions exist for older people and Luxembourgers living abroad.

The Act of 4 February 2005 does not contain any further indication on the effects of a referendum. It simply provides in Art. 58 that the referendum would be deemed successful if a majority of voters who have been issued with a valid ballot paper have voted in favour of the question.

The use of referendum has remained exceptional in Luxembourg's history

Though the possibility of holding referendum was introduced in Luxembourg's constitution almost a century ago, the possibility offered by Art. 51(7) of the constitution has only been used on three – rather extraordinary – occasions. None of the three referendums that took place in 1919, 1937 and 2005 was held in order to consult the people on a constitutional amendment. But, as we will see, all three of them were held in relation to questions that can be considered of constitutional relevance or which are about constitutional change in the broadest sense.

The first referendum was held on 28 September 1919 against the backdrop of internal and external tensions. It consisted of two separate consultations that had been convened by two separate legislative acts adopted on 3 April 1919 and 4 July 1919. The first one touched on the dynastic question and the form of the state, and

11 Loi du 4 Février 2005 relative au referendum au niveau national, Memorial A, n° 27 of 3March 2005, 548.

12 Loi électorale of 18 February 2003, consolidated version published in Mémorial A-31, 17 February 2011.

the second was about a possible economic union to be concluded with France or Belgium. Both referendums were finally held on the same day and were organized by a single grand-ducal decision of 19 September 1919.

Both the so-called political and the so-called economic referendum allowed the voters to make a real choice between several options. They did not only consist of a single question to be answered 'yes' or 'no'. The 'political' referendum offered the voters the possibility of choosing between four options: to keep the Grand Duchess Charlotte, who had taken over the throne a few months before; to retain the dynasty, but replace Charlotte; to retain the monarchy, but replace the dynasty; or to change the form of the state to a republic. Though the vote was not yet compulsory at that time, there was an electoral turnout of over 72 per cent. The vast majority, almost 78 per cent of valid votes, chose the first option, to retain the grand duchess in her role. Almost 20 per cent were in favour of establishing a republic.[13] As the outcome of the referendum confirmed that both the dynasty and the form of the state were to remain in place, no constitutional reform needed to be implemented. The 'economic' referendum required the electors to indicate their preference with regard to an economic union to be concluded either with France or with Belgium. Almost 73 per cent of the valid votes turned out to be in favour of entering into an economic union with France rather than with Belgium (27 per cent).[14] The French Republic refused, however, to negotiate such a union with Luxembourg, and finally, in 1922, the Chambre approved the treaty on the 'Union économique belgo-luxembourgeoise' (UEBL). Thus, the vote of the Luxembourgish people did not produce the desired effect.

The second referendum took place on 6 June 1937 in a context of heated political debate. Following an initiative of the government, the Chambre had adopted on 23 April 1937 the so-called muzzle bill, an Act 'on the defence of the political and social order' allowing de facto the dissolution of the Communist Party as well as other associations considered to militate violently against the constitution. In the Chambre, the bill passed with a broad majority of 34 against 19. Under pressure from trade unions and at the demand of the Liberal party, the Chambre decided very rapidly, on 7 May 1937, to submit this Act to a referendum in order to ask the people whether they 'agreed to its entry into force'. With a very slim majority of 50.67 per cent, the electors answered 'no' to this question. The difference between the number of negative and positive votes was only 1,929.

The legal nature of this consultation is difficult to appreciate. According to the predominant interpretation of Art. 51(7), it could have had a consultative value only. This time, however, the referendum took place after the final vote of the bill by the Chambre. The 'muzzle bill' only needed to be enacted by the grand duchesse and to be published in the official journal (*Mémorial*) in order to come into force.[15] The question was thus not so much whether – in a representative

13 cf. Fayot (n. 4) 35.
14 Ibid. 36.
15 cp Heuschling (n. 5) 21 ff.

democracy such as Luxembourg – a 'decision' of the people could bind the Chambre but whether it could bind the executive power. In this sense, the outcome of the 1937 referendum was certainly considered binding by all actors. Consequently, the bill was apparently never enacted by the grand duchesse and was certainly never published in the official journal, and the government resigned.

After these two national referendums, which had been convened during the period between the two world wars, it took more than 70 years before the third one was organized regarding a matter of EU integration. The referendum on the ratification of the treaty establishing a constitution for Europe was held on 10 July 2005, shortly after the negative voting outcomes of the French and the Dutch electorate.[16] The result of the referendum was that 56.52 per cent of the voters said 'yes'. Luxembourg is indeed regarded as one of the EU's most enthusiastic member states, and the most prominent political figures supported the constitution for Europe, with both the governing coalition and the main opposition parties campaigning for a 'yes' vote. On 28 June 2005, the Chambre had already approved the ratification of the treaty on its first reading. The poll was consultative in nature but the Chambre agreed – before the second reading – to abide by the people's majority vote. The then prime minister, Jean-Claude Juncker, said that he would resign if the referendum resulted in a 'no' vote.

In connection with this referendum, a question arose as to whether EU citizens other than Luxembourgish ones were allowed to vote, to which the reply was negative.[17] The statement of reasons set out in the Act organizing the referendum in June 2005 does not refer to any specific rationale regarding the constitutional procedure chosen to approve the treaty establishing a constitution for Europe. However, the draft Act concerning this referendum notes:

> If the referendum is, from the legal point of view, of advisory character, the legislature will nevertheless feel politically bound by the popular verdict. Therefore, it is necessary to measure the challenges raised by the consultation to be held on 10 July 2005. Due to the exceptional nature of referendums in our history, the results will leave a lasting imprint on the political life of our country.

Are there any conclusions to be drawn from these three precedents? At first glance the differences in terms of historical context, subject matter, type of question, outcome and effect seem to prevail. The only thing they have in common is that they were organized in times of heated political debates. It appears notably

16 La loi du 14 avril 2005 portant organisation d'un referendum national sur Traité établissant une Constitution pour l'Europe, signé à Rome, le 29 Octobre 2004. For a discussion concerning this referendum see P. Dumont, F. Fehlen, R. Kies and P. Poirier, *Le référendum sur le Traité établissant une Constitution pour l'Europe, Rapport Elaboré pour la Chambre des Députés* (STADE–Études sociologiques et politiques sur le Luxembourg Université du Luxembourg, Février 2007) 212.

17 cf. p. 3 of the Projet de loi portant organisation d'un référendum national sur le Traité établissant une Constitution pour l'Europe, signé à Rome, le 29 Octobre 2004, parl. doc. no. 5443.

difficult to detect any consistent practice, especially with regard to their consultative or decisional effect. This question has never been subject to any Luxembourgish case law either.

None of the three (or four if the two in 1919 are counted separately) referendums were linked to formal amendments of the constitution, but all them were held on matters of constitutional change in the broadest sense. The 'political' referendum of 1919 would indeed have required a major constitutional reform if the people had voted in favour of having a republic or in favour of another grand-ducal dynasty. The three other consultations were held on questions that formally belong to the field of ordinary legislation. The 1937 referendum prevented a major breach of public freedoms while no constitutional court existed to censure the legislative power. The 'economic' referendum of 1919 and the 2005 referendum on the EU constitution touched upon the question of international integration, which is crucial for a small state such as Luxembourg and certainly constitutes a matter of a constitutional nature.

The Luxembourgish tradition of holding referendum does not allow an easy conclusion to be drawn on the question of whether a referendum held on the basis of Art. 51(7) can only be of consultative force or whether it could, under some conditions, have a decisional character. One should not overestimate the fact that the 'economic' referendum of 1919 and the EU referendum of 2005 have not been followed by the effect desired by the Luxembourgish people. In the field of international treaties, national referendums can, understandably, only influence the position of one of the concluding parties.

The moment at which a referendum is scheduled seems to be an important element in terms of the appreciation of its effects. In Luxembourg's constitutional practice there have been three different scenarios: the referendum was held at a preparatory stage, well before the Chambre could take a formal decision on the issue (1919); the consultation took place after the final vote of the Chambre and allowed the people to veto the entry into force of an approved bill (1937); or the referendum was inserted between the first and second reading in the Chambre (2005), which only makes sense if the Chambre declares that it will be bound by the outcome. According to these scenarios, therefore, the referendum can be considered purely consultative, as in the first case (1919), legally binding on the executive power, as in the second case (1937), or, at the very least, politically binding on the Chambre, as in the third case (2005).

The pending proposal for a new constitution will be submitted to referendum twice

The constitution of the grand duchy, one of the oldest constitutional documents in Europe still in force, is currently undergoing a far-reaching revision procedure aiming at a general overhaul.[18] According to the parliamentary committee in

18 cf. J. Gerkrath, 'Some Remarks on the Pending Constitutional Change in the Grand Duchy of Luxembourg' (2013) 19(3) *European Public Law* 449.

charge, this revision will finally give birth to a 'new' constitution, meaning that a modified and updated edition of the constitution will be published in the official journal and the current constitution will be repealed.

The present amendment procedure started officially in April 2009 with the submission of a formal revision proposal by the parliamentary committee on constitutional amendment.[19] The proposal aspires to realize a general renovation and updating of the constitution and to rearrange the whole document. It has been evaluated in depth by the Venice Commission, which delivered an opinion in December 2009, and by the Conseil d'Etat, which published its extensive opinion in June 2012.[20] This text of 216 pages is set out like a true 'counterproposal' and is completed by a table that allows the reader to compare the current wording of the constitution with the initial revision proposal and the version favoured by the Conseil d'Etat.

In the light of this opinion, the parliamentary committee significantly modified its initial proposal and in January 2013 established an internal working document containing a first consolidated version that included all the future amendments to the constitution.

After the breaking up of the coalition government formed by the conservative Christian Democrats of Jean-Claude Juncker (CSV) and the Social Democrats (LSAP), the Chambre was dissolved by the Grand Duke and parliamentary elections took place on 20 October 2013. Though the CSV remained, with 23 seats, the strongest party in the Chambre, three smaller parties formed a new coalition government. This coalition of the Democratic Party (DP), led by the new Prime Minister Xavier Bettel, the LSAP and the Green party (Dei Greng) is supported by a slim majority of 32 seats out of 60.

Under the new majority, the renewed committee on constitutional revision went back to work and managed to agree on most of the chapters and provisions of the draft constitution during 2014. In March 2015, the committee's draft was finally published on the website of the Chambre on a special page dedicated to the referendum that was held on 7 June 2015.[21]

It must be emphasized that there was absolutely no direct popular involvement in the drafting process of the new constitution until this stage. The work of the parliamentary committee could be followed by reading the minutes of its numerous meetings, which are regularly published on the Chambre's website.[22] These minutes show that the committee has a strong tendency to find solutions that are acceptable to a large majority within the Chambre. The document that had the highest impact on the work of the committee was clearly the opinion delivered

19 See 'Proposition de révision portant modification et nouvel ordonnancement de la Constitution' of 21 April 2009, doc. parl. N° 6030, www.chd.lu, accessed 16 May 2015.

20 Avis du Conseil d'Etat du 6 juin 2012, no. 48.433, doc. parl. 6030/06.

21 See http://www.referendum.lu/Uploads/Nouvelle_Constitution/Doc/1_1_Proposition-NouvelleConstitution.pdf, accessed 16 May 2015.

22 cf. http://www.chd.lu/wps/portal/public/RoleEtendu?action=doDocpaDetails&backto=/wps/portal/public&id=6030, accessed 16 May 2015.

by the Conseil d'Etat in June 2012. Opinions and positions introduced by other bodies, such as the judiciary, the Venice Commission and the professional chambers, only played a secondary role.

The question of whether the amended constitution should be submitted to a referendum had often been raised in the past, but the different political parties changed their positions over time. In 1999 Prime Minister Juncker (CSV) still considered that a more participatory society was needed: 'We have therefore decided that, in the case of a substantial revision of the constitution, we would proceed to a referendum. A fundamental and substantial revision of the constitution represents a historical work and would need the consent of the sovereign people.'[23] Ten years later, in 2009, the coalition agreement concluded between the Christian Democrats (CSV) and the Social Democrats (LSAP) no longer mentioned this ambition. In November 2010, the chairman of the committee on constitutional revision, Paul-Henri Meyers (CSV), openly expressed his doubts on whether a referendum would be appropriate. In January 2011, Prime Minister Juncker himself considered that it is 'not as a good idea'. Since December 2013, however, the project of consulting the Luxembourgish people on the new constitution has reappeared on the agenda of the new coalition government and was vigorously supported.

A first referendum was thus scheduled for 7 June 2015 by an Act of 27 February 2015 'on the organization of a national referendum on different questions related to the working out of a new Constitution'.[24] The members of the parliamentary majority, which authored the proposal of this Act, justified this first referendum, based on Art. 51(7) of the constitution, by referring to the need to consult the people on several essential questions that had remained controversial during the preparatory work on the draft constitution.[25]

Both the authors of the proposal and the Conseil d'Etat insist on the point that this referendum was purely consultative and must not be confused with the referendum foreseen by Art. 114 of the constitution.[26] It was a consultative referendum scheduled well before the first vote of the Chambre on the final text was due to take place. Though the outcome of this referendum will not be legally binding on the Chambre, it will strongly influence the final discussions within the parliamentary committee on constitutional amendment, which has to 'translate' this outcome into constitutional provisions.

23 Déclaration de M. Jean-Claude Juncker, Premier Ministre, Ministre d'Etat concernant le programme gouvernementa, doc. parl. n° C-1999-W-002-000, <http://www.chd.lu>, p. 68 (in Luxembourgish language).

24 Loi du 27 Février 2015 portant organisation d'un référendum national sur différentes questions en relation avec l'élaboration d'une nouvelle Constitution, Mémorial A-35, 4 March 2015, 358.

25 See Proposal of an act on the organization of a national referendum on issues related to the making of a new Constitution, doc. parl. 6738, 2.

26 See the Opinion of the Conseil d'Etat of 13 January 2015, doc. parl. 6738/1, 2.

The initial proposal suggested submitting four questions to the referendum: first, whether the voting age should be lowered to 16; second, whether foreigners should be allowed to vote in the Chambre elections; third, whether mandates of members of the government should be limited to ten years; and, fourth, whether the obligation of the state to pay the salaries and pensions of religious officials should end. As the result of an agreement reached between the state and the religious communities and a consensus reached within the parliamentary committee to introduce a new article in the draft constitution on the neutrality of the state in religious matters and the separation between the state and the religious communities, the fourth question was eventually withdrawn from the proposal.[27]

The Act of 27 February 2015 'on the organization of a national referendum on different questions related to the working out of a new Constitution' thus finally called the voters to answer 'yes' or 'no' to the following three questions:

'1. Do you agree with the idea that Luxembourgers aged between sixteen and eighteen have the right to optionally enrol in order to participate as voters in elections for the Chamber of Deputies, European and local elections as well as referendum?
2. Do you agree with the idea that non-Luxembourgish residents have the right to optionally enrol in order to participate as voters in elections for the Chamber of Deputies, under the double particular condition of having resided for at least ten years in Luxembourg and of having previously participated in local or European elections in Luxembourg?
3. Do you agree with the idea of restricting to ten years the maximum time a person can continuously be part of the government?'

All three questions are replicated in French, Luxembourgish and German, the three official languages of the grand duchy. The referendum was organized according to the conditions laid down in the Act of 4 February 2005 relating to a national referendum. As the questions refer to 'ideas' rather than to written draft articles, the Chambre and its committee on constitutional amendment conserved a margin of appreciation with regard to the outcome of the three questions. Once the drafting of the new constitution is finished it will need to be approved in a first reading of the Chambre by a majority of two-thirds of its members.

A second decisional referendum, planned for October 2017, will be organized in order to approve the new constitution by a direct popular consultation rather than a second vote within the Chambre. As the governmental majority has announced this referendum, it is very likely that the members of the majority will vote in favour of it. The necessary number of at least 16 members of the Chambre asking for it, as foreseen by Art. 114 of the constitution, should thus easily be reached.

27 See doc. parl. 6738/2 of 23 January 2015.

The significance of this 'sudden eagerness' to consult on constitutional change

It is, first of all, remarkable that for the very first time in its constitutional history the grand duchy will hold a direct popular consultation on constitutional change in the sense of a formal amendment of the constitution. Considering the exceptional character of referendums in the past and the absence of any consistent practice, the current political situation seems to be promoting a renewed interest in the instruments of direct democracy. There is, however, a distinction to be made between the eagerness to consult on the new constitution and the coincident eagerness to broaden the scope of popular consultations within this process. In the first case, it is the current governmental majority alone that decided to proceed in this direction. In the second case, a wide consensus already existed between the political parties that such a broadening of scope was desirable.

Eagerness to consult on the new constitution

The decision of the current political majority to achieve the current constitutional amendment process through the combination of a preceding consultative referendum and a conclusive decisional referendum seems at first glance to have been motivated by the will to strengthen the direct involvement of the people. When looking more closely, however, the first referendum appears rather as an attempt to call on the people in order to overcome the controversy between the governmental coalition DP–LSAP–Dei Greng and the main opposition party CSV. Within the parliamentary committee on constitutional amendment, no consensus and indeed not even a majority of two-thirds could be reached on the three controversial points. Thus, the referendum was used to put popular pressure on the Christian Democrats (CSV) in particular, who still hold 23 seats out of 60 within the Chambre.[28]

This situation is rather unusual for Luxembourg. All previous constitutional amendments have been adopted in the Chambre by consensus of a very broad majority. The political system is strongly characterized by stability, proximity to the citizens and a common desire to take decisions based on consensus. This is particularly true for decisions on constitutional revision, which are mostly supported by much stronger parliamentary majorities than are necessary and are very often supported unanimously. The modification of the revision procedure, for instance, was adopted in November 2003 by 59 votes in favour and one abstention, and the most recent amendment of Art. 34, depriving the Grand Duke of his power to 'sanction' legislative acts, was adopted in March 2009 by a unanimous vote.[29]

28 The remaining five seats are held by two members of a left-wing party (Dei Lenk) and three members of the right-wing party (ADR).

29 cf. L. Frieden, 'Luxembourg: Parliament Abolishes Royal Confirmation of Laws' (2009) 7(3) *International Journal of Constitutional Law* 539.

One of the smaller opposition parties, the right-wing ADR, argued that organizing a consultative referendum on constitutional questions before the first vote on the amendments by the Chambre is contrary to the spirit and the wording of the constitution. According to this reasoning, Art. 114, which governs the referendum within the constitutional amendment procedure, constitutes a *lege speciale* prohibiting the application of the 'legislative referendum' in connection with an amendment of the constitution. This is not a convincing interpretation. It must be admitted, however, that a popular consultation under Art. 51(7) of the constitution may be organized on any question that the Chambre decides to submit to the voters by adopting an ordinary legislative Act.[30]

It is true that the constitution does not articulate the relationship between Arts 51(7) and 114. On the other hand, a referendum based on Art. 51(7) may certainly not violate the procedure of constitutional amendment. It has to respect in particular the competences that both provisions reserve exclusively to the Chambre. This is still the case in relation to the situation that is being discussed here. The Chambre elected to consult the people on three controversial questions; it will have to adopt the draft constitution on a first reading by a majority of two-thirds, and after this first reading the decisional referendum can be held.

Eagerness to broaden the place of popular consultations within the new constitution

The Luxembourgish people will not only be consulted twice on the new constitution; the place of popular consultations will also be broadened within the new constitution. The consolidated working document of the draft constitution introduces a constitutional basis for a citizens' initiative and clarifies somewhat the rules on referendums. A large majority within the parliamentary committee in charge has agreed upon these amendments to the current constitution.

The first innovation results from Art. 74 of the draft constitution. It reads as follows:

> Voters may take the initiative to transmit a reasoned proposal to legislate to the Chamber of Deputies. The law determines the conditions and procedures of this citizens' initiative.[31]

The introduction in the pending revision draft of a basis for popular initiatives in legislative matters will enable the Chambre to resume discussions on the establishment of a right for citizens to introduce legislative proposals. The detailed

30 cf. Opinion of the Conseil d'Etat of 13 January 2015, doc. parl. 6738/1, 2; L. Heuschling, 'Illégal? Consultatif?, Deux questions juridiques à propos du premier référendum constituant' (2014) 345 *Forum* 7.

31 'Des électeurs peuvent prendre l'initiative de transmettre à la Chambre des Députés une proposition motivée aux fins de légiférer. La loi détermine les conditions et procédures de cette initiative citoyenne'.

procedure for such an initiative will have to be regulated by a legislative Act. Juncker, the prime minister, tabled a proposal on the legislative popular initiative and the referendum on 20 May 2003, intending to introduce such a right.[32] However, this aspect of the proposal was held in abeyance after the Conseil d'Etat formally opposed it because it lacked a constitutional basis. The Act of 4 February 2005, which was adopted on the basis of this proposal, therefore only regulates the national referendum.

The future constitutional basis for a national popular initiative will, at any rate, coexist with the possibility of all European citizens living in Luxembourg participating in a European citizen's initiative in accordance with Regulation (EU) No. 211/2011 of the European Parliament and of the Council of 16 February 2011, which establishes the procedures and conditions required for a citizens' initiative as provided for in Art. 11 TEU and Art. 24 TFEU.

The second innovation results from a new Art. 76 of the draft constitution. Replacing the current Art. 51(7), it states:

> The Chamber may decide to have recourse to referendum in the cases, under the conditions and with the effects to be determined by law.[33]

In comparison with the current Art. 51(7), three comments can be made. First, the new provision is still part of the chapter dedicated to the Chambre. Second, the possibility of holding a referendum is explicitly designed as a faculty of the Chambre, which remains the responsible constitutional organ. Third, the Chambre is obviously invited to determine the effects of future referendums by ordinary legislation. This additional element can only be understood as a discretionary power given to the Chambre in order to decide on a case-by-case basis whether future referendums will be merely consultative or truly decisional.

The position of the ratification-referendum within the amendment procedure is transferred from the current Art. 114 to Art. 125 of the constitution without any notable changes. Some questions remain, however, with regard to the exercise of the people's constituent power within a traditional parliamentary system.

The exercise of the people's constituent power in Luxembourg's parliamentary system

In a democratic state, the source of sovereign power lies with the people. This is also the case in Luxembourg despite the formulation of the current Art. 32 of the constitution declaring that 'the sovereign power resides in the Nation'. Furthermore, such a small state offers good prerequisites for the introduction of

32 Doc. parl. 5132.

33 'La Chambre des Députés peut décider d'avoir recours au référendum dans les cas, sous les conditions et avec les effets à déterminer para. la loi'.

elements of direct democracy.[34] The process of the democratization of its constitution led to a clear choice in favour of a system of parliamentary democracy with a small dose of direct popular involvement. The objective of finding a 'third way' between a purely representative system and a direct democracy had been announced by the very ambitious legislative proposal of 20 May 2003. This proposal of an Act 'on popular initiative in legislative matters and on the referendum' aimed not only to establish the legislative rules on referendum under Arts 51(7) and 114, as it finally did, but also to allow popular initiatives concerning legislative Acts and popular requests to hold referendum on the Acts adopted as a result of such initiatives.[35] The last two elements have, however, been abandoned due to the opposition of the Conseil d'Etat, which rightly pointed out that there was no constitutional basis for their introduction.

As such a constitutional basis will probably be created by the draft constitution, at least with regard to citizens' initiatives, the idea of encouraging the direct participation of citizens within the traditional system of representative democracy is again on the agenda. The procedural combination of the Chambre retaining the power to amend the constitution with the possibility of the people, first, being consulted during the amendment procedure and, second, actively calling for a referendum in order to ratify or veto the amendment finally adopted by the Chambre raises challenging questions. The resulting coexistence of a representative system and elements of direct democracy has to be carefully organized, especially when it comes to constitutional amendments.

In Luxembourg's parliamentary system, it is the Chambre that 'represents the country', as stated in Art. 50 of the current constitution, or rather 'the Nation', as foreseen by Art. 60 of the draft constitution. The same provisions prohibit at present, as well as in the future, imperative mandates and indicate that the members of the Chambre vote on behalf of 'the general interest'.[36] This provision has often been quoted to explain why referendum held under Art. 51(7) can only have consultative value. It is, however, difficult to explain to the voters that their vote has no more than a consultative effect despite voting having been made compulsory by the electoral law. Article 76 of the draft constitution will permit the Chambre to determine the effects of future referendums organized on this basis, including in theory the possibility of making them binding, at least, one might think, if they are held after the final vote of the Chambre.

In the field of constitutional amendment, referendum preceding the vote of the Chambre will certainly remain consultative. Only a referendum based on Art. 114 (Art. 125 of the draft constitution) gives the people the final word. Does the draft

34 cf. C. Hemmer, 'Für das Referendum: mehr Direktdemokratie!' *Letzeburger Land* (24 July 1987), 10.

35 See 'Projet de loi relative à l'initiative populaire en matière législative et au référendum', 205.2003, doc. parl. 5132.

36 See Art. 60 of the draft Constitution: 'La Chambre des Députés représente la Nation. Elle exerce le pouvoir législatif. Les députés votent sans en référer à leurs commettants et ne peuvent avoir en vue que l'intérêt général'.

constitution allow citizens' initiatives for constitutional amendments? The answer must be negative. Article 74 of the draft explicitly confines the scope of these initiatives to proposals 'to legislate'. It is true that, besides the majority requirements of the amendment procedure, revision acts in Luxembourg follow the legislative procedure. But amending the constitution is not the same as 'legislating'.

The future will show whether the practice of holding referendum and citizens' initiatives will become less exceptional than in the past. As the role of the Chambre in this context is still pivotal, one might expect that it could persist in having a preference for consultative referendums, especially when it comes to constitutional amendments. Why should it take the risk that the people, at the end of a long and laborious amendment procedure, might reject by a slim majority a compromise that has been accepted by more than two-thirds of its members?

The most challenging question with regard to popular involvement in the constitutional amendment procedure touches the composition of the electorate. Luxembourg's constitution does not mention 'the people'; it refers to the Nation (Art. 32), to Luxembourgers (Art. 9), to non-Luxembourgers (Art. 9), to foreigners (Art. 111) and to electors (Arts 51(7) and 114). Only those who fulfil the conditions for voting in the elections of the Chambre are also entitled to vote in national referendums. The second question of the referendum of 7 June 2015 therefore touched not only the question of whether foreigners would be allowed to vote in the Chambre's elections. Once they were allowed to register as electors on the national electoral lists, they would automatically be allowed to vote in referendums as well.

As the resident population of the grand duchy currently consists of 54 per cent of Luxembourgers and 46 per cent of foreigners – with an ongoing growth in the latter group – the issue is of the utmost importance.[37] It seems unacceptable that in a democratic state half of the population could be indefinitely disqualified to vote in national elections and referendums. Only Luxembourgers voted, however, on the three referendum questions, and the 'no' vote prevailed in all questions by a wide margin.

37 See M. Finck, 'Towards an Ever Closer Union Between Résidents and Citizens? On the Possible Extension of Voting Rights to Foreign Résidents in Luxembourg' (2015) 11 *European Constitutional Law Review* 78.

9 The role of the people in constitutional amendment in Greece

Between narratives and practice

Alkmene Fotiadou

> Sir, with no intention to take offence,
> I deny your right to put words into my mouth.
>
> *Robert Louis Stevenson*, Treasure Island

Introduction

In the last few years Greece came very close to experiencing in a schematic form the most representative scenarios of strong popular involvement in constitutional change. For a considerable time such plans were not materialized and this failure, although less dramatic than their success would have been, is characteristic of the constitutional culture. It appears that the more distant the people are becoming from the constitutional revision process, the stronger the narratives for more involvement get.

A cancelled referendum and a never materialized constituent assembly conveyed for a long time through negation, the image of absence of movement and of vague and unfulfilled democratic promises linked to the impact of the financial crisis. This inertia came to an abrupt end by an unexpected snap referendum, which wounded the participatory potential of referendums in Greece even more than the prior state of disuse.

In the first part of this chapter we shall explore the two unaccomplished attempts to involve the people in matters of constitutional change, that is the abandoned Papandreou referendum and the dialogue about convening a constituent assembly in 2011. In the second part we shall analyze the Greek bailout referendum, questioning whether it fulfilled the criteria of a democratic, participatory process. In the third part we shall discuss the current amendment formula and the proposals about enshrining a constitutional referendum. To do so, we shall consider the lack of any referendum practice in Greece from 1974 until 2015, and the features of the only referendum held under the current Greek constitution enacted in 1975. The future constitutional legislator, who wishes to consider the possibility of enhancing participatory constitutional procedures, is faced with the experience of a long period of disuse followed by a snap undemocratic referendum. The question is what this experience has to offer to constitutional design.

Disuse and narratives

The cancelled referendum

Following the collapse of the military regime in Greece, a referendum was held in December 1974 on the status of the head of state, and the monarchy was abolished. The 1974 referendum had posed a straight-forward choice between a crowned republic and a republic. In reality this referendum could be viewed as a plebiscitum, because the dilemma entailed more than a choice between forms of government. If the monarchy was restored, this would mean the return of King Constantine II, that is the choice entailed a specific person.

The current constitution came into effect in June 1975 and although it included a provision enshrining referendums (Art. 44 para. 2), no referendum had been held prior to the 5 July 2015 bailout referendum. Referendums seemed to be part of scholarly research, not part of the constitutional culture. Nonetheless, after the outbreak of the financial crisis referendums made a comeback marked by a cancelled bailout referendum and a snap bailout referendum.

The first attempt at direct recourse to the people regarding bailout agreements was the referendum planned by the then prime minister George Papandreou on a EU debt rescue package in October 2011. This would have been the first referendum in Greece since the restoration of democracy in 1974. However, it was promptly called off. In retrospect it is challenging to detect what this referendum would have been about. Even if the Papandreou referendum had been held, it would have taken place after the passage of the 2010 bailout and the 2011 austerity package that his government had imposed without any thought of asking the people their opinion. The first bailout agreement and the austerity measures resulting from it had been a source of enormous informal constitutional change. An acceptance vote in favour of the new bailout would in practice have been an ex post approval of already accomplished constitutional change.

The reasons about the cancellation are more or less known. Sanford Levinson lamented in a blog post the 'death of the Greek democracy'.[1] The saga got even more captivating due to the comments made by foreign leaders and publications about how upset markets were. Eloquently expressed by Jean-Claude Juncker, 'The Greek prime minister has taken this decision without talking it through with his European colleagues'.[2] In other words, it was thought self-evident that a prime minister in order to call a referendum should have first discussed it with foreign leaders. This was but a first sign of the involvement the president of the European Commission would have in the 2015 bailout referendum, when he directly addressed the Greek people.

1 S. Levinson, 'The Death of Democracy in Greece' *Balkinization* (3 November 2011), http://balkin.blogspot.gr/2011/11/death-of-democracy-in-greece.html, accessed 11 November 2011.

2 D. Schwartz, 'ANALYSIS: Papandreou's Referendum Gamble' *CBC News* (1 November 2011), http://www.cbc.ca/m/touch/news/story/1.994167, accessed 11 November 2011.

The dialogue that took place on the question that would be put to referendum is also interesting, because it offers an oversimplification of the dilemmas posed on how to articulate and pose referendum questions. Would it be 'Do you agree with the bailout plan', or 'do you wish to remain in the Eurozone', or as put by Sweden's foreign minister '"Do we want to be saved or not?" Is that the question?'[3] These wordings bring forth, in its roughest version, the issue of clarity in framing the substantive issue. It would possibly have been an excellent case study on how different variations of the referendum question can lead to different outcomes.[4] In addition, the above dialogue and the course of events is an excellent example of placing state sovereignty within an international context. Was it an issue that could be played out within the confines of state sovereignty, or it had to be placed within the European normative environment? Constitutional control appeared to have clearly slipped away from the hands of national political actors and moved to a context with more players and far more complicated stakes.[5] The cancelled Papandreou referendum and the issues it posed proved to be a dress rehearsal for the bailout referendum, which set forth the same issues only in a more compelling way.

The narrative of re-awakening the constituent power

Throughout the crisis constant calls for radical constitutional change accompanied total lack of formal constitutional change. Frequent discussions about constitutional reforms that would remedy flaws of the past treated constitutional change as a path towards recovery.[6] With the eyes fixed on Iceland's crowdsourcing experiment, and in total ignorance of the problems faced there, or of the political culture that allowed it to happen,[7] several prominent members of the political elite in Greece put forth the idea of re-drafting the constitution from bottom-up. A constituent assembly would also allow a renegotiation of the form of government, which is among the material limits of the Greek constitution.[8]

3 H. Schneider and M. Birnbaum, 'Greek Referendum Call Upends Euro-Plans' *The Washington Post* (2 November 2011), https://www.washingtonpost.com/business/economy/greek-referendum-call-upends-euro-plans/2011/11/01/gIQAxQGZdM_story.html, accessed 11 November 2011.

4 S. Tierney, *Constitutional Referendums: The Theory and Practice of Republican Deliberation* (Oxford University Press 2014) 230.

5 Tierney (n. 4) 153.

6 X. Contiades and A. Fotiadou, 'On Resilience of Constitutions: What Makes Constitutions Resistant to External Shocks?' (2015) 1 *Vienna Journal on International Constitutional Law* 3.

7 B. Thorarensen, 'The Impact of the Financial Crisis on Icelandic Constitutional Law: Legislative Reforms, Judicial Review and Revision of the Constitution' in X. Contiades (ed.), *Constitutions in the Global Financial Crisis: A Comparative Analysis* (Ashgate 2013) 263; B. Thorarensen, 'Why the Making of a Crowd-Sourced Constitution in Iceland Failed' *Constitution Making & Constitutional Change* (26 February 2014), http://constitutional-change.com/why-the-making-of-a-crowd-sourced-constitution-in-iceland-failed/, accessed 20 February 2015.

8 On unamendability see Y. Roznai, 'Unamendability and the Genetic Code of the Constitution', *European Review of Public Law* (Forthcoming), New York University School of Law, Public Law Research Paper 15–13, http://ssrn.com/abstract=2569279, accessed 24 February 2015.

Greece seemed ideal for becoming a test case for theorists who crave for mild constitutional revolutions. Were we witnessing the creation of the conditions that stimulate the emergence of constituent power? The often discussed, but never attempted, constitutional replacement became a disturbing reminder of the pending question whether radical change lies within the people's control, or adversely the loci of power are increasingly moving away.

Joel Colón-Riós in 'Weak Constitutionalism' detects and then sides with the emergence of popular constituent power that sprung, as he believes, during the protests against the austerity measures and the occupation of Syntagma Square (which means constitution square) in the centre of Athens and in other cities by a group of people calling themselves 'indignant'.[9] Colon-Rios was not the only enthusiast about the possibility of a constitutional revolution in progress. Professor Douzinas of the Critical Legal Studies movement revelled in the idea of 'the meaning and limits of democracy [being] renegotiated in the place it was born'.[10] Still, nothing happened. Greece remained at the still point of a turning world. Was this because strong constituted powers, such as the powers of the EU and credit-rating agencies got in the way of popular deliberation,[11] or because it is a mistake to read into protests the conditions for a full-fledged constitutional revolution?[12] Perhaps a crucial parameter for understanding the contradiction between narratives and praxis is that during the first phase of the recession it was constitutionally impossible to initiate a constitutional amendment, due to the procedural limits of the amending formula that provided for a mandatory five-year time lapse. Nonetheless, even after the mandatory time lapse expired in May 2013 and Greece could embark on a constitutional reform journey, it has remained in a state of reform anticipation. No intentional formal constitutional reform has been materialized since the beginning of the crisis. The contrast between proposals for radical constitutional reforms and the reality of inertia produces an intermittent disillusionment with the dynamics of constitutional change.

Bad practice: The snap bailout referendum

At the point when referendums seemed to be but a democratic narrative about the potential of a dormant constitutional procedure, a snap referendum forced an abrupt change of scenery. Greece has now referendum experience under the

9 J. Colon-Rios, *Weak Constitutionalism* (Routledge 2012) 180.

10 C. Douzinas, 'Greece and the future of Europe' *Critical Legal Thinking* (3 December 2012), http://criticallegalthinking.com/2012/12/03/greece-and-the-future-of-europe/, accessed 12 December 2012.

11 See Zoran Oklopcic review of Colon-Rio's Weak Constitutionalism in http://www.iconnectblog.com/2012/10/joel-colon-rios-weak-constitutionalism-democratic-legitimacy-and-the-question-of-constituent-power-london-routledge-2012/, accessed 31 December 2012.

12 M. Tushnet, 'Peasants with Pitchforks, and Toilers with Twitter: Constitutional Revolutions and the Constituent Power' (2015) 13(3) *International Journal of Constitutional Law* 639.

current constitution and a remarkably awkward one.[13] On 5 July 2015 Greek citizens went to the polls to answer a question characterized by oracular ambiguity. More than that, it was an unavailing question, which could not lead to a binding result.

A chronicle of the events that took place in the days following the announcement of the referendum is indicative of various serious problems. The timeline of the short pre-referendum period would begin with the announcement of the referendum on Friday 26 June, when the Greek prime minister made a statement that a referendum would be held on Sunday 5 July. The vote would be on the 'Reforms for the completion of the Current Program and Beyond' and on the 'Preliminary Debt sustainability analysis', the then latest offer of the international lenders. The referendum was officially declared by the president of the republic on 28 June, after a parliamentary vote held on 27 June. On 28 June the European Commission published these latest proposals 'in the interest of transparency and for the information of the Greek people'. On 28 June, an Act of Legislative Content (A′ 64 28/6/2015) altered several of the pre-existing rules regarding referendums. The first official translation of the two documents appeared on 29 June containing a mistake and was replaced by the corrected version on 30 June. On 30 June this offer expired and Greece did not pay its dues to the IMF. On 3 July the Supreme Administrative Court unanimously rejected a complaint against the constitutionality of the referendum, as it lacks competence to decide on this question, while the referendum object being a governmental act is not subject to judicial review. On 5 July the referendum was held with a 62.5 per cent turnout. The no vote prevailed with 61.31 per cent. On 8 June, three days after the 'no' vote, Greece officially requested a three-year bailout agreement and on 13 July the Greek government accepted a bailout package containing severe austerity measures.

Two crucial questions emerged. The first is whether the bailout referendum was constitutional. The second is whether it met the standards of a democratic referendum.[14] The answer to these two interrelated questions is important for two distinct reasons. Being the only referendum held under the current constitution it impacts the future practice of referendums in Greece, as well as any discussion about enhancing their use. Furthermore, viewed from the aspect of multi-level constitutionalism this peculiar undemocratic referendum is now part of the EU referendums history.

13 See X. Contiades and A. Fotiadou, 'The Greek Referendum Unconstitutional and Undemocratic', in Constitutional Change through Euro Crisis Law, EUI Law Department Papers, 7 July 2015, http://eurocrisislaw.eui.eu/news/the-greek-referendum-unconstitutional-and-undemocratic-by-xenophon-contiades-and-alkmene-fotiadou/, accessed 10 July 2015.

14 M. Suski, *Bringing in the People: A Comparison of Constitutional Forms and Practices of the Referendum* (Martinus Nijhoff Publishers 1993); M. Mendelson and A. Parkin (eds), *Referendum Democracy: Citizens, Elites and Deliberation in Referendum Campaigns* (Palgrave Macmillan 2001); and A.H. Trechsel, 'How Democratic is the Greek Referendum?' *European Union Democracy Observatory* (3 July 2015), https://blogs.eui.eu/eudo-cafe/2015/07/03/how-democratic-is-the-greek-referendum/, accessed 20 July 2015.

To begin with, focus must be placed on the provisions of the Greek constitution (Art. 44 para. 2) that was put into use for the first time. The referendum provisions had never been applied under the current constitution and after 40 years of non-use seemed to lie in between being dormant or disused.[15] In other words the constant and conscious disuse of referendums by political actors appeared to have rendered the constitutional provisions obsolete. Still, although there seemed to be clear signs of constitutional atrophy[16] suggestive of informal amendment through disuse, it turned out that provisions enshrining referendums were just dormant. Due to dormancy, discussions about referendums had been purely theoretical. Thus, there was no referendum practice to draw interpretative guidance from. What followed shows that awakening dormant provisions might trigger malfunctions. It is probable that constitutional apparatus that has been out of use for long may fail to operate smoothly straight away.

According to Art. 44 para. 2 of the Greek constitution:

> The President of the Republic shall by decree proclaim a referendum on crucial national matters following a resolution voted by an absolute majority of the total number of Members of Parliament, taken upon proposal of the Cabinet. A referendum on Bills passed by parliament regulating important social matters, with the exception of the fiscal ones shall be proclaimed by decree by the President of the Republic, if this is decided by three-fifths of the total number of its members, following a proposal of two-fifths of the total number of its members, and as the Standing Orders and the law for the application of the present paragraph provide.

It is obvious that only the first option was available, since the matter (at least that of the proposed question) was clearly fiscal, at least for the most part, and no bill passed by parliament existed. The question here is whether a fiscal matter can be put to referendum as a crucial national matter, or adversely the ratio of the exclusion applies to the first option as well. The *ratio legis* of excluding fiscal issues is that referendums are not considered the appropriate tool for deciding whether or not to impose taxes in the Greek legal order. This is a clear choice made by the Greek constitutional lawmaker. Fiscal referendums involve citizens in decisions about taxes, the tax state and redistribution.[17] Such an involvement would require a balance between the participatory elements inserted in the constitution through the constitutional enshrinement of fiscal referendums and representative

15 On constitutional desuetude see R. Albert, 'Constitutional Amendment by Constitutional Desuetude (1 March 2014) 62 *American Journal of Comparative Law* 641, Boston College Law School Legal Studies Research Paper 328, http://ssrn.com/abstract=2461509, accessed 10 October 2015.

16 A. Vermuele, 'The Atrophy of Constitutional Powers' (2012) 32 *Oxford Journal of Legal Studies* 421.

17 M. Freitag and A. Vatter, 'Initiatives, Referendums, and the Tax State' (January 2006) 13(1) *Journal of European Public Policy* 89.

democracy. Can this clear choice with regard to tax legislation be bypassed through the application of the first type of referendum, that is, by considering a fiscal issue as an issue of crucial national importance? What are the criteria that differentiate this particular package of fiscal issues from previous measures and even from future fiscal measures? It is noteworthy that Greek constitutional scholarship, with regard to the meaning of the abstract notion of crucial national matter, has interpreted them as matters above social and political antagonism, such as foreign affairs and issues of national defence.[18]

The issue becomes even more complex, since the financial alternative to the proposed fiscal measures was not clear. A second complication in the bailout referendum is that beneath the wording of the question lay a far more crucial question; still one left unspoken. Exiting the Eurozone is an issue of national importance with potential far-reaching repercussions. This stresses the multiplicity of the problems created by the ambiguity of the question: The conformity of the matter with the constitution can only be determined on the basis of the actual wording of the question and not in light of its underlying connoted content.

It is true that the constitution says nothing about time or about the clarity of the question. According, however, to the law enacted to regulate referendums (Law no. 4023/2011) the question must be clear and precise, while the poll must take place within 30 days following the presidential decree proclaiming the referendum. Should such details be part of the constitutional text? That is, should the constitutional provisions explicitly state that the referendum question must be clear, comprehensible and concise, allowing voters to understand the choice they are called to make, and where such a description is absent the relevant provisions can be taken to allow ambiguity and vagueness?

By the time the referendum was held, the referendum question, as put on the ballot paper, had no object. The offer had expired and had already been followed by other unsuccessful negotiations. What was left was an implied question, which was ambiguous and unclear. Furthermore, it was an ineffective question, which could not elicit a specific and applicable result. Its answer was incapable of leading to a foreseeable closure. Nonetheless, the wording of the question is a governmental act, and thus, according to the jurisprudence of the Council of State, not subject to judicial review. This, however, does not mean it cannot be in violation of the constitution and the legislation that regulates referendums. The text of the constitution does not spell out that referendum questions must be clear. However, the implementation law that interprets it does. Should we demand this level of detail in the constitution? Is it necessary for the constitution to spell out that referendum questions must be clear, in the sense that in any other case it allows ambiguity? This would be a far-fetched interpretation, implying that the Greek constitution should display the ultimate

18 P.C. Spyropoulos and T.P. Fortsakis, *Constitutional Law in Greece* (Kluwer Law International 2009) 129.

level of distrust toward constitutional actors.[19] But then again perhaps it should, judging from the result.

The ambiguity of the question was tremendous.[20] The most obvious reading should be 'yes or no' (or rather 'no or yes' according to the ballot paper) to the implied question 'should Greece remain in the Eurozone?' On 29 June Jean-Claude Juncker addressed the Greek people asking them to vote 'yes', since voting 'no' would mean willingness to exit the Eurozone.[21] Adversely, the Greek prime minister had repeatedly and clearly stated that the 'no' vote did not mean exiting the Eurozone, but would instead lead to a solution within the euro area. The 'no' vote, thus, for some voters meant 'yes' to Europe but with a better deal, whereas to others 'no' meant Grexit. Referendum questions are not meant to be in application of the subjective reader response theory, according to which everyone can read their own things into the text. They are supposed to be understood in the same way by all voters. And after the vote they are supposed to be understood in the same way by all actors. However, the 'no' vote was open to multiple interpretations by voters, as well as by international actors and entities.

The basic condition for elite manipulation is thus fulfilled: the question was unclear. A second characteristic that may render a referendum susceptible to elite manipulation is lack of time for deliberation. One week for deciding on bailout terms, that are written in a language inaccessible to most citizens, could only lead to a farcical referendum. Deciding on an underlying question is equally farcical; and if the underlying question had to do with the country's place in the EU, the deliberation that took place in other member states with regard to their membership cannot even be compared with the hurried Greek referendum.[22]

The most striking characteristic of the proposed snap referendum is that it was a shock referendum, which took voters as well as political actors by surprise. Lack of time for deliberation was more than apparent. Actually there was no time to even realize what is at stake. As far as referendums go, this was not an expression of deliberative democracy; unless deliberation was unnecessary and it was presumed that the people had already decided and all they had to do was to express their pre-existing will. Did the stunned opposition make a good choice deciding to take part in the referendum campaign, or should it have refused to take up the challenge and refuse to participate in a non-deliberative procedure?[23] The

19 T. Ginsburg, 'Constitutional Specificity, Unwritten Understandings and Constitutional Agreement' in A. Sajo and R. Uitz (eds), *Constitutional Topography: Values and Constitutions* (Eleven International Publishing 2010) 69–93.

20 Tierney (n. 4) 226.

21 Available at http://europa.eu/rapid/press-release_SPEECH-15-5274_en.htm, accessed 5 July 2015.

22 F. Mendez, M. Mendez and V. Triga, *Referendums and the European Union: A Comparative Inquiry* (Cambridge University Press 2014).

23 J. Suiter, E. O'Malley and D. Farrell, 'When Do Deliberative Citizens Change Their Opinions? Evidence from an Irish Citizens' Assembly' (2014) *International Political Science Review* 1, http://ips.sagepub.com/content/early/2014/09/08/0192512114544068, accessed 10 October 2015.

acceptance of this referendum process by the political forces sets a bad precedent for future referendums.

Could it be possible that a democratic constitution allows holding a referendum on a matter of crucial importance a week after it is proclaimed? Or that the 30-day period prescribed by law allows a one-week pre-electoral period? This time frame leaves no time for expert elaboration of the question or for informing the public; no time to deliberate and no time for serious campaigns; no time for an independent committee to revise the question or the ballot. This absence became conspicuous not only in the wording of the question, but also in the way in which the question appeared on the ballot paper, where the 'no' box was above the 'yes' box.

A possible way to treat the snap bailout referendum is to consider it a symptom of the financial crisis and place it within the context of the impact the crisis has had on constitutions. One of the characteristics of the financial crisis has been that it accelerated law making.[24] The question is whether the importance and urgency of the matter can be used as an argument in favour of holding a hurried referendum, in the same manner with decree-laws used to speed up law making at the cost of deliberation in parliament. Still, it is unclear what rendered the matter urgent. Does an unexpected failure in negotiations, or a sudden realization by the government that it could not fulfil its promises, qualify as a reason for holding a fast-track referendum after 40 years of disuse? Does the importance of an issue offer an argument in favour of speeding up procedures, or instead it dictates that a longer deliberation period is required?

The campaigns, that lasted for five days only, were doomed to focus on narratives rather than information. The amount of time available for reflection did not allow making rational choices based on information, but rather sentimental ones. It is noteworthy that the usual head start the 'yes' campaigns normally have, being perceived as positive and as such easier to support, did not apply in the Greek case. The 'no' answer was fraught with the connotations of heroic resistance against foreign occupation. It reflected the rejection by the Greek prime minister in 1940 of an Italian ultimatum demanding the occupation of Greek territory. Still, this 'no' for many stood for 'no to austerity', whereas for others it was a 'no to the EU'. The whole campaign was not conducted in terms of reason versus reason, but in the form of slogans versus slogans.[25]

Does merely giving the people a sudden opportunity to express themselves suffice to view this referendum as an expression of democracy? Or were a clear question and an opportunity to deliberate also necessary? Were closed banks, following the imposition of capital controls, an environment that could allow sober reflection and debate?

24 X. Contiades and A. Fotiadou, 'How Constitutions Reacted to the Financial Crisis' in X. Contiades (ed.), *Constitutions in the Global Financial Crisis: A Comparative Analysis* (Ashgate 2013) 14–17.

25 On the relationship between feelings and reason in voting behaviour see M. Lodge and Ch.S. Taber, *The Rationalizing Voter* (Cambridge University Press 2013).

The lack of referendum practice experience had the side-effect of creating a strange blurred mixture with representative democracy. The prime minister campaigning for 'no', implied that he would resign where 'yes' prevailed, which added an extra parameter to the referendum dilemma.[26] Were the people giving a precise answer to the question posed, or a more general mandate to the freshly elected government? On the other hand, the referendum being a novel experience for many made it easier for citizens to feel empowered by the very participation in a democratic procedure. Absence of an independent electoral committee to elaborate the question, to monitor the campaigns and so on, seemed like legal technicalities, trivial before the chance of popular expression. No prior referendum experience meant that the people had nothing to compare this referendum process with, in which case the wording of the question, the lack of time, the absence of an electoral committee and so on would be visible to all.

In the aftermath of the referendum the result was, and still is, open to multiple interpretations. In order to answer whether the outcome was respected there ought to be a unanimous interpretation of the question. Nonetheless, the ambiguity of the question lead to open-ended readings of the outcome. The 'no' vote won by a 61.31 per cent with a 62.5 per cent turnout, while it prevailed in all Greek electoral constituencies. German Chancellor Angela Merkel and French President Francois Hollande made statements that the result of the referendum would be respected. Subsequently Greece submitted a request for a third bailout, which was agreed upon at the euro area summit on 12–13 July, that is a few days after the referendum, and was finalized following further negotiations concluded in August. Given that the 'no' vote has won a sweeping victory, the signature of a new bailout leads to the hypothesis that where the 'no' meant 'no to the Eurozone' the result was not respected, whereas where 'no' meant 'no to the particular measures but acceptance of another bailout', a juxtaposition of the measures put to vote with the measures finally agreed upon is necessary.

To answer whether the deal taken had better or worse terms one would have to engage in economic analysis, where different criteria could lead to competing answers. Still, the two deals appear to have striking similarities, enough to suggest that respect for the win of an anti-austerity 'no' must also be ruled out. Pension cuts and tax increases are part of the new bailout package. A very narrow reading of the referendum dilemma could suggest that any differentiation between the two bailout agreements would be sufficient to support that the outcome of the referendum was respected. Another option would be to seek answers in the snap general election held on Sunday 20 September, where Syriza, the left-wing party responsible for proclaiming the referendum, won despite the remarkably low turnout at 56.6 per cent. Nonetheless, it is too strained to presume that the election result can be interpreted as a sign that the referendum result was respected. Instead, it enhances the arguments in favour of the mix up between representative and direct democracy caused by the referendum. What respect for the referendum

26 See Trechsel (n. 14).

result meant to international leaders like Chancellor Angela Merkel and President Francois Hollande, to the Greek prime minister, to the opposition and to the voters is still vague. The obscure question led to a result that was open to interpretation and manipulation. Narratives about the referendum dilemma were replaced by narratives about respect and disrespect for the will expressed by the people. These narratives are no longer central to the political discourse, that swiftly moved away from the referendum in order to focus on the new bailout terms.

In retrospect the Greferendum looks like a counterfeit direct-democratic episode, which should better be forgotten. Still, from the aspect of constitutional design, referendum provisions must be viewed through the lens of the only referendum experience Greece has had under the current constitution. The fact that the constitutional order had no safety valve against an undemocratic referendum became conspicuous. Collective narratives about enhancing participation and deliberation have been rendered far less innocent. Is the recurrence of a referendum desirable? Does this referendum create a precedent, and if so what kind of precedent?

Perhaps there are important lessons to be learned about the wake from hibernation of a constitutional provision enshrined before modern theory and practice of referendums developed into their contemporary notion. This referendum could prove useful for the discussion on enshrining constitutional referendums. The question whether the current referendum provisions are rational and well-designed and how they relate to constitutional change must be addressed before any attempt to amend them. Had the referendum led to Grexit, it would have been a source of immense informal constitutional change. Instead, the potentiality of such change, occurring through the side-path of referendums, became visible.

Turning political narratives into constitutional design

Throughout the crisis and until the bailout referendum popular constitutional amendment narratives and frequent proposals for the adoption of more direct democratic procedures were part of the political discourse, being a reaction towards the crisis-induced feeling that the people have been left outside the deliberation process on most issues that matter. Although it is too soon to evaluate whether the referendum experience will be the end of such narratives through disillusionment, it does create a precedent.

Beyond that, Greece is actually left with what it already had: over-stringent formal amendment rules operating in a context of political distrust. The amending formula provides for intervening elections between the two parliaments responsible for the revision. These elections can be mistaken for a means of allowing the electorate to have a say on the revision.

Moreover, the amendment mechanism provides for a mandatory time lapse, that is initiation of the revision process is not permitted until five years have passed from the completion of the previous revision (Art. 110 para. 6). This means in practice that a temporary lack of consent may block change for an extended period of time, which influences the initiation of constitutional revision processes. What is more, the constitutional provisions to be revised are determined during the first phase of the revision procedure. During the second phase the parliament has the power to decide whether or not to amend the proposed provisions and the substantive content of the revisions as well. In other words, the first parliament proposes en masse the amendable provisions. As a result, taking into consideration the combination of time lapses and the culture of distrust, the possibility of the electorate to vote in light of one particular proposed amendment, or changing its vote in the general elections because it is convinced by this amendment's opponents, simply does not exist.[27]

Tom Ginsburg and John Melton have recently used the example of the Greek amending formula to discuss the impact of lengthy procedures on constitutional amendment, considering popular participation as an important aspect of the outcome. Nonetheless, this understanding of how the process works is totally mistaken. Ginsburg and Melton's analysis is based on the procedural prerequisite of the Greek constitution, which dictates that constitutional revision takes place in two phases, between which, general elections are held. In the Greek experience, however, the intervening elections adding time to the process hardly influence 'public opinion towards the amendment', which 'might change over time',[28] as Ginsburg and Melton suggest. This view is based on the possibility of voters changing their opinion on a proposed amendment due to the passage of time, or due to a successful opposition to the amendment.

This is very distant to what happens in reality.[29] The prerequisite of popular elections was designed to enhance the role of the people in constitutional revision, but it led to a totally different and unintended consequence. People in elections do not vote about amendments. They vote in accordance to their political convictions and the general agenda of political parties or for their favourite candidate. Within a polarized political system, distrust among political actors is the major obstacle to achieving flexibility through consent, while polarization does not leave room for voters to reflect on constitutional amendment issues. The distrust culture explains the distance between the ratio of the Greek amendment formula and its unintended consequences. What's more, the intervening general elections requirement adds length to the procedure, but the concept of people deliberating about amendment proposals, changing their opining about them and voting in accordance, is purely imaginary.

27 X. Contiades and A. Fotiadou, 'The Hellenic Republic' in L. Besselink, P. Bovend'Eert, H. Broeksteeg, R. de Lange and W.J.M. Voermans (eds), *Constitutional Law of the EU Member States* (Kluwer 2014) 703–771.

28 T. Ginsburg and J. Melton, 'Does the Constitutional Amendment Rule Matter at All? Amendment Cultures and the Challenges of Measuring Amendment Difficulty' (2015) 13 *International Journal of Constitutional Law* 707.

29 This brings forth some concerns about relying solely on the text of constitutions to draw conclusions on issues that require awareness of history, constitutional culture and political context.

Another parameter that cannot be ignored is that throughout the crisis normal lawmaking was transformed into fast-track legislation usually passed by way of decree-laws. Thus, even deliberation in parliament became a luxury.[30] The question is, would the introduction of constitutional referendums as part of the amendment process render the process more participatory? Is it possible that by adding a hurdle (the term used would be 'prerequisite', which could end up as a euphemism for hurdle) we might enhance the rigidity level, rendering an already difficult to change constitution even more rigid? How easy is it to promote citizen engagement by introducing referendums in a constitutional order where citizens are not accustomed in such forms of participation? Would providing for an additional veto player[31] in the amendment process enhance participatory constitution-writing, or instead augment the rigidity level of the constitution?

Currently the Greek constitution prescribes a system of representative democracy (Art. 51 para. 2), but also incorporates referendums considered to be an infusion of direct-democratic elements. (Art. 44 para. 2). The recent referendum demonstrated that this mixture opens up the possibility for elite manipulation, while also renders it possible for referendums to be used as a means to 'shift governmental responsibility to the people as a whole'.[32] The addition of a constitutional referendum to the amendment formula would have to consider such possible malfunctions. According to the current text of the constitution, the referendum author is a minimum of the two-fifths of members of parliament, the initiator a minimum three-fifths of members of parliament, and the designated decision maker is the electorate.

The financial crisis impacted the Greek constitution in many ways.[33] Absence of formal amendment and lawmaker-driven informal changes affected constitutional normativity and the constitution appears to have been submissive to whatever the crisis demanded, without however being able to adapt.[34] The cancelled debt referendum and the materialized one are part of the overall difficulty of the Greek constitution to respond effectively toward the crisis.

The tendency to enhance participatory procedures as a reaction to the financial crisis must be put into perspective in view of the recent lesson in referendum

30 Contiades and Fotiadou (n. 6). On the deliberative role of Parliaments during the financial crisis see C. Fasone, 'Taking Budgetary Powers Away from National Parliaments? On Parliamentary Prerogatives in the Eurozone Crisis' (2015) EUI Department of Law Research Paper 37/2015, http://ssrn.com/abstract=2665216, accessed 12 December 2015.

31 G. Tsebelis, *Veto Players: How Political Institutions Work* (Princeton University Press 2002) Chapter 5; S. Hug and G. Tsebelis, 'Veto Players and Referendums Around the World' (2002) 14(4) *Journal of Theoretical Politics* 465.

32 Trechsel (n. 14).

33 X. Contiades and I. Tassopoulos, 'The Impact of the Financial Crisis on the Greek Constitution' in X. Contiades (ed.), *Constitutions in the Global Financial Crisis: A Comparative Analysis* (Ashgate 2013) 195.

34 X. Contiades and A. Fotiadou, 'How Constitutions Reacted to the Financial Crisis', in X. Contiades (ed.), *Constitutions in the Global Financial Crisis: A Comparative Analysis* (Ashgate 2013) 49–50.

practice, in the absence of referendum culture, and following a long period of disuse. This is important for the future of the existing provisions and also for any proposal to enshrine constitutional referendum. Expelling referendums from the constitutional text would carry high political cost, especially in light of the strong narratives in favour of adopting more direct-democratic practices. Still, the constitutional law textbook mantra of 'representative plus some direct-democratic infusions' is no longer convincing. By contrast, constitutional designers must take into consideration what facilitates political actors to manipulate procedures instead of seeking to enforce participation and deliberation.

Introducing a referendum as part of the formal amendment rules could perhaps be a major step in the direction of popular involvement, and even toward reviving lost constitutional faith. Nonetheless, the manner in which constitutional design can make such a major change of practice workable, that is, starting off from virtually no popular participation and achieving to render the people key players in constitutional change, is far from clear. The culture of distrust is a given, while the recent malpractice event of referendums suggests no direct-democratic culture exists at the moment.

Lack of referendum culture is not in itself a convincing argument against enhancing popular involvement in constitutional amendment. Constitutional design can aim at changing the culture. We should however consider the danger of adverse results. If the prerequisites set to ensure popular participation are not met, then the constitution would be rendered even more difficult to change than it already is; which in turn would deliver it in the hands of whomever can effect informal constitutional change. In Greece that would be the lawmaker, and in the current situation the executive. It must be noted that in the Greek context the judiciary has not taken the lead in the realm of informal constitutional change. Thus, constitutional design could end up producing the exact opposite consequences than the ones intended; in which case, the 'deliberative turn'[35] will never be achieved in the crisis context, giving a true voice to the people, and popular involvement shall remain but a narrative.

It is true that the crisis appears to create a distinct setting for the rise of referendums. If we look at the conditions that foster the adoption of such democratic tools we might be tempted to diagnose the conditions for what Tierney calls the new wave of referendums.[36] Trust between government and citizens has been disrupted, problems of representative democracy has become acute, people have witnessed the power moving away from the sovereign state to supranational entities (not in the optimistic manner EU integration had suggested, but by the austerity dictated by international lenders). On the other hand, the inherent risk

35 D.M. Farrell, 'The 2013 Irish Constitutional Convention: A Bold Step or a Damp Squib?' (Draft chapter for inclusion) in J. O'Dowd and G. Ferrari (eds), *Comparative Reflections on 75 Years of the Irish Constitution: The 2013 Irish Constitutional Convention* (Clarus Press 2013) <http://www.openpolitics.ro/wp-content/uploads/UCD_Mar13_final1.pdf>.

36 S. Tierney, 'Whose Political Constitution? Citizens and Referendums' (2013) 14 *German Law Journal* 2185.

referendums carry for constitutionalism are also enhanced in such conditions. When sovereignty is an implied issue in referendums and not an explicit one, this may produce consequences the voters had never even imagined. Beyond the apparent danger of elite manipulation, incorporating referendums without damaging constitutionalism[37] is even more difficult in a context of disenchantment and turmoil. Culture largely determines the success of such endeavours.

Conclusion

Adopting constitutional referendums now and in Greece would require a leap of faith; and possibly a common understanding of the timing and the reason for their adoption, which is something quite different from an abstract belief that they shall enhance democratic deliberation. However, at this point it is difficult to say even whether the idea of enhancing deliberation has survived the recent referendum. It is thus hard to predict whether following the non-deliberative bailout referendum it will be still easy to put forth narratives about participatory processes.

Although political parties occasionally present constitutional reform proposals, general elections that have been taking place (at an augmented rate) in the crisis context do not evolve around constitutional issues. A change of the political scenery is what the stakes are about. With political polarization at its peak, the initiation of a constitutional revision process has been announced several times but has never actually begun. The revision process has been halted more than once. In other words, the need to revise the constitution is being repeatedly invoked for purposes other than genuine constitutional change. Constitutional revision in the course of the crisis has failed to pass the 'words vs. actions' test. Still, once again the prime minister has announced in October 2015 a constitutional revision and the enhancement of direct-democratic elements including the enshrinement of popular initiative.

Both the cancelled referendum and the one that materialized have been lessons in lost sovereignty and in the pitfalls of putting the question. The rise of constituent power detected by many scholars in street protests was disproved by total inertia. The 'no' vote that could have led to sweeping constitutional changes, triggered by exiting the Eurozone, led to a new memorandum, the third one since 2010. It is possible that the initiation of the revision process shall turn out to be another lesson in constitutional rigidity fostered by political distrust.[38] In the near future we shall find out how this scenario shall be played out. Until then the notion of citizen engagement in constitutional change shall remain in a state of limbo, caught in between narratives and practice.

37 A. Sajo, *Limiting Government: An Introduction to Constitutionalism* (Central European University Press 1999) 68.

38 See X. Contiades and A. Fotiadou, 'Models of Constitutional Change' in X. Contiades (ed.), *Engineering Constitutional Change: A Comparative Perspective on Europe, Canada and the USA* (Routledge 2012) 458–463.

Part VI

EU aspects of popular participation

European integration, national sovereignty and direct-democratic procedures

10 The use of referendums on European topics in the integration process of the European Union

Dario Elia Tosi

Europe and referendums: The story of a long-time relationship

Direct democracy is often perceived as being a very important issue in the current stage of Europe's integration process. In particular, in recent years it can be noted that there is increasing support for the idea of using referendums for European topics.[1] In fact, in the public's opinion such mechanisms could be used to overcome problems relating to a democratic deficit that has characterized the European experience until now (2015). In this sense, the importance of the ballots launched for the Treaty establishing a Constitution for Europe (TEC) of 2004 or for the Lisbon Treaty is often underlined. Indeed, these votes have been seen as a reaffirming moment for the sovereignty of the people of the European Union. In the same way, nearly all reports have stated that the most recent referendum held in Greece on the approval of the 'troika' proposal on economic reforms was important proof of democracy. Last but not least, the current debate on the referendum on the future of the UK's European membership focuses on the right of the people to express their willingness to remain part of a form of union that is very far from the one that was voted on in the ballot of 1975.

Although in the public's opinion referendums are usually associated with the most recent steps in the European process, it seems that the option of popular ballots on European topics has a long-standing history. From the popular vote held in France in 1972 regarding the enlargement of the EC to the Greek ballot of 2015 for approval of the EU–IMF–ECB proposal on economic reforms, European states have turned to a popular vote more than 40 times in 40 years. Given this framework, an analysis of the use of this kind of poll in the European experience assumes a self-evident relevance.

In this regard a preliminary observation shows that, despite recent pressures at the political level for the creation of a European referendum, until now no

1 On the relationship between referendums and the EU integration process, see S. Tierney, 'The People's Last Sight? Referendums and European Integration' (2012) 18 *European Public Law* 683.

consultation has ever been established nor regulated by European institutions. Ballots have always been held by national governments in accordance with the provisions of their domestic legal systems and have always involved only the nationals of their respective countries.

It is therefore the national framework that we have to look at in order to understand the different rationales for the use of this instrument and how it gives effect to the electorate's expression. In this context, it is difficult, if not impossible, to lay down a systematic classification and, subsequently, to carry out an analysis of ballots along a single line of inquiry. Given the diversity of the explicit subject matters of polls, the wide variety of constitutional models and the different political and constitutional environment which consultations were held in, it seems to be of greater interest to investigate only some of the multiform peculiar profiles of analysis that are prepared and that are examined by scholars, reserving some overall assessments to the concluding remarks section.

Thus, an examination of the first phase of the use of referendums can coincide with an examination of the different consultations from a chronological point of view. In fact, in relation to an overall analysis, it can be seen that the use of the referendum is concentrated in well-defined phases of the European integration process. The first phase of the use of referendums coincides with the first enlargement process of the European Community, which occurred in the early 1970s. On the one hand, during this period it can be observed that the option of referendums was provided by countries that wanted to join the Community or, as was the case with Switzerland, by countries that expressed a willingness to sign cooperation agreements with the Community institutions. On the other hand, during the same period popular consultations concerning the future of the integration process were launched, such as the French one in 1972 on the project of allowing the accession of new European countries or the British one in 1975 on the permanence of the UK within the group.

The second phase of the use of referendums, longer than the first, coincides with the radical change in the European integration process that emerged from the move towards a form of political union that could replace, or at least elevate, the original economic roots of the Community treaties. The referendum held in Italy in 1989, as well as several consultations on the Treaties of Maastricht, Amsterdam and Nice, can be included in this second phase. In addition, even during this phase, numerous ballots can be observed that were organized by some of the countries that had applied for accession or new cooperation agreements.

The third phase of European referendums runs from 2003 to 2005. Although it is very close in terms of time to the period covered by the second phase, this third phase nevertheless takes on an independent character. In fact, it is in this historical environment that two of the most important steps of the current process of European integration happened. The first step was the negotiations and consultations that led to the accession to the EU of many states of central and eastern Europe; consequently, this triggered a deep transformation of the functioning dynamics of EU institutions. The second step was strictly associated with the enlargement of the EU to 27 (28 by 2015) member states, and it

Table 10.1 Referendums on European issues

Year	*Country*	*Issue*	*Result*
1972	France	Enlargement of EC	Yes
1972	Ireland	EC Membership	Yes
1972	Norway	EC Membership	No
1972	Denmark	EC Membership	Yes
1972	Switzerland	EC-EFTA Treaty	Yes
1975	Great Britain	Continuation of EC membership	Yes
1986	Denmark	Single European Act	Yes
1987	Ireland	Single European Act	Yes
1989	Italy	Mandate for MEPs	Yes
1992	Denmark	Maastricht Treaty	No
1992	Ireland	Maastricht Treaty	Yes
1992	France	Maastricht Treaty	Yes
1992	Switzerland	European Economic Area Treaty	No
1992	Liechtenstein	European Economic Area Treaty	Yes
1993	Denmark	Maastricht Treaty	Yes
1994	Austria	EU Membership	Yes
1994	Sweden	EU Membership	Yes
1994	Finland	EU Membership	Yes
1994	Norway	EU Membership	No
1998	Ireland	Amsterdam Treaty	Yes
1998	Denmark	Amsterdam Treaty	Yes
2000	Denmark	European Monetary Union	No
2001	Switzerland	Resume accession talks with EU	Yes
2001	Ireland	Nice Treaty	No
2002	Ireland	Nice Treaty	Yes
2003	Sweden	European Monetary Union	No
2003	Lithuania	EU Membership	Yes
2003	Latvia	EU Membership	Yes
2003	Estonia	EU Membership	Yes
2003	Poland	EU Membership	Yes
2003	Czech Republic	EU Membership	Yes
2003	Slovakia	EU Membership	Yes
2003	Slovenia	EU Membership	Yes
2003	Malta	EU Membership	Yes

(*Continued*)

Table 10.1 (Continued)

Year	*Country*	*Issue*	*Result*
2003	Hungary	EU Membership	Yes
2003	Romania	Adjusting National law to EU acquis	Yes
2005	Spain	European Constitutional Treaty	Yes
2005	France	European Constitutional Treaty	No
2005	Netherlands	European Constitutional Treaty	No
2005	Luxembourg	European Constitutional Treaty	Yes
2005	Switzerland	Free movement of persons	Yes
2005	Switzerland	Schengen	Yes
2008	Ireland	Lisbon Treaty	No
2009	Ireland	Lisbon Treaty	Yes
2009	Switzerland	Free movement of persons	Yes
2012	Croatia	EU Membership	Yes
2012	Ireland	Fiscal Compact Treaty	Yes
2015	Greece	EU–IMF–ECB Agreement Proposal on economic reforms programme	No

must be stressed that the drafting process of the Treaty of Rome in 2004 and, consequently, the radical changes that the approval of a constitution for Europe could have prompted in the overall integration process and in the nature of the Union were very important. These two steps were submitted to popular scrutiny in several countries. Owing to the complex outcomes of the different national polls, since 2005 a significant change has emerged in the attitude of national governments towards the use of referendums on issues related to the development of the European integration. That's not to say, as we will consider later, that a referendum is an unavoidable choice in the forthcoming stage of European integration, nor does it represent a dangerous solution that it is advisable to avoid.

For a simpler view of the chronology that has been briefly discussed, it seems useful to present a table summarising the consultations launched to date (2015) on European issues.[2]

2 The table is based on the one published in S. Seeger, 'From Referendum Euphoria to Referendum Phobia–Framing the Ratification Question' (2008) 4 *European Journal of Law Reform* 439. A relevant point to note in relation to the referendum period that ran from 2003 to 2005 is that there are no references to the popular ballots on the TEC of 2004, scheduled by various governments (in particular Ireland, Denmark, Poland, Portugal, Czech Republic and the UK) but never held because of the negative result of the French and Dutch referendums. For a more detailed discussion, see A. Di Gregorio, 'La ratifica della Costituzione europea tra "vecchia" e "nuova" Europa' (2005) 4 *Diritto Pubblico Europeo e Comparato* 1610.

The problem of the subject matter submitted to the ballot

In addition to the chronological analysis of electoral ballots on EU issues, the first focus of an investigation of this issue can be the different specific subject matters of popular votes. Public opinion perceives that referendums on European topics concern fundamental decisions of the electorate on the Union and, in the end, the destiny of the integration process itself. It is certainly true that these subjects have been the main focus of several polls. Examples of such polls include popular consultations held on the ratification of the revision of the Communities and of the EU treaties. All of the referendums on the reform of the original treaties, from the ballots launched in Denmark and Ireland to decide on whether to sign the Single European Act of 1986 to the second Irish consultation on the Lisbon Treaty of 2009, have focused on the role and powers of EU institutions and on the idea of strengthening the Union. In addition, referendums are held regarding the accession of new members. Although the subject matter of the referendums does not include deciding on a transformation of the EU's institutional system or whether there should be a division of powers between the member states and Brussels, because they focus only on the extension of EU jurisdiction to new national communities, these voting exercises inexorably include fundamental assessments of the fate of the EU's integration process and the will to be part of it. The French referendum of 1972 on the enlargement of the Community to include new members illustrates this point, as it clearly involved the electorate in deciding on the choices to make on the future of the European experience.

Among these kinds of polls, consultations organized by countries that applied to become members of the EU represent the biggest part. Apart from in Norway, where the outcome of the consultation was negative, 16 of the current 28 governments set up a popular ballot to give legitimacy to their decision to be part of the EU system. The figures are even more interesting if we consider that six of the 12 members that did not opt to hold a referendum are the founding countries of the Community; therefore, in 16 of 22 cases of new entry, governments deemed it necessary or desirable to make the electorate directly express its will.

This contrast in the figures is extremely interesting in the context of the different trends of the Communitarian era and the Union one. In fact, it might be considered that the significant transformation of the integration process over the last 20 years and the consequent changes in the division of powers between national governments and EU institutions has prompted several countries to involve the Community in the fundamental decision on the limitation of their original sovereignty.

National governments have often chosen to call popular ballots on specific and circumscribed EU issues. In this regard, consultations on the European Monetary Union that took place in Denmark and Sweden, in 2000 and 2003 respectively, represent the most important examples. Similarly, there are the recent episodes of the use of a referendum vote, which took place in Ireland in

2012, when Irish citizens were called to express themselves on the Fiscal Compact Treaty, and in Greece in 2015, when the government prompted the people to make a definitive decision on the approval of the proposals of international creditors for severe economic reforms. Though very important aspects of the Union were affected by these referendums, in both of these cases the electorate did not get involved in deciding on a definitive resolution regarding continuing or not continuing to be part of the EU; nor was the ultimate destiny of the Union itself called into question. People were asked to decide only on the degree of their participation in the integration process. Similar types of referendums have been held in Switzerland and Lichtenstein on the European Economic Area Treaty, as well as referendums on bilateral agreements on the freedom of movement of people and on the extent of the application of the Schengen Treaty. Like the consultations on the monetary union, in these cases the *thema decidendum* was not so much the future of the Union itself, but the desirability of a closer cooperation on specific issues.[3]

Value and character of popular votes on EU topics

The evaluation of the different types of referendums that, from time to time, national governments have organized is firmly connected with the theme of the subject matters submitted to the popular ballot. Scholars and public opinion traditionally frame referendums on European topics in the overall category of constitutional referendums.[4] Nevertheless, this classification seems to be the outcome of a transposition at the European level of the value that a popular vote takes on at the national level. In other words, it is generally accepted that referendums on the European integration process, whatever the direct subject matter of the vote, ultimately deal with sovereign powers.

However, such a categorization cannot be entirely supported. First, even on an analysis of the phenomenon only from the European point of view, it seems fair to say that not all popular consultations held have had a constitutional dimension in the ongoing integration process. In an attempt to classify different consultations, it can be assumed that referendums organized in relation to the ratification of the Treaty on the European Constitution definitely had real constituent value, representing the ultimate legitimacy of a text deliberately identified as the *Grundnorm* of a new political reality. In contrast, constitutional,

3 For a more accurate analysis of the evolution of relations between EU and Switzerland, see C. Bonte, *La Suisse e l'Union européenne: entre space économique européenne et accords bilateraux* (Institut européen de l'Université de Genève 1999); P. Macchia, 'Confederazione elvetica ed Unione europea: accordi di (non) integrazione' (2009) 1 *Diritto Pubblico Comparato ed Europeo* 94.

4 For a common classification of different kinds of referendum and, in particular, constitutional referendums, among others, see M. Volpi, 'Referendum' in *Digesto Delle Discipline Pubblicistiche*, vol. 12 (Utet 1997) 500; S. Tierney, *Constitutional Referendums: The Theory and Practice of Republican Deliberation* (Oxford University Press 2012).

but not constituent, value can be recognized in popular votes that called for the revision of the founding treaties.

However, as can clearly be seen in Table 10.1, these two kinds of referendum are not the only ones that have characterized the life of the Union so far. From the perspective of the EU legal system, consultations launched by national governments that had applied to become new members have no constitutional value. Indeed, unlike referendums organized for the purpose of gaining agreement to a revision of treaties, these types of popular vote do not aim to create or change a constitutional contract, but have as their focus the will of a community that is outside the community of the Union but that can decide on whether it wants to take part in the covenant that already binds other political communities.[5] Similarly, there is no constitutional value in those referendums launched both by member states or third countries that focus on the desirability of some form of cooperation with the EU. Thus, for example, both the Swedish ballot on the European Monetary Union and the Swiss one that aimed at extending the freedom of movement of people, far from questioning the fundamental elements of the 'constitutional' pact signed by 28 member states, prompted the electoral bodies to accept or reject specific measures and regulations.

Observations can also be made from a fully domestic perspective. However, from this point of view the analysis becomes more articulated and complex. Indeed, the overall outline depends on the domestic environment of the different countries concerned. Thus, there are certainly national systems in which referendums on European issues take always on a constitutional value.

The Irish experience can definitely be included in this category. As generally known, the Constitutional Charter provides that a referendum can be held as an essential step in the constitutional amendment procedure (Art. 46 Const.). Thus, due to the lack of opening clauses limiting the possible forms of sovereignty in favour of supranational organizations, when the government applied to become a member of the EC, it was urged to launch a referendum with the purpose of inserting in the constitutional text a clause that directly permitted communitarian laws to be enacted in the Irish legal system (Art. 29.4 Const.). Despite this general provision, the government was also compelled to call popular consultations on the ratification of the Single European Act of 1986 and the Treaties of Maastricht, Amsterdam, Nice and Lisbon as well as the ratification of the Treaty on the Fiscal Compact of 2012. A referendum was also scheduled in relation to the ratification of the Treaty of Rome in 2004. In fact, on the ground of the *Crotty Rule*, outlined by the High Court in response to the government's aim of ratifying the approval of the Single European Act without the involvement of the electorate, any change of the original treaties triggering further limitations of national sovereignty inevitably needs a change in the constitutional

5 For a discussion of this point, see J. Ziller, *Diritto delle politiche e delle istituzioni dell'Unione europea* (Mulino 2013) 86.

structure and, as such, must be compulsorily approved by popular vote.[6] Hence, there is an inherent constitutional value in each referendum held in Ireland on European issues.

On closer inspection, the Gaelic experience is an exception in the European landscape. Indeed, in other national systems, the choice of the referendum on issues relating to the European integration process does not always have a constitutional value. In this regard, by way of example, the Swiss and French experiences can be mentioned. The Swiss system is of particular interest because the electorate has been repeatedly involved in order to express its will on European issues. As is well known, the Swiss constitution envisages the use of referendums for a variety of circumstances. In addition to mandatory referendums, which have an inherent constitutional value, the constitutional charter provides for optional referendums on subject matters that, although they are of political interest, do not relate to constitutional matters. Consultations on international relations fall within one of these two categories depending on whether they concern the membership of supranational communities, which triggers limitations of national sovereignty, or treaties and agreements, which only require ordinary cooperation without any limitation of sovereignty. In this framework, although Switzerland has never formally applied for EU membership, some of the referendums launched were considered mandatory, since they aimed at creating an organic and institutionalized association between the EU and Switzerland that would result in an inherent loss of domestic sovereign powers. In contrast, referendums on issues such as the extension of the Schengen Treaty area or the enactment of workers' freedom of movement were considered only optional, because they only affected matters of political, not constitutional, concern.

The experience of France, whose system is very different from that of Switzerland, is characterized by a limited use of referendums on European issues. In fact, the French people were only called to express their will on European topics in 1972, when they had to decide whether or not to agree to the enlargement of the Communities and the ratification of the Maastricht and Rome treaties, in 1992 and 2004 respectively.[7] Nevertheless, with regard to the analysis of the character of EU referendums, the French case is of particular relevance because of the solutions that were adopted in such a constitutional framework.

As is widely known, the constitution of 1958 provides for the use of referendums in two different cases. On the one hand, Art. 89 of the constitution envisages popular vote as the ordinary procedure for constitutional amendment,

6 *Raymond Crotty v An Taoiseach & Others* [1987] IR 713. On the use of referendums on European topics in Ireland, see G. Barrett, 'Building a Swiss Chalet in an Irish Legal Landscape? Referendums on European Union Treaties in Ireland & the Impact of Supreme Court Jurisprudence' (2009) 5(1) *European Constitutional Law Review* 38; G. Hogan, 'The Lisbon Treaty and the Irish Referendum' (2009) 15(2) *European Public Law* 163.

7 For a general overview of the use of referendums on European issues, see I.M. Cantos Padilla, 'El referéndum francés de ratificación del Tratado que establece una Constitución para. Europa, de 29 de mayo 2005' (2006) 65 *Revista de derecho politico* 259.

making it possible for the president of the republic to replace the ballot with a qualified majority vote of parliament convened in Congress. On the other hand, Art. 11 contemplates the possibility that the head of state or, after the 2008 reform, a parliamentary minority, launch a referendum on a bill which deals with the organization of the public authorities or with reforms relating to economic, social or environmental policy, or which provides for authorization to ratify a treaty. In this framework, constitutional reforms were normally achieved by way of the parliamentary vote, and sometimes referendums ex Art. 11 of the constitution were used to make changes that had constitutional value, but we must observe that the system explicitly gives these two kinds of consultation a different value: while the first takes on a constitutional nature, the second apparently focuses on questions of political concern.[8]

This distinction is of specific importance in this context. Indeed, in all the cases of popular ballot on European issues, referendums were launched on the ground of the provision of Art. 11 of the constitution. This circumstance is of even greater significance if one considers that both when France had to ratify the Treaty of Maastricht and when it signed the Treaty of Rome, the Conseil Constitutionel stressed the need to amend the constitution to permit limitations of domestic sovereignty resulting from the enactment of these agreements. Thus, both in 1992 and in 2004 the ratification procedure was characterized by previous constitutional revisions. Nevertheless, all these amendments were achieved by the vote of the parliament convened in Congress, without the involvement of the people. By contrast, the president of the republic chose to replace the parliamentary vote with popular ballots for the subsequent ratifications of the treaties. The main reason for this solution seems to be based on the constitutional environment of the French system, in which referendums are traditionally regarded not as a means of expression of the people on matters of fundamental significance, but as instruments of plebiscitarian approbation of the head of state and his political orientations.[9]

In fact, this thinking seems to be confirmed by the analysis of the procedures followed on the ratification of other European treaties. Even in those cases, such as that of the Lisbon Treaty of 2007, when the Conseil Constitutionel was compelled to amend the constitution, the president chose the parliamentary procedure, both for the revision and the ratification. The negative effects that a renewed popular rejection of the treaty could have had on the political legitimacy, both domestic and international, of the president prompted Sarkozy to confirm that he was in favour of parliamentary ratification.

The fact that referendums on European issues may have a constitutional significance or a merely political value, can be seen from an analysis of ballots launched

8 For a discussion of this, see M. Calamo Specchia, 'Il referendum in Francia ovvero la démocratie représentative alla prova' (2005) 3 *Diritto Pubblico Europeo e Comparto* 1259.

9 Among others, see S. Wolff and G. Mounier, 'France: The Come-Back of Political Parties' (2005) 1(3) *European Constitutional Law Review* 383.

by different countries for the same situation. In this regard, the ratification process of the treaty for the enlargement of the EU, signed in 2004, is of particular interest. In fact, in that case, nine of the ten countries which were to become full members of the EU decided to directly involve the electorate in order to reach their final decision. Nevertheless, although in almost all cases accession to the EU represented a step in the complex transition to a liberal democratic system, the value that referendums took on was very diverse.

In some cases, the choice of involving the people seems closely linked to the particular country's purpose of breaking with their recent past. This seems to be true of, for instance, the reason for the decision made by the Hungarian Parliament in 2002, which was to amend the constitution by providing a special and binding referendum on the accession to the EU. The constitutional value of this ballot is seen clearly in the fact that the amendment expressly indicated the wording of the question and, moreover, the date of the poll. Similarly, a constitutional significance can be attributed to the referendum organized in the Czech Republic, in which the accession process was characterized by a previous constitutional reform which established the need to proceed with the ratification of international treaties through special parliamentary proceedings or by a specific law only, by means of a popular vote.

Although they had different features, the experiences of the three Baltic republics seem to have followed a similar pattern. Indeed, on the one hand, a constitutional reform explicitly affirmed that the EU membership of Latvia was to be approved by a referendum; on the other hand, the choice of popular ballot in Estonia clearly contravened the provisions of the constitution, which generally prohibited (and still prohibits) the use of referendums for the ratification and denunciation of international treaties. Although in the case of Latvia the constitutional content of the vote is grounded on the constitutional provision, in the Estonia example the fundamental significance of the poll emerges from the contravention of the Constitutional Charter. A similar value can be attributed to the popular ballot launched in Lithuania, in which, because of the lack of specific provisions or prohibitions, the juridical basis of the referendum resides in the wording of Art. 9 of the constitution, which affirms that the most significant issues concerning 'the life of the State and the Nation' have to be decided by means of a direct consultation of the electorate.

By contrast, in other countries the option of holding a referendum in relation to accession to the EU was not driven by the constitutional content of the decision. In this regard, the Slovak and Maltese experiences can be cited. In the first case, in addition to the ordinary parliamentary procedure provided for by the constitution, the parliament decided to launch a 'consultative' ballot. Similarly, in the case of Malta, in view of the silence of the constitution, the government chose to organize an advisory referendum, deciding to proceed to the approval of a constitutional amendment and, later, the ratification of the accession treaty only by means of parliamentary procedure, without any involvement of the electorate.

The problem of the legal effects of referendums

The reference just made to the experience of Malta leads to another issue of interest in the overall analysis of the role of referendums in the European integration process: the topic of the legal effects of consultations. Indeed, it is clear that the significance that referendums can take on in the European framework largely depends on the legal force that constitutional systems attribute to the popular vote. Once again in this regard, far from being outlined in equivalent terms, every legal system has adopted different choices, sometimes even moving away from the general rules concerning the referendum. Some referendums had only advisory and non-binding characteristics, and Malta's referendum on accession could be characterized in this way. As an aside, notwithstanding obvious differences, this characteristic seems to be consistent with the constitutional tradition that had inspired the Anglo-Saxon legal system of Valletta. Indeed, even the popular ballot of 1975 held in the UK on its permanence in the European Community had had merely an advisory and non-binding character.

Urged to make a ruling on the use of an instrument that had never before been used at national level, among several other issues to deal with, the legislator of the Referendum Act of 1975 in the UK had to tackle the problem of what legal force a tool of direct democracy should have within the country that first developed and placed at the foundation of its system the representative democracy model. Approving the use of referendums would mean moving from the principle of Parliamentary supremacy, so it was difficult, if not impossible, to admit the likelihood that the freedom of the House of Commons could be limited, though only on a specific point, by the decision of the electorate. Thus, it was said that the referendum would have only a 'pre-legislative' nature, i.e. an advisory value. In other words, the popular vote could force the executive power to adopt its preferred programme, but could not in any way limit the action of the parliamentary Assembly, which would be free to vote for a measure that was not consistent with, or was even openly contrary to, the government's policy.[10]

A non-binding character must also be ascribed to the referendum held in Italy in 1989. In this regard, it should be noted that, similarly to the experience of the UK, this ballot represented a break with, or at least an exception to, the framework outlined by the constitutional charter. Unlike the legal system of the UK, the Italian legal system already provided for different kinds of referendum that had binding force. Nevertheless, perhaps due to the nature of the question to be submitted to the electorate, which was the transfer to the European Parliament

10 In this respect, one can recall the position expressed by Edward Short, reported in J.O. Frosini and G.Tagiuri, 'Il referendum del 1975: quando I britannici decisero di rimanere nella Comunità economica europea' in A. Torre and J.O. Frosini (eds), *Democrazia rappresentativa e referendum nel Regno Unito* (Maggioli 2012) 165. For a more detailed discussion on British parliamentary supremacy and its consequences, see J. Goldsworthy, *The Sovereignty of Parliament: History and Philosophy* (Oxford University Press 1999).

(and not to Italian institutions) of a general mandate to 'prepare a draft European Constitution', the legislator considered it necessary to regulate the effects of the popular vote, moving away from the domestic framework of the sources of law. In fact, despite the polls provided for in Arts 75 and 138 of the constitution that, while performing a repeal and a confirmatory function respectively, had (and still have) a binding legal force, the Constitutional Law 1/1989 gave the referendum a purpose that was merely advisory.

Although these cases that have been briefly discussed are characterized by the non-binding nature of the referendum, in most of them implementing the result of the poll is inexorably compulsory. An example of this is the constitutional amendment process of Ireland. The French system can be included in this category too, in relation to referendums organized with the purpose of reforming the constitution and those launched by the president on the ground of Art. 11 of the constitution concerning issues of primary political concern. In the same way, votes cast on the latest accessions to the Union, including the recent consultation held in Croatia but with the exceptions of those held in Malta and Slovakia, constrained governments and parliaments in their freedom of action.

In addition, although they were held within frameworks that differ deeply with regard to the use of referendums, the vote held in Spain for the ratification of the Treaty of Rome of 2004, and the consultations launched in Switzerland, as well as in Denmark, were strictly binding.

Other experiences were affected in a similar way when, notwithstanding the silence of the constitutional charter, all the institutions considered the popular vote compulsory, irrespective of the view supported throughout the electoral campaign.

In this respect the case of Norway should be mentioned. The government applied to become a member of the EC in 1970, together with UK, Ireland and Denmark. Although it strongly upheld the undertaking to accede to the EU, the executive power had to deal with the deep-rooted division in the parliament. Due to the constitutional provision that demanded the approval of a qualified majority of three-quarters of the members of the Storting, this situation could have represented an insurmountable problem. Thus, in order to overcome this deadlock, the government majority deemed it necessary to launch a popular consultation, like the one that took place at the beginning of the century on the occurrence of Norway's separation from Sweden and the decision that followed about the form that the government should take. Notwithstanding this, because of the silence of the constitution, referendums established by ordinary Acts could only have an advisory value, similar to those that had been held before, but in 1970 both government and parliament affirmed that they would comply with the result of the ballot. Along the same lines, the government decided to hold a referendum in relation to the application for accession that was made in 1994. It seemed that the choice of the referendum did comply with a constitutional convention. In other words, in a complex political framework, the solution of having the poll seemed to be prompted by common thinking on the need to directly involve the people in fundamental decisions regarding the life of the nation.

Similar experiences to the Norwegian ones seem to have affected the Netherlands' experience.[11] In fact, as in the case for Norway, the constitution of the Netherlands does not contain any reference to instruments of direct democracy. This element, in addition to a political framework that is strongly against the use of popular consultations, meant that, at national level, the electorate was never directly involved until 2005. In fact, only on the occasion of the ratification of the TEC of 2004 did the pressure of the opposition lead to the approval of an ad hoc statute that expressly provided for a referendum on the Treaty. As in the Norwegian system, from a strictly legal point of view, because the constitution was silent on this issue the vote should have been merely advisory. Nevertheless, just like what happened in Norway, problems associated with the 'political management' of the European dossier drove the government, which upheld the ratification of the treaty, to avow that it would comply with the sovereign decision expressed by the people.

The latest Greek experience of a popular ballot on the approval of the proposal of international creditors (EU–IMF–ECB) for severe economic reforms could assume a particular value. Indeed, the constitution affirms that, further to a proposal of the government and a resolution approved by the absolute majority of the parliament, the president can call for a referendum on matters of 'crucial national' concern. Despite the silence of the constitution and the fact that after 1974 no referendum was ever launched, it seems that such a vote would be compulsory. That said, we must note that the economic reforms plan approved by the Greek parliament in the days subsequent to the ballot substantially replaced the former proposal of international creditors. In this context, the fundamental avoidance of the popular will is raised as an issue. Therefore, the contrast between the Greek experience and the Norwegian and Netherlands ones is self-evident.

Moreover, in addition to national effects, this research of the legal value of referendums on EU issues also has a particular interest in the heterogeneous consequences generated by homogeneous kinds of poll. In fact, the analysis stresses that referendums of an apparently similar character had a quite different impact on the European framework. In fact, from the perspective of a more distinctly political evaluation, cases from all over Europe show that the consequences of direct consultation can be very different, depending both on the country that is voting and on the *thema decidendum*. On an initial analysis, there is a self-evident difference between the effects generated by ballots held in EU countries and those produced by polls held in non-member states. Similarly, the consequences of referendums on particular aspects of the integration process are dissimilar from those engendered by consultations on draft revisions of original treaties. In so far as European institutions may attempt to widen their jurisdiction, even from a geographical point of view, unpredictable refusals of specific measures or

11 For a general analysis, see A. Nijeboer, 'The Dutch Referendum' (2005) 1(3) *European Constitutional Law Review* 393; L.F.M. Besselink, 'Double Dutch: The Referendum on the European Constitution' (2006) 12(3) *European Public Law* 345.

failed applications for accession do not seem to have the same impact that may be engendered when projects relating to organic reform of the overall institutional framework are called in question.

In addition, in either case we must remark that the ultimate consequences of a negative vote are very different depending on the countries directly involved. In this regard, the most recent events related to the ratification process of the Lisbon Treaty and the TEC of 2004 stress how, though both of them needed the approval of all EU member states, EU institutions and national governments reacted differently to the negative vote in Ireland than to the ones in France and the Netherlands. In fact, further to the negative result of the Irish ballot the common political view urged the government to go on with the process of ratification. Therefore, European institutions were prompted to 'bargain' with the Irish government for 'exemptions' that could ensure, in a new referendum, the final approval of the European project. By contrast, the rejection of the TEC by the Netherlands and, above all, France, led to a stalemate that, in the end, called into question the future of the Union. In this case, the importance of the negative result of consultations held in two of the EC's founding countries, especially in terms of the significance of the project submitted to the electorate and the political weight that France had always played in the European framework, prompted national governments and EU institutions to consider that it was not suitable to minimize popular dissent and instead to try to overcome the deadlock by means of ad hoc concessions.[12]

The place of direct democracy instruments in the EU integration process between national constitutional roots and European impetuses: Some concluding remarks

The analysis seems to confirm the initial reflection on the significant impact that, since the early stage of their use, referendums have had on the European integration process. From a political perspective it can first be pointed out that the experience of the 40 years that have been considered in this chapter emphasizes that referendums can both strengthen or diminish the legitimacy of the EU. From a chronological point of view, this ambivalence has historically led to an alternation of periods of 'referendum euphoria' and 'referendum phobia'.[13] Indeed, such a sequence seems to be related to factors of a different nature. On the one hand, a decisive circumstance rests in the economic environment in which different referendums are grounded. In fact, during an economic crisis, because of the worries of the electorate about the negative effects engendered by a supranational integration process and, therefore, the more likely opposition to European projects, the use of popular ballots is perceived with greater circumspection by the national governments concerned.

12 For a discussion of this, see Ziller (n. 5) 86.
13 For a discussion of these concepts, see Seeger (n. 2).

On the other hand, the political orientation of public opinion towards national and supranational issues is a crucial element. Indeed, the traditional ambivalence that still characterizes people's attitude towards the development of the European integration project drives different national communities to express themselves in a different direction on the basis of the idea of Europe that at a particular time widely prevails. When the vision of Europe is associated with the idea that a stronger union can improve well-being of the overall community, it can be noted that there is substantial support for the integration process. By contrast, the prevalence of the conviction that a stronger integration would represent the final loss of national sovereignty clearly affects the view of the electorate.

From a different perspective, the analysis of popular consultations held to date (2015) and the respective domestic political debates related to them highlight the opportunity to differentiate between cases in which referendums are provided for by the constitutional system as a mandatory and binding instrument, or represent the ordinary solution dictated by constitutional convention, and those in which the use of the referendum appears to be an exception in institutional life. Indeed, while the first cases show that the referendum can be merely an instrument of direct democracy, i.e. a means complementary to those of the representative democracy model, in the second circumstances the use of the referendum seems to be grounded on reasons of political concern. In the first category, for instance, the Irish system can be included to the same extent as the Danish or the Norwegian ones.[14]

The Dutch experience can be included in the second category. Indeed, the involvement of the people that occurred in 2005 in relation to the ratification of the TEC represents the first national consultation after 1797. In this context, the circumstances suggest, that the choice of giving the electorate the final say resulted from the pressure exerted by the opposition and the political weakness of the parliamentary majority, and not from the belief that the fundamental law of the Union had to be legitimized directly from the people.

The Greek experience was motivated along the same lines. In fact, beyond the political campaign on the need to give people the last word, the decision to launch the referendum on the proposal of international creditors was a result of the need for legitimacy of the current parliamentary majority. From abroad, it seems that the prime minister, Tsipras, won the last polls by grounding the campaign on a promise to struggle against austerity plans and to make a radical change in the European agenda. Given the negative result of previous negotiations, and aware of the fact that, on the one hand, beyond the severe bailout plan of international creditors, no one could produce any other solutions to prevent

14 Recalling what has been said about Ireland and Norway, it is of interest to mention the Danish experience. The constitutional charter provides for the referendum as an alternative instrument that can be used to ratify international agreement on sovereign powers. Notwithstanding this, given that the normal procedure requires parliamentary approval with a five-sixths majority, the popular ballot ends up representing the ordinary way of making decisions that are of fundamental significance for the life of the nation.

default and, on the other hand, it would be hard to make public opinion and his parliamentary coalition accept a proposal forced by 'external' subjects, the prime minister referred the final decision to the people. Incidentally, the fact that the involvement of the people found its basis in the political weakness of the government seems to be confirmed by the fact that, according to analysts, despite the negative result of the referendum, in an effort to prevent the 'Grexit', in the days subsequent to the referendum the parliament approved, with the consent of a majority larger than that of the government coalition and rejection by part of the Premier's party, a 'domestic' plan of economic reforms that was very much like the EU–IMF–ECB proposal.

Although it has different nuances, even the British attitude towards the use of the referendum on the issues of European integration seems directly influenced by the contingent political framework. In fact, the only case in which the government decided to consult the electorate on issues directly related to Europe coincided with a phase of serious political crisis. Firstly, the launch of the popular vote in 1975 followed the first brief experience of a coalition government. Secondly, the Labour Party, which won the second election in 1975, decided to call a popular consultation on the continuation of British EC membership, not so much on the ground that it had promised to do so during the electoral campaign, but because the parliamentary majority was deeply divided within itself. In other words, far from being the consequence of a belief in the need to involve the electorate in fundamental decisions regarding the life of the national community, the use of referendums seemed to be dictated by the inability of the executive power to take all the consequences of a troublesome political position upon itself.

Nowadays, it is undeniable that the British framework is undergoing such profound changes that it is possible to imagine the consolidation of new constitutional conventions that impose the use of a referendum in relation to all matters of constitutional value.[15] Nonetheless, with regard to the issue of European integration it seems that the current political phase is still following the traditional pattern. In fact, on the one hand, it is true that the previous coalition government repeatedly promised that, if they won the next national election, they would provide for a consultation on British EU membership in 2017. But in the meantime, the parliamentary majority approved the European Union Act of 2011,[16] which forces the use of a referendum for any European project with tangible effects on the interests of the United Kingdom. On the other hand, it must be noted that, similarly to in 1975, the previous government was supported by a majority of the coalition. Thus, it seems that both the approval of the Act and the proposition of

15 On this theme, D. Kavanagh, 'Referendums in British Politics' in A. Torre and J.O. Frosini (eds), *Democrazia rappresentativa e referendum nel Regno Unito* (Maggioli 2012) 122.

16 On this issue, see L. McEldowney, 'UK Membership of the European Union: The Relevance of the European Union Act 2011—Dilemmas and Debates' *Constitution Making and Constitutional Change* (25 April 2014), www.constitutional-change.com, accessed 12 July 2015.

a popular ballot was a response to the pressure from opposition parties[17] and the weakness of the governmental majority.

The observation that in the UK decisions on the use of referendum strictly depend on the contingent political framework seems to be confirmed by an examination of the different positions held in 2004 and 2007 in relation to the ratification of the TEC and the Lisbon Treaty respectively. In the first case, the general feeling of euphoria towards the completely renewed system pushed the government to uphold the solution of the direct involvement of the people. The radical change of direction driven by the negative results of consultations held in the Netherlands and France prompted the government (led by the same majority and by the premier that had governed in 2004) to move away from the previous choice and assume the burden of a parliamentary ratification of the Treaty of 2007.

Similar suggestions arise from the current political debate on the EU membership referendum that shall be held on 23 June 2016. Indeed, the present government is no longer supported by a coalition, but by a single party. However, one of the most significant commitments that was discussed during the electoral campaign was the obligation to hold a referendum on the permanence of the UK's EU membership. In this context, given the impossibility of simply turning his back on his promises, the prime minister, Cameron, seems to want use the popular ballot as a political lever to achieve his ultimate goals at EU level. In a similar way to what happened recently with the Irish government after the negative result regarding the Lisbon Treaty, EU institutions and member states appeared not likely to risk the exit of the UK.[18] Thus, they will probably negotiate with Great Britain with the aim of coming to an agreement.

Conclusion

Hence, this conclusion can focus on the role of referendums in the European integration process. It can certainly be suggested that this instrument ought to be ruled in an organic way and governed by the European institutions.

However, this chapter reveals how referendums are deeply tied to the national framework within which they are held and, consequently, can cause profoundly different effects depending on the country concerned and the issue that is focused on. The possibility of a binding or only consultative vote, as well as the political value or the constitutional character of the decision taken by the electorate, makes it difficult to outline definitive conclusions about the same ballot. Thus, in this context it seems more appropriate to give national systems the greatest freedom

17 In this context, a significant role can be attributed to the position held by UKIP and the possible effects that its Eurosceptic campaign could have on the final result of the recent national elections.

18 However, it must be noted that domestic stakeholders seemed not to want an exit, and a consequent isolation of the economy, of the UK.

to find ways in which each nation can express itself regarding the complex issues of the integration process. Indeed, in areas so closely linked to crucial issues concerning the sovereignty of the national political community, it does not seem particularly valuable to have a European-level regulation, at least until such time as Europe cannot be perceived as a unified political community that, despite clear differences within itself, represents a new national, not supranational, experience. For the time being, both the electorates'[19] and the national governments' attitudes throughout Europe are much too different to suggest the possibility of giving EU institutions jurisdiction over an instrument such as the referendum. As a matter of fact, in more than 60 years of the European experience, the people of the Union, considered in its entirety, have never been called to express themselves directly on a common issue. It should be noted that it was this lack of perception of the people of EU countries as a unique community and the diversity in the attitudes towards instruments of direct democracy that prompted governments to limit the forms of involvement of the electorate that are included in the current text of the TEU. Provided for in Art. 11 TEU and currently governed by EU Regulation 211/2011, the 'European Citizen Initiative' (ECI) is the only qualified means of direct participation recognized by the European system. Furthermore, the general will to preserve domestic jurisdiction drove constituent parties to give such an instrument only an advisory value.

This does not lead to the conclusion that things will not change. In fact, referendums already play a significant role in the European integration process, but for the time being they are inexorably perceived of as a matter of national concern. Thus, given the current framework, the granting to EU institutions of jurisdiction on this issue could raise problems that are too complex to be tackled in an efficient way.

19 Points of investigation that could be very significant for a complete analysis of this matter are the different rates of participation of the electorate and how the question that is submitted to the people is drafted. The first element plays an especially fundamental role, because countries in which the people's attitude to this kind of political instrument is more favourable could have a stronger position than those in which referendums are not ordinary instruments of the political life of the community.

11 Sovereignty, constitutional identity, direct democracy? Direct democracy as a national strategy for upholding the nation state in EU integration

Helle Krunke

Introduction

Europe seems to be undergoing a democratization process at the moment. The UK has recently reformed the House of Lords. A Scottish referendum regarding independence from the United Kingdom took place on 18 September 2014 and in Catalonia a non-binding vote on the political future of Catalonia took place on 9 November 2014. As this book shows, the people are increasingly involved in constitutional reform. For instance, Iceland, Ireland and Romania have all recently experimented with new democratic processes when reforming their constitutions. In Luxembourg a citizens' initiative is part of a proposed constitutional amendment which was the object of a consultative referendum in June 2015 and a decisional referendum in 2016. These examples raise the question of what has triggered these initiatives. Other chapters of this book discuss these developments from the perspective of an economic or political crisis. Even though there is no doubt that the financial and political crises have played a direct or in some cases perhaps an indirect role in the democratic developments in some of the European countries, it seems that this is not the only explanation for the recent trend of democratization in Europe. The picture is more complex and more factors seem to be involved. Each country must be viewed in its specific context, and it is probably not possible to give one exhaustive explanation for the development. The purpose of this chapter is to discuss whether the strengthened direct democracy trend can also be explained by a factor other than the financial and political crisis, namely one that is related to EU integration[1] and is maybe even part of

1 In 2004 Bruno Kaufmann and M. Dane Waters pointed to the democratic revolution taking place in Europe in the form of a trend towards more referendums. According to them, this trend was built on two main reasons. First, the democratic revolutions in eastern Europe have led to 27 new constitutions which were in most cases approved by popular referendum. Second, the accelerated integration process within the EU which has launched a direct democratic wave with transnational consequences means that no other set of issues internationally has resulted in as many referendums as European integration. See B. Kaufmann and M. Dane Waters, *Direct Democracy in Europe: A Comprehensive Reference Guide to the Initiative and Referendum Process in Europe* (Carolina Academic Press 2004) 3.

a competition between the EU and the nation states for democratic legitimacy among the 'people'.

The EU is looking for more democratic legitimacy through projects such as the introduction of citizens' initiatives. At the same time, many member states are taking action that directly involves direct democracy. Can these national initiatives be seen as a way of preserving the sovereign nation states that are in competition with an increasingly integrated European Union? Is direct involvement of the people a new strategy as regards sustaining the concept of 'nation states' and in reality part of the ongoing power struggle between the EU and the member states? This struggle has involved 'sovereignty' and 'constitutional identity', and now we seem to have entered the era of 'direct democracy'. Since the development of a stronger involvement of the people seems to be a general tendency that is also taking place in countries outside the EU, the explanation just introduced is of course not an exhaustive explanation of the trend we are witnessing. However, this explanation could explain part of the picture, at least in the EU context and some member states.

Direct democracy

It is difficult to define democracy. Much has been written in this field and many different understandings of the concept exist. March and Olsen have formulated it in the following way:[2]

> The practices of democratic governance differ among contemporary democratic systems, as each differs from its own antecedents. Democracy is culture, a faith, and an ethos that develop through interpretation, practice, wars, and revolutions. It discovers new meanings and new possibilities in new experiences and ideologies. As a result, democratic traditions involve a richly evolving collection of diverse beliefs, processes, and structures that are neither easily characterized in concise terms nor summarized in a single systematic philosophy of governance.

Hence, instead of defining democracy, it might be more useful to highlight some often-existing elements or visions (the term used by March and Olsen) of it or criteria (the term used by Dahl) for it, such as the commitment to personal liberty and individual responsibility in its exercise; the idea of popular sovereignty and political equality; faith in the role of the individual and collective reason in human affairs; and an emphasis on procedural reliability and stability, the rule of law and the regulation of arbitrary power.[3]

2 See J.G. March and J.P. Olsen, *Democratic Governance* (Free Press 1995) 1–2. See also R.A. Dahl, *On Democracy* (Yale University Press 1998) 36–37.

3 See March and Olsen (n. 2) 1–2, and Dahl (n. 2) 37–38. The four mentioned visions come from March and Olsen (n. 2) 2–3.

As regards the concept of 'direct democracy', Ian Budge has formulated an abstract definition of the term:

> a regime in which the population as a whole votes on the most important political decisions.[4]

In a later work, the focus is not only on the voting but also on the debate related to political decisions:

> a regime in which the adult citizens as a whole debate and vote on the most important political decisions, and where their vote determines the action to be taken.[5]

Operationally, he translates this into:

> the operational requirement that the body of adult citizens discusses and votes authoritatively on most of the matters on which, in representative systems, parliament now debates and votes.[6]

However, even within such a broad definition, direct democracy can take many different institutional forms, and there are 'halfway houses' in between the two polar types of 'unmediated popular voting' on the one hand and 'party-based direct democracy' on the other hand.[7] Interestingly, Budge's definition of direct democracy does not seem to include citizens' initiatives unless they are designed in such a way that the electors vote on the proposal at a later stage.

As was the case with the concept of democracy, one possibility other than posing a definition is to point out some elements that are frequently associated with direct democracy. Such elements could be, citizen initiatives and, in a US context, recalls.[8] Bruno Kaufmann and M. Dane Waters focus on citizens' initiatives and referendums (on constitutional amendments, new EU treaties and other issues) when discussing direct democracy in Europe. In a study of civic constitutionalism in central and eastern Europe, Paul Blokker explores three dimensions: civic influence on constitutional amendment or constitutional reform, the existence of channels of direct democracy on various levels, and decentralization and local self-government.[9] In this chapter we include elements such as citizens' initiatives and referendums on constitutional amendments, new EU treaties and other issues

4 See I. Budge, 'Direct Democracy: Terms of Debate' in D. Held (ed.), *Prospects for Democracy: North, South, East, West* (Polity Press 1993) 137.
5 See I. Budge, *The New Challenge of Direct Democracy* (Polity Press 1996) 35.
6 Ibid.
7 See Budge (n. 5) 138–139.
8 See Th.E. Cronin, *Direct Democracy: The Politics of Initiative, Referendum, and Recall* (Harvard University Press 1989). See also Kaufmann and Waters (n. 1).
9 See P. Blokker, *New Democracies in Crisis?* (Routledge 2014) Chapter 5.

that are included in the discussions of current trends towards a higher degree of direct democracy. Direct democracy initiatives at both national and regional levels are of interest, since a new trend will in some cases start at the local level and then spread to the national level. Finally, citizens' initiatives are included even if no referendum follows the proposed initiative.

Direct democracy is often associated with Rousseau.[10] However, in ancient Greece, direct participation of citizens in the legislative functions was already an important element of the political culture, though citizenship was very restricted.[11] In contemporary times, direct democracy as a form of government is normally associated with countries such as Switzerland. Even Rousseau did not believe that direct democracy in its clear form was possible outside a small city-state.[12] In practice, elements of direct democracy are normally combined with representative democracy. In relation to the EU, the concept of direct democracy is stretched and challenged even further since we are dealing with a supranational setting.

Direct democracy initiatives at the national level

As already mentioned in the introduction and as reflected in the other chapters of this book, we are currently witnessing a democratization process in Europe.[13] Part of this process is being carried out through more direct involvement of the people in constitutional amendment, through an increased use of referendums in general and through the introduction of citizens' initiatives. Since other authors of chapters in this book focus on the increasing involvement of the people in constitutional change and the increased use of referendums has been pointed out elsewhere,[14] we shall move directly on to initiatives of direct democracy at the EU level and to establishing a link between EU integration and the direct democracy developments we see at the national level.

Direct democracy initiatives at the EU level

Direct elections for the European Parliament

The first huge step as regards a transnational democratic involvement of the people of the EU took place in 1979 when the first election for the European

10 See V. Gourevitch (ed.), *Rousseau, The Social Contract and Other Later Political Writings* (Cambridge University Press 1997) 24.

11 See D. Held, *Models of Democracy* (Polity Press 1996) 15–28.

12 Ibid. 60.

13 In relation to this trend, see also Kaufmann and Waters (n. 1); B. Kaufmann, 'Prospects for Transnational Direct Democracy – Exploring the New European Approach to Citizens' Power beyond the Nation-State' in Z. Tibor Pállinger, B. Kaufmann, W. Marxer and Th. Schiller (ed.), *Direct Democracy in Europe* (VS Verlag für Sozialwissenschaften 2007) 149. Bruno Kaufmann also points to the fact that the increasing importance of citizens' initiatives and referendums is a global trend and not just a European trend.

14 See Kaufmann and Waters (n. 1).

Parliament took place. Since 1979 the competences of the European Parliament have been continuously strengthened, which has strengthened the democratic legitimacy of the EU. As a result of the Lisbon Treaty, the European Parliament is now on an almost equal footing with the Council as EU legislator. Though an election at the national level must clearly be viewed as indirect democracy, a direct EU election in the member states – as contrary to national elections in which the politicians who will be representing a member state in the EU are elected – seems to carry a certain quasi direct democratic element because of the transnational character of the election. In relation to this, it is also interesting that EU citizens who are living in another EU member state can vote in the elections for the EU Parliament in this member state, and furthermore they can vote in regional elections.

The introduction of a citizens' initiative

With the Lisbon Treaty's introduction of the citizens' initiative in 2009, the EU moved one big step closer to implementing elements of direct democracy. According to Art. 11, part 4, of the Treaty of the European Union:

> Not less than one million citizens who are nationals of a significant number of member States may take the initiative of inviting the European Commission, within the framework of its powers, to submit any appropriate proposal on matters where citizens consider that a legal act of the Union is required for the purpose of implementing Treaties.

The procedures and conditions required for such a citizens' initiative are determined in accordance with the first paragraph of Art. 24 of the Treaty on the Functioning of the European Union.

More detailed rules on the citizens' initiative can be found in Regulation No. 211/2011 of The European Parliament and the Council of 16 February 2011.

The citizens' initiative was originally part of the Constitutional Treaty, Art. I–47, Part 4. The idea of an EU citizens' initiative was fostered in the Convention on the Future of the Union. At the Laeken Intergovernmental Conference it was decided that a European Convention would be formed, which could consider key issues arising from the Union's future development and could try to identify the various possible responses.[15] The idea of the European Convention was that a process that worked as 'broadly and openly' as possible was to be promoted.[16] The Convention was established in 2001 by the European Council and consisted of 102 members with Valéry Giscard d'Estaing as its chairman.

15 See Laeken Declaration on the future of the European Union, Paragraph III Convening of a convention to the future of Europe.

16 See Ibid.

During the proceedings at the Convention, several members put forward suggestions for a citizens' initiative, among them Professor Dr Jürgen Meyer, Delegate of the German Bundestag. According to him, a citizens' initiative would bring Europe closer to the people, as recommended in the Laeken Declaration, and it would be a big step in the democratization of Europe. Caspar Einem and Maria Berger also proposed a citizens' initiative as part of the Constitutional Treaty.

On 12 June, 2003 the citizens' initiative was inserted into the Draft for a Constitutional Treaty.[17] The European Convention's proposal for a citizens' initiative was close to the final wording in the Constitutional Treaty and later on the Lisbon Treaty:[18]

> No less than one million citizens coming from a significant number of Member States may invite the Commission to submit any appropriate proposal on matters where citizens consider that a legal act of the Union is required for the purpose of implementing the Constitution. A European law shall determine the provisions for the specific procedures and conditions required for such a citizens' initiative.

The proposal was adopted at a meeting of the European Council in June 2004.

The introduction of the citizens' initiative was mainly driven by interest groups lobbying the members of the Convention.[19] However, it is also important to emphasize the purpose of the Laeken Declaration. The Laeken Declaration had a strong focus on democracy, how the European institutions could be brought closer to the citizens and the wishes of the European citizens for a democratic Europe. Obviously, the citizens' initiative was consistent with the values and aims expressed in the Laeken Declaration, though the Declaration did not mention a citizens' initiative.

Furthermore, a citizens' initiative had already been discussed during the Amsterdam governmental conference. However, it was not backed by the governmental conference. The discussion was initiated by the European Parliament which, together with the Commission, has been supportive of the introduction of direct democratic elements since 1988.[20]

17 The citizens' initiative was not part of the draft of 10 June 2003. Together with six other last-minute amendments it was inserted into the draft on 12 June (the eve of the last convention session). See Kaufmann and Waters (n. 1) 21; V. Cuesta-López, 'A Comparative Approach to the Regulation on the European Citizens' Initiative' (2012) 13(3) *Perspectives on European Politics and Society* 258. Behind the proposal lay a long process of lobbying by different interest groups such as 'Mehr Demokratie'. See http://www.citizens-initiative.eu/how-the-convention-got-convinced/, accessed 15 May 2015.

18 See Art. 48, part 4, of the Draft Treaty establishing a Constitution for Europe, CONV 850/03.

19 See http://www.citizens-initiative.eu/how-the-convention-got-convinced/, accessed 15 May 2015.

20 See Kaufmann and Waters (n. 1) 21–22. See also EP (1988). Resolution on ways of consulting European citizens about the EU, Brussels: JO C 187/231, EP institutional commission, DOC A2–0332/88 and EP Commission, DOC A3–0031/94.

Direct democracy and EU constitutional change: A European referendum on the constitutional treaty?

The citizens' initiative was not the only element of direct democracy that was discussed by the convention. Interestingly, during the discussions held by the working groups of the convention, the question of a European referendum on the Constitutional Treaty and/or future changes to the Constitutional Treaty was put forward by, for instance, Alain Lamassoure.[21] And Caspar Einem and Maria Berger noted:

> 4) Any fundamental changes of the constitution decided on by the relevant organs of the European Union must be submitted for approval by the citizens of Europe in a referendum.
>
> 5) A European Citizens' Referendum is accepted if the majority of those voting were in favour and a majority was also in favour in more than half of the member states. For changes to the constitution, there must be a majority in at least half of the states representing two-thirds of the population of the Union.

Furthermore, European referendums in general as a tool that could be used to achieve more direct democratic involvement of the EU citizens were on the agenda in the discussions held at the convention.[22]

One might view a European referendum's process on the Constitutional Treaty and later amendments of the treaty as direct democracy in relation to EU constitutional change. However, the final Draft for a Constitutional Treaty did not directly recommend a European referendum on the Constitutional Treaty. The convention took note of a resolution signed by a large group of members, alternates and observers demanding such a referendum, though.[23] In general, EU referendums on treaties or treaty changes highlight problems in relation to the national ratification procedures and traditions which differ from one member state to the other, ranging from those in Ireland, where a national referendum on EU treaties always takes place, to those in countries such as Britain, where no referendum on new EU treaties has taken place (though there might be a

21 The stated reasons for the proposal were as follows: 'Il s'agit d'introduire les procédures de la démocratie directe dans la vie de l'Union. Combinées avec l'amendement déposé sur la révision constitutionnelle, ces propositions ouvrent quatre possibilités différentes: droit des citoyens d'obtenir un débat; droit de proposer une loi nouvelle ou l'abrogation d'une loi existante; droit d'être consultés para. référendum sur un projet de loi ou de traité (par exemple un traité d'adhésion); droit d'obtenir le recours au référendum pour ratifier une révision de la Constitution.'

22 Such propositions were put forward by, for instance, Borrell and Carnero y López Garrido, Voggenhuber, Einem and Berger.

23 Kaufmann and Waters (n. 1) 25, and Contribution 291 by Alain Lamassoure and others on 31 March 2003.

referendum on EU membership within the next two years after the recent UK elections).[24]

The idea of a European referendum on the Constitutional Treaty had already been anticipated in the Laeken Declaration and was formed as one of a number of questions raised about how more democracy, transparency and efficiency could be achieved in the European Union: 'Should a European electoral constituency be created. Or should constituencies continue to be determined nationally?'[25]

Why is the EU interested in developing new elements of direct democracy at the EU level?

In relation to the development and support of ideas concerning more elements of direct democracy in the EU, the Laeken Declaration, which lay behind the establishment of the European Convention which led to the Constitutional Treaty and later on the Lisbon Treaty, is essential. However, one might ask what interest the EU has in more direct democracy. According to the Laeken Declaration, the Union is facing a democratic challenge within its borders. The image of a democratic, engaged Europe must be well matched to the wishes of the citizens. European institutions must be brought closer to their citizens, and they must be more open, subject to better democratic scrutiny and not too bureaucratic:

> In short, citizens are calling for a clear, open, effective, democratically controlled Community approach, developing a Europe which points the way ahead for the world.

According to the Laeken Declaration, the Union therefore needs to become more democratic, more transparent and more efficient. One of the aims is to meet the expectations of the citizens. Accordingly, this will strengthen the democratic legitimacy of the European Union, and this is probably the real pay-off for the Union:

> The European Union derives its *legitimacy* from the democratic values it projects, the aims it pursues and the powers and instruments it possesses. However, the European project also derives its *legitimacy* from democratic, transparent and efficient institutions. The national parliaments also contribute towards the *legitimacy* of the European project . . . The first question is thus how we can increase the democratic legitimacy and transparency of the

24 On how an 'All-Europe referendum' could be designed, see N. MacCormick, 'The Convention and Its Constitution: All a Great Mistake?' in H. Petersen, A.L. Kjær, H. Krunke and M. Eask Madsen (eds), *Paradoxes of European Legal Integration* (Ashgate 2008) 17–27.

25 See Laeken Declaration on the future of the European Union, Paragraph II Challenges and reforms in a renewed Union, subtitle 'More democracy, transparency and efficiency in the European Union'.

present institutions, a question which is valid for the three institutions . . . A second question, which also relates to ***democratic legitimacy***, involves the role of national parliaments.

(italics inserted by the author)

The Laeken Declaration's focus on how the national parliaments can be strengthened shows at the same time that direct democracy through, for instance, direct elections of the president of the Commission or the creation of a European electoral constituency, should be combined with strengthening what one would at the national level refer to as representative democracy. This must also be seen in light of the Constitutional Treaty's and Lisbon Treaty's introduction of the early warning system[26] and the more informal 'Barosso initiative' from 2006.[27] This also shows that the EU is concerned with democratic legitimacy in general, both through elements of direct democracy and through elements of representative democracy. One might even add through greater transparency, for instance a strengthened access to EU documents.

Finally, another impact of introducing the European citizens' initiative could be the creation of more transnational public debate and the construction of 'supranational discourses in an emerging European public space'.[28]

The discussions on why the EU is interested in introducing new elements of direct democracy naturally leads to the discussion on whether we are witnessing a competition for democratic legitimacy through direct democracy between the EU and the member states. However, before we turn to that discussion, we shall look into whether EU integration in general can be linked to the developments at the national level towards more direct democracy.

Searching for coherence between EU integration and direct democracy developments at the national level

As previously mentioned, national developments as regards direct democracy can be explained by many factors, such as the financial and political crisis. However, can national developments be viewed in isolation from EU integration? Or is there coherence between EU integration and national direct democracy developments? Below we shall try to establish some tentative links between the two levels as regards direct democracy.

We shall attempt to identify a number of possible links between the European and the national level. The first observation is that the number one country in Europe, when it comes to direct democracy, is Switzerland, which is not a

26 See Protocol (No. 2) on the Application of the Principles of Subsidiarity and Proportionality.

27 See Commission of the European Communities, COM(2006) 211, A Citizen's Agenda–Delivering Results for Europe (10 May 2006).

28 See Cuesta-López (n. 17); Kaufmann, 'Prospects for Transnational Direct Democracy' (n. 13) 156, 159.

member of the EU. Hence, one might tentatively put forward the idea that a very high degree of national direct democracy at the national level is normally not associated with EU membership.

The next observation is that, at least in some cases, there seems to be a temporal convergence between direct democracy initiatives (and other democratic initiatives) at the national level and EU treaties that have resulted in further surrender of national sovereignty. For instance, Portugal became a member of the EU in 1986, and in the 1990s, at the same time as Portugal was adapting the Treaties of Maastricht and Amsterdam, a citizens' initiative was introduced along with a strengthening of the Assembly of the Republic's exclusive legislative powers. Poland became a member of the EU in 1994 and introduced a citizens' initiative in 1997. In general in the 1990s, a number of the central, eastern and Baltic European countries introduced a citizens' initiative after regaining their independence from the Soviet Union while entering the EU at the same time. Each country must of course be seen in its unique context; however, at the same time these countries obviously had something in common. They shared a historic past and a desire to create new democratic constitutional systems (though their new constitutions ended up differing from each other in many ways).[29] Hence, countries such as Poland, Slovenia, Lithuania, Latvia, Romania, Slovakia and Hungary (until the constitutional changes in 2011) all introduced a citizens' initiative roughly within the same period as they negotiated membership with and entered the EU. The introduction of direct democratic elements such as a citizens' initiative could, on the one hand, reflect the fact that these countries believed that by strengthening their democratic constitutional structure they would live up to the EU's democratic values. On the other hand, it could reflect that these countries, having just regained their independence, held on to the notion of a nation state by introducing elements of direct democracy, while at the same time entering into the supranational EU cooperation which, in the 1990s with the Maastricht Treaty, took a huge step forward towards an 'ever closer European cooperation'. An interesting observation is that some member states strengthened their national parliamentary democracy when they signed the Lisbon Treaty. Hence, in France and Portugal the national parliaments were given an enhanced role in the national constitutions in relation to the ratification of the Lisbon Treaty.[30] Furthermore, one impact of the German Lisbon judgment was that new competences were given to the German parliament.[31] In this way, new democratic initiatives at the national level can in general be linked to further EU integration. A study of which countries have (or are in the process of getting) direct democratic elements such as a citizens' initiative, etc. and of ECJ

29 See Blokker (n. 9).

30 See J.-C. Piris, *The Lisbon Treaty* (Cambridge University Press 2010) 125–126.

31 Ibid.

case law on constitutional and national identity[32] seems to show an interesting coherence. Apparently, there is quite a good match between EU member states which have been involved in cases on constitutional identity and national identity and EU member states which at the time of these cases already had (or are currently introducing) elements of direct democracy. In general, there are not many ECJ cases on constitutional and national identity, which strengthens the thesis that there could be a link.

Austria and Italy have a long tradition of citizens' initiatives. In Austria, a right to a citizens' initiative was introduced as early as the 1920s, and in Italy the citizens' initiative dates back to 1947 (just before Italy entered into the Coal and Steel Union). Austria also has a strong tradition of referendums.[33] Austria entered the EU in 1995. One of the so-called leading cases on identity is the Austrian *Sayn-Wittgenstein* case.[34] However, more identity case law involving Austria exists.[35] Italy has also been involved in identity cases.[36] Besides the citizens' initiative, which has been actively used over a long period of time, the Italian electors may also play a role in constitutional amendment by referendums.

Spain introduced a right to a citizens' initiative in 1978; however, a number of issues, such as taxation and constitutional reform, are excluded from this initiative

32 The current legal basis of the constitutional identity clause is Art. 4, part 2, TEU. However, in 1992 a national identity clause had already been introduced into the Maastricht Treaty in Art. F.I: 'the Union shall respect the national identities of its Member States, whose systems of government are founded on the principle of democracy'. In the Amsterdam Treaty the provision was changed to 'the Union shall respect the national identities of the Member States', detaching identity from democracy. Finally, in the Lisbon Treaty the term national identity is linked to constitutional identity: 'The Union shall respect the equality of Member States before the Treaties as well as their national identities, inherent in their fundamental structures, political and constitutional, inclusive of regional and local self-government'. Furthermore, the preamble of the Charter of Fundamental Rights states: 'The Union contributes to the preservation and to the development of these common values while respecting the diversity of the cultures and traditions of the peoples of Europe as well as the national identities of the Member States and the organization of their public authorities at national, regional and local levels.' For an exhaustive discussion of this development in the provisions, see, for instance, M. Claes, 'National Identity: Trump Card or Up for Negotiation?' in A. Saiz Arnaiz and C. Alcoberro Llivina (eds), *National Constitutional Identity and European Integration* (Intersentia 2013) 109–139; R. Toniatti, 'Sovereignty Lost, Constitutional Identity Regained' in A. Saiz Arnaiz and C. Alcoberro Llivina (eds), *National Constitutional Identity and European Integration* (Intersentaia 2013) 49–73; and B. Guastaferro, 'Beyond the Exceptionalism of Constitutional Conflicts: The Ordinary Functions of the Identity Clause' (2012) Jean Monet Working paper 01/2012, 12ff. See also E. Elander Duque, 'United in Diversity or Through Diversity? National identity as a Flexibility Clause–Granting Member States a Margin of Appreciation' (2013) 2 *Lund Student EU Law Review* 36.

33 See Kaufmann and Waters (n. 1) 33.

34 Case C-208/09 Sayn-Wittgenstein [2010].

35 Case C-205/08 Umweltanwalt von Kärnten [2009].

36 Case C-180/04 Vasello ECR [2005] in which the General Advocate referred to an identity argument while the ECJ did not, and Case T-185/05 *Italy, Spain and Latvia v Commission* [2008].

right.[37] Spain entered the EC after many years of negotiation in 1986. Spain has also been involved in a number of identity cases.[38]

Some of the Baltic countries also have a right to a citizens' initiative. Baltic countries entered the EU in 2004. After its independence from the Soviet Union, Latvia reinstated its original constitution in 1991. Latvia has a right to a citizens' initiative. It has also been involved in an identity case at the ECJ.[39] As regards Lithuania, from 1992 its new constitution has included the right to a citizens' initiative. Lithuania has been involved in an identity case too.[40]

Ireland does not have a right to a citizens' initiative. However, it has other interesting elements of direct democracy, such as obligatory referendums on all EU treaties and referendums in connection with amendments of the constitution. Ireland has been characterized as a referendum-friendly country.[41] Furthermore, Ireland is at the moment carrying out a process of constitutional amendment based on the work of a convention on the constitution. This convention had 100 members, of which 66 were ordinary citizens. Ireland entered the EU in 1973. It dealt with one of the very first identity cases, at a stage when no identity clause even existed concerning Ireland.[42] In 2004 Germany was involved in the *Omega* case.[43] This case is quite famous in the identity literature even though the judgment does not explicitly refer to identity.[44]

Germany has played a special role in relation to the identity rhetoric, starting with *Solange I* in 1974 and later on in the *German Lisbon* judgment in 2009.[45] Hence, in the German context the German Federal Constitutional Court has played an important role in relation to identifying German identity. The court has also argued along the line of democratic self-determination.[46] However, Germany has also had a strong tradition of direct democracy at the regional level since the reunification in 1990.[47] Bavaria has been especially active in this regard, and a

37 See Kaufmann and Waters (n. 1) 111.

38 See Case C-160/03 *Spain v Eurojust* [2005] and Case T-185/05 *Italy, Spain and Latvia v Commission* [2008]. See also Case C-399/11 Melloni [2013] in which the General Advocate, contrary to the ECJ, based his argumentation on the identity clause.

39 Case T-185/05 *Italy, Spain and Latvia v Commission* [2008].

40 Case C-391/09 *Malgozata Runevic-Vardyn and Lukasz Pawel Wardyn v Vilniaus miesto savivaldybės administracija and Others* [2011].

41 See Kaufmann and Waters (n. 1) 70–73.

42 Case C-379/87 *Anita Groener v Minister for Education and the City of Dublin Vocational Educational Committee* [1989].

43 Case C-36/02 *Omega* [2004].

44 See Claes (n. 32) 132.

45 Federal Constitutional Court–BvL 52/71–BverfGE 37, 271 ff. and Federal Constitutional Court–2 be 2/08–BverfGE 123, 267 et seq.

46 See K.P. Sommermann, 'The Theory of "Essential National Policies" in the Lisbon Judgment of the German Federal Constitutional Court' in Th. Giegerich, O.J. Gstrein and S. Zeitsmann (eds), *The EU Between 'an Ever Closer Union' and Inalienable Policy Domains of Member States* (Nomos 2014) 52–55.

47 See Kaufmann and Waters (n. 1) 63.

general trend towards more direct democracy seems to have taken place.[48] As shown earlier, German members of the convention were also active in promoting the inclusion of a European citizens' initiative in the Constitutional Treaty. However, as regards referendums at the national level, Germany has a weak tradition.

Luxembourg has been involved in a number of identity cases.[49] Traditionally, Luxembourg has not had a strong tradition of direct democracy, neither through referendums nor through citizens' initiatives. However, Luxembourg is experiencing a development in this field. Since 2001 an 'Initiative for Direct Democracy' has worked for more direct democracy and political initiatives have been taken.[50] According to Art. 114, which was amended in 2003, the electorate may in some cases be consulted through a referendum when the constitution is amended. Furthermore, in 2003 there was an attempt to introduce a right to a citizens' initiative by an ordinary legislative Act; however, the Conseil d'Etat objected that there was no legal basis for such an initiative in the constitution. A new attempt is currently being made since a citizens' initiative has been introduced as part of a proposed constitutional reform. In general, Luxembourg is currently experiencing a trend of consulting the electors on constitutional change.[51]

Greece has no strong tradition of direct democracy.[52] During the financial crisis referendum on whether or not Greece was to accept the conditions put forward by the EU, the IMF and the ECB were considered, leading to the July 2015 referendum. Greece has been involved in an identity case at the ECJ,[53] and has been a member of the EU since 1981.

It seems that many countries with quite a strong tradition of direct democracy or a current trend towards the introduction of direct democratic elements have been involved in identity cases. As already mentioned, there are not many cases in this field and therefore the link is interesting. We should also tentatively mention that countries without a citizens' initiative or with a weak element of direct democracy have not been involved in identity cases, for instance Britain, Finland and Sweden. Though we cannot make a conclusion that is 100 per cent certain as regards the link between a member state's interest in and position as regards constitutional/national identity on the one hand and direct democracy on the other hand, a pattern does seem to appear.

Another relevant observation is that the initiative to extend the identity clause in the Constitutional Treaty came from a Danish member of the convention, Henning Christophersen, who was chairman of Working Group 5 on

48 See Ibid.

49 Case C-473/93 *Commission v Luxembourg* [1996], Case C-193/05 *Commission v Luxembourg* [2006], and Case C-51/08 *Commission v Luxembourg* [2011].

50 See Kaufmann and Waters (n. 1) 91.

51 See the chapter by Jörg Gerkrath, in this book.

52 See X. Contiades and I. Tassopoulos, 'Constitutional Change in Greece' in X. Contiades (ed.), *Engineering Constitutional Change: A Comparative Perspective on Europe, Canada and the USA* (Routledge 2013) 161–163.

53 Case C-213/07 Michaniki [2008].

'Complementary Competence'.[54] Hence, the identity clause was consistently referred to as the 'Christophersen Clause' in the working documents of the European Convention.[55] Denmark has not a right to a citizens' initiative; however, it has other elements of direct democracy in its constitution. For instance, the electors play an important role in constitutional change. In order to amend the Danish constitution, the electors must be involved twice, first through an election and second through a referendum on the proposed amendment (Art. 88). In this referendum, a majority of those voting and not less than 40 per cent of all those entitled to vote must vote in favour of the amendment.[56] Furthermore, when ceding sovereignty to international institutions, a referendum must be held unless five-sixths of parliament votes in favour of the proposal (Art. 20). Finally, a minimum of one-third of parliament can (with a few exceptions) demand a binding referendum on bills that have been adopted by parliament (Art. 42).

Hence, we have pointed out a number of tentative links between EU integration and national direct democracy. It seems that the introduction of citizens' initiatives can in some cases be linked to entering the EU or to new EU treaties that will entail extensive transfer of sovereignty. It also seems that member states with strong direct democratic elements (or those in the process of introducing them) are involved in cases at the ECJ concerning national/constitutional identity more often than other member states. Switzerland, which is the European country that comes closest to direct democracy, has chosen not to join the EU. Elements of direct democracy at EU level are introduced and promoted by member states that have elements of direct democracy. Further studies could be conducted to strengthen the thesis and to formulate the links more precisely. However, it seems that the EU context and the national context do not function in isolation from each other as regards national direct democracy initiatives. The two levels have an ongoing impact on each other.

Competition between the EU and the member states for democratic legitimacy through direct democracy?

Another interesting aspect of this issue is that while a number of member states are developing towards more direct democracy at the national level, the EU

54 See Working Group V, Working Document 5, Highlighting the limits of the EU competence, Henning Christophersen, Brussels, 11 July 2002.

55 See Guastaferro (n. 32). See also Elander Duque (n. 32).

56 An interesting feature of the Danish system of constitutional amendment, among others, is that because of the difficult amendment procedure, which requires extensive popular participation, the constitution is rarely amended. The last revision of the Danish constitution took place in 1953. So although formal constitutional change is a very democratic process which requires much direct participation of the electors, in reality constitutional change seldom takes place, leaving it up to the politicians and the courts to interpret the constitution without direct democratic participation. See H. Krunke, 'Formal and Informal Methods of Constitutional Change in Denmark' in X. Contiades (ed.), *Engineering Constitutional Change: A Comparative Perspective on Europe, Canada and the USA* (Routledge 2013) 73–92.

is, at the same time, striving for democratic legitimacy; this is reflected in the Laeken Declaration as well as in other agreements. This is being obtained both by strengthening the national parliaments and the EU Parliament (representative democracy at different levels) and by strengthening direct democracy through the European citizens' initiative. This is how a competition for democratic legitimacy through direct involvement of the citizens is created.

That a link between democracy, democratic legitimacy and identity exists in the EU frame of reference is reflected in the Laeken Declaration. According to the declaration, the need for the EU to bring the EU institutions closer to the citizens is linked to a feeling at the national level that the EU is a 'threat to their identity'.[57] Furthermore, it is stated that citizens feel that the Union is behaving too bureaucratically in numerous areas and that the 'member states' individuality' should not be jeopardized.[58]

Sovereignty, constitutional identity, direct democracy?

In the legal literature it has been stated that the concept of constitutional identity has replaced the concept of sovereignty.[59] However, according to Monica Claes, identity does not 'replace' sovereignty:[60]

> While there may be some truth in this, and academics and constitutional courts rally round the concept of constitutional identity, the reality of the political debate as well as the case-law demonstrates that 'sovereignty' has not left the building. The rise of 'national or constitutional identity' seems to coincide with the persisting or renewed concern for sovereignty. The concepts seem to be mutually reinforcing, as they both express the same underlying sense of a (national) 'we' – a feeling of community – that seems to be in need of protection in the face of European integration.

Even though national direct democracy might have a slightly different character to that of sovereignty and constitutional/national identity, which are understood as legal arguments used at national courts and the ECJ for protecting national competences (one might even refer to this as judicial dialogue),[61] the concept of direct democracy can be compared to sovereignty and identity in that they can all be considered rhetorical and strategic tools for maintaining a nation state. Direct democracy provides the nation state with a deep democratic legitimacy, and the concept of national direct democracy presupposes that there is a national competence that the people can decide upon. Though judicial dialogue might

57 See Laeken Declaration on the Future of the European Union, 2.

58 Ibid. 3.

59 See, for instance, J.H.H. Weiler, 'A Constitution for Europe? Some Hard Choices' (2002) 40(4) *Journal of Common Market Studies* 563ff.

60 See Claes (n. 32) 109.

61 Ibid. 109–139; Toniatti (n. 32).

not fit national direct democracy initiatives as well as 'sovereignty' and especially 'identity', direct democracy initiatives certainly fall under the term 'constitutional dialogue'. In fact, both national direct democracy initiatives and EU direct democracy initiatives can be said to be part of a constitutional dialogue between member states and the EU and vice versa.

As has been shown, direct democracy and identity are linked to a certain extent – just as identity and sovereignty are too. European countries focused on direct democracy elements also seem to be interested in identity. This means that we might be able to see sovereignty, constitutional/national identity and national direct democracy as a 'three-stage rocket' (in which the layers interact and support each other) of national strategies and tools that can be used to maintain national competence in a process that is integrating Europe more than ever before.

A changing notion of the 'people'

We have now identified two movements towards more direct involvement of the citizens through the introduction of elements of direct democracy: one at the national level and one at the EU level. Furthermore, one might view this as a competition between the EU and the member states for democratic legitimacy. We have also tried to show that there is a link between EU integration in general and the developments at the national level.

Yet another interesting democratic development concerns the notion of the 'people'. In this respect, a democratization process seems to be taking place in the sense that the notion of 'people' in a number of European countries has been broadened. Hence, the voting age seems to be moving from the age of 18 towards the age of 16. For instance, since 2008 the voting age in Austria has been 16 compared to the former voting age of 18. Furthermore, some of the countries that are currently undergoing constitutional change that entails the direct involvement of the people are considering lowering the voting age from 18 to 16. This includes Ireland and Luxembourg.[62] Iceland also considered lowering the voting age from 18 to 16 in 2015. Scotland can now regulate the voting age for election to its parliament from 2016. In the referendum on independence from the UK, the voting age was lowered from 18 to 16. In the UK, the voting age was part of the election campaign during 2015. The Isle of Man (2006), Jersey (2008) and Guernsey (2007) have lowered the voting age to 16. In Germany, whether the voting age should be lowered has also been discussed. However, so far there has not been enough political support for this. Interestingly, a number of Bundesländer have lowered the voting age for Landtagswahlen to the age of 16, among them Bremen (2009), Brandenburg (2011), Hamburg (2013) and Schleswig-Holstein (2013). Furthermore, a number of Bundesländer have lowered the voting age for Kommunalwahlen to 16, among them Lower Saxony (1996),

62 In Luxembourg, lowering the voting age is part of the consultative referendums in relation to the proposed constitutional amendments, whereas in Ireland lowering the voting age is not part of the planned referendums on constitutional amendments.

Saxony-Anhalt (1998), Schleswig-Holstein (1998), Mecklenburg-Vorpommern (1999), Bremen (2007), Brandenburg (2011) and Baden-Württemberg (2013).

At EU level, we are also witnessing a growing focus on the inclusion of young people in democratic processes.[63] This is also reflected in the Laeken Declaration, in which it is stated:

> The Union needs to become more democratic, more transparent and more efficient. It also has to resolve three basic challenges: how to bring citizens, and *primarily the young*, closer to the European design and the European institutions.
>
> (italics inserted by author)

In general, the EU has now a greater focus on future generations. This is, for instance, reflected in the Preamble of both the Constitutional Treaty and the Lisbon Treaty and in the Preamble of the European Chart of Human Rights. Furthermore, Art. 3, Part 3, TEU, mentions solidarity between generations as one of the goals of the European Union.[64]

However, broadening the notion of the 'people' by lowering the voting age is not the only development taking place. Another trend is the widening of the right to vote because of Europeanization and globalization. For instance, in the EU it is possible for EU citizens to vote in local elections and for the elections to the European Parliament in the member state in which the person is living even if he or she is not a national citizen of that member state. One of the proposed constitutional amendments in Luxembourg is to allow non-Luxembourgish residents the right to optionally enroll in order to participate as voters in elections for the Chamber of Deputies, under the double condition of having resided for at least ten years in Luxembourg and having previously participated in local or European elections in Luxembourg. This proposition is part of the referendums on constitutional amendments.

Hence, the growing trend of introducing more elements of direct democracy through the involvement of the people in constitutional change, through referendums in general and through citizen initiatives, is accompanied by a trend towards a broader perception of who the 'people' are.

Conclusion

We are witnessing a complex, multi-faceted democratization process that geographically includes a general democratization process in large parts of Europe,

63 See, for instance, Resolution 1826 (2001) on Expansion of democracy by lowering the voting age to 16 and Resolution 1630 (2008) on Refreshing the youth agenda of the Council of Europe.

64 On this development see H. Krunke, *Pensionsreform. De Retlige grænser og Muligheder. Berettigede Forventninger. Generationsfordeling. Demokrati* (Jurist-og Økonomforbundets Forlag 2010) 195–199, 263–268.

where the process takes place at many levels, including the national and local levels and even the EU one. A significant feature of this process is the development of further involvement of the people through elements of direct democracy. Finally, the perception of the 'people' itself is undergoing a democratic change. The different processes cannot be viewed in isolation since the interaction between, for instance, the EU and the member states is so close and projects that encourage direct democracy both at the national level of member states and at the EU level can be seen as part of a constitutional dialogue between the national and the EU level and vice versa. In this way, direct democracy can also be seen as yet another rhetorical and strategic tool that can be used to keep the concept of a nation state in line with the more well-established theory on 'sovereignty' and 'national/constitutional identity'. While the member states are introducing elements of direct democracy at the national level, the EU is looking to strengthen democratic legitimacy by, among other things, introducing elements of direct democracy. Hence, it seems that a competition between the EU and the nation states for democratic legitimacy among the people is taking place.

Index

For Product Safety Concerns and Information please contact our EU representative GPSR@taylorandfrancis.com Taylor & Francis Verlag GmbH, Kaufingerstraße 24, 80331 München, Germany